Hidden Markets

The past decade has witnessed an unprecedented expansion in the influence of the private sector in all aspects of public education. Across the United States, test publishers, software companies, virtual charter school operators, and other industries are rapidly moving to take advantage of the significant revenues made available by public education funds. As these private companies are garnering billions of dollars in public revenues they have assumed a central place in the day-to-day governance and administration of public schools—but, while drawing on public money and on the authority of public policy, the work of the new privatization has been kept relatively hidden from view.

Hidden Markets suggests that much more transparency is needed around what exactly these firms are doing in our schools, the influence of the market on their work, and the implications of these dynamics for the goals claimed by federal policy designers. Drawing on analytic tools such as investigative financial accounting, Patricia Burch maps the financial and operational reach of some of the largest for-profit firms in the K–12 education industry, offering a close look at how these activities are unfolding on the ground and the roles being transferred from the public to the private sector. Ultimately, Burch's careful analysis demonstrates that only when we subject the education industry and its strategies to systematic and in-depth critical examination can we begin to demand more corporate accountability.

Patricia Burch is Assistant Professor of Educational Policy Studies at the University of Wisconsin—Madison.

The Critical Social Thought Series

Edited by Michael W. Apple,
University of Wisconsin—Madison

Hidden Markets

The New Education Privatization

Patricia Burch

Routledge
Taylor & Francis Group

NEW YORK AND LONDON

First published 2009
by Routledge
270 Madison Ave, New York, NY 10016

Simultaneously published in the UK
by Routledge
2 Park Square, Milton Park, Abingdon, Oxon OX14 4RN

Routledge is an imprint of the Taylor & Francis Group, an informa business

Typeset in Minion by Evs Communicaton Networx, Inc.
Printed and bound in the United States of America on acid-free paper by Edwards Brothers, Inc.

Library of Congress Cataloging in Publication Data
Burch, Patricia.
Hidden markets : the new education privatization / Patricia Burch.
p. cm. — (The critical social thought series)
Includes bibliographical references and index.
1. Privatization in education—United States. I. Title.
LB2806.36.B87 2009
379.1—dc22
2008029468

ISBN 10: 0-415-95566-1 (hbk)
ISBN 10: 0-415-95567-X (pbk)
ISBN 10: 0-203-88394-2 (ebk)

ISBN 13: 978-0-415-95566-9 (hbk)
ISBN 10: 978-0-415-95567-6 (pbk)
ISBN 13: 978-0-203-88394-5 (ebk)

To my family:

For all of their love, support, and inspiration

Contents

Series Editor's Introduction
to *Hidden Markets*

In an interesting quirk of fate, I am writing the Introduction to this fine book in London, just a few days after I have had a meal at the Houses of Parliament with a New Labour MP. She was thoughtful and articulate—and deeply committed to expanding the role of the private sector in education and in the entire public sector. The distinction between public and private seemed not to be a major concern of hers. Efficiency and accountability were her watchwords.

She is not alone either in England or in the United States. But should we be concerned that so many people now feel this way? Should we be concerned that a number of groups go even further, seeing "private" as necessarily good and "public" as necessarily bad? With neoliberalism now driving a good deal of policy in many parts of our economic and social worlds, there may be reasons for worry.

For example, we are witnessing a situation where important parts of education are being steadily, but radically, transformed. In many ways, education is being commodified, turned into something that is bought and sold on a market as if it was bread, cars, or plasma screen TVs. It is being treated internally as a business and put on a market like other businesses.

As I show in *Educating the "Right" Way*,[1] these things are part of a much larger set of changes. It is not an easy process to transform parts of our lives and institutions that were not totally integrated into market relations so that they are part of a market. To do this, at least four significant things must be worked on.[2]

1. The services or goods that are to be focused upon must be reconfigured so that they can indeed be bought and sold.
2. People who received these things from the state must be convinced to want to buy them.

3. The working conditions and outlook of the employees who work in this sector must be transformed from a model based on collective understandings and providing service to "the public" on the one hand to working to produce profits for owners and investors and subject to market discipline on the other.
4. When business moves into what were previously non-market fields, as much as possible their risks must be underwritten by the state.

I noted earlier that this is a world-wide phenomenon. As Stephen Ball and Deborah Youdell have shown, in a considerable number of nations what they call "hidden privatization" is occurring at an ever increasing rate.[3] Ball describes the policies that both lie behind these changes and that support them as "policy technologies." That is, they are sets of interrelated reforms that provide new ways of thinking about education, new languages for describing what it does and does not do, new roles for the people who work in it or use it, and new identities for the teachers, students, parents, and "managers" involved in it. As he says,

> Targets, accountability, competition and choice, leadership, entrepreneurism, performance-related pay, and privatization articulate new ways of thinking about what we do, what we value, and what our purposes are. They work together to render education as like a "commodity" rather than a public good … They bring into play now roles and relationships, those of client/consumer and competitor, manager/managed, appraiser/inspector/monitor, and they exclude or marginalize previous roles, loyalties, and subjectivities. They change what is important and valuable and necessary.[4]

With the focus on being "business-like" and on highly prescriptive systems of accountability, schools are rated and compared. And this is done almost totally in terms of testing. Each school and school district is under immense pressure to carefully prepare its students for these tests. This is straightforward enough and is seen throughout our nation and so many others. But because of this situation, once more Ball's worries are important here and give what Burch has accomplished in this book even more salience. As Ball puts it,

> But the question that is avoided here is whether these indicators actually stand for and thus represent valid, worthwhile or meaningful outputs. Does increased emphasis on preparation for the tests and the adaptation of pedagogy and curriculum to the requirements of test performance constitute worthwhile effects of "improvement"? In terms of economic competitiveness, is what is measured here what is needed?[5]

These kinds of policies are perhaps best exemplified in No Child Left Behind, and this is one of the reasons that *Hidden Markets* devotes a good deal of its attention to its effects. But while No Child Left Behind provided the context for the extension of these tendencies, at times making them mandatory, many of them were in existence before No Child Left Behind was put into place. No Child Left Behind and the policies that both led to it and that it has sponsored have their supporters, but they have also been subjected to some very powerful empirical, political, and educational criticisms from multiple groups.[6] However, even if No Child Left Behind is substantially changed and/or its policies and mandates made more flexible, there can be little doubt that much that it signaled is now accepted as common-sense. The private sector is now a very large player in education. Mandatory comparative testing is now so institutionalized that it will be very difficult to remove. The need to be competitive, to be seen as business-like, to employ the strategies of business in restructuring public institutions such as schools, and thus to be seen as lean and efficient and to incorporate managerial ideologies and technical resources to support all of this—all of these things seem to have been cemented in place.

Not all of this is necessarily bad. After all, we spend billions of dollars on schooling. Evidence of success is needed, as is accountability in where the money goes and whether it is well spent. Of course, issues such as what the goals of schooling should be, what the knowledge that we teach should be, who decides, what counts as evidence, accountability to whom, and similar kinds of things are not easy to ask or to answer. But they can get forgotten in the midst of our search for efficiency, measurability, and business-like procedures.

Too often our analyses of neoliberalism in education have been at such a general level as to make it hard to see what is actually happening and what is actually at stake when schools are turned into sources of profit. This is exactly where *Hidden Markets* enters and where it makes a significant contribution. Burch brings together approaches taken from critical policy analysis and new institutional theory to help explain not only what is happening, but how and why it is happening.

Burch's account is well-balanced. Her task is not to condemn. She understands the demands and complexities of schools and on the people who work in them in times such as these. She does not romanticize what goes on educational policy or in the daily life of schools currently. Rather, she succeeds in showing what the costs are of the transformations that are occurring in these policies and practices right now. *Hidden Markets* doesn't answer the question of whether these kinds of reforms lead to higher test scores, often the only question that many people tend to ask. Rather, she asks questions about things that are occurring below the radar screen, so to speak. In essence, the questions she raises can be summarized this way: What are the important hidden effects of our insistent focus on commodification, marketization, accountability, and performance as measured by standardized test data on the entire school system? This is a question that is absolutely essential that we ask. As Burch shows, the answers to this question may be more than a little discomforting to those of us who truly want a school system that is effective and responsive.

Her examples of the hidden effects of the growth of for-profit relations in the daily workings of schools provide us with a picture that has exceptional clarity. She examines the growth of large and small firms that sell expertise, technology, tests, tutoring services, curricula, and all kinds of managerial resources to schools. But Burch also wisely understands that in the current context our very understanding of what counts as a school is undergoing major changes. Virtual schools and home schooling are helping to redefine who the teacher is, what the curriculum is and from where it comes, and who is in charge of its selection, evaluation, and use. This is something that I too have weighed in on elsewhere.[7] But in *Hidden Markets* Patricia Burch markedly extends a number of my and others' arguments and analyses and does so in truly illuminating ways. She has done her homework empirically, carefully searching out data that are not usually readily available to the public. In the process, she teaches all of us a good deal about both how all of these policies operate in real schools and real communities and how these changes can and do create opportunities for profit.

At the end of this Introduction, it is wise to give Patricia Burch the last words. The final paragraphs of the book both summarize Burch's arguments and, just and importantly, issue words of caution that must be taken very seriously.

> In this book, I have argued for more attention to hidden developments in K-12 education contracting. We do not expect for-profit, private firms to have the same level of accessibility and transparency as public agencies. Yet, these private, for-profit firms draw on public funds that are designed to serve common interests. Of course, it is important to recognize that private firms have a role to play in public education. They long have acted as suppliers to education and will continue to do so. Under certain conditions, they can contribute to the democratic purposes of education.
>
> But, right now, the center of gravity in public policy is shifting. Ideologies of neoliberalism are remaking education policy to fit the needs of the market. The ideas are pushed as helping public education although the arguments have little empirical basis. The governance of public education is not just another education market. The distinction between public policy and private markets in education, as in other sectors, is very important, and it is worth defending.

With its rich sources of data and careful analysis of what is happening on the ground as schools increasingly become sources of profit, *Hidden Markets* demonstrates why these issues count. It deserves to be read by anyone who cares about the real effects of educational policies both in the United States and elsewhere.

Michael W. Apple
*John Bascom Professor of Curriculum and Instruction
and Educational Policy Studies
University of Wisconsin—Madison*

Notes

1. Michael W. Apple (2006), *Educating the "Right" Way: Markets, Standards, God, and Inequality*, 2nd edition. New York: Routledge.
2. Colin Leys (2003), *Market-Driven Politics: Neoliberal Democracy and the Public Interest*. New York: Verso, p. 4.
3. Stephen Ball and Deborah Youdell (2008), *Hidden Privatization in Education*. Brussels: Education International.
4. Stephen Ball (2008), *The Education Debate*. Bristol, UK: Policy Press, pp. 43-44.
5. Ball (2008), p. 150.
6. For support of NCLB, see for example, Frederick Hess and Chester Finn, eds. (2004), *Leaving No Child Behind? Options for Kids in Failing Schools*. New York: Palgrave, and Paul Peterson and Martin West, eds. (2003), *No Child Left Behind? The Politics and Practice of School Accountability*. Washington, DC: Brookings Institution Press. For some of the varied criticisms, see Deborah Meier and George Wood, eds. (2004), *Many Children Left Behind: How the No Child Left Behind Act is Damaging Our Children and Our Schools*. Boston: Beacon Press, Angela Valenzuela, ed. (2005), *Leaving Children Behind: How "Texas-style" Accountability Fails Latino Youth*. Albany: State University of New York Press, and Michael W. Apple (2006).
7. Michael W. Apple (2006).

Acknowledgments

Many people have contributed to the development of this book. I am particularly grateful to my colleagues, Michael Apple and Mary H. Metz, for their tremendous support and valued feedback. I also have benefited from conversations with Nancy Kendall, Harry Brighouse, Beth Graue, Jeffrey Henig, Alex Molnar, Michael Olneck, Simone Schweber, Gail Sunderman, Carolyn Heinrich, and Robert Meyer. Numerous graduate students at the University of Wisconsin-Madison collaborated in the project and gave generously of their time. This includes Joy Connolly, Joseph Donovan, Annalee Good, Jocelyn Huber, May Hara, Tracy Hayes, Kathy Price and Matthew Steinberg. My special thanks are due to Annalee Good, who provided expert research assistance at all stages of the work. James Spillane and Milbrey McLaughlin have offered encouragement and friendship throughout the years.

I also am deeply appreciative of the time and insights of all who participated in the study. The University of Wisconsin Graduate School and the Wisconsin Center for Education Research provided critical financial support for the work.

CHAPTER 1

Trends and Origins

The New Privatization

The center of gravity in public policy has shifted. Once considered relatively fringe, market principles of competition, consumerism, and incentives linked to performance, have become accepted policy strategies for improving social outcomes. Proponents of the market model claim that problems such as unsafe highways and crowded jails stem from government-run programs and government monopolies. Their idea is that if policy making is modeled after market relationships, government will become more cost efficient; government services will improve and society will benefit.[1]

This book examines an aspect of this trend within American public education—a trend that I call the new privatization.[2] In the new privatization, education policy and the market have become more closely linked. The No Child Left Behind Act (the 2002 revision of the Elementary and Secondary Education Act of 1965) has helped private firms make inroads into local education markets. The firms gaining prominence under the new privatization are drawing on political networks, new technologies, and capital investments to become major suppliers to school systems for a vast array of educational services. This includes services such as test score data storage, remedial instruction for the poor, online curriculum, and online school management.

Public monies including Federal, state, and local dollars intended for schools help fund the operations of the businesses that I describe. While drawing on public money and on the authority of public policy, the work of the new privatization is relatively hidden from view. The activities are largely invisible to taxpayers and general citizens. The firms keep a low profile. They work with school districts through a complex web of contracts and subcontracts. They sell their services under different brand names. Further, many are privately held and thus have little obligation to report their finances and operations.

The new privatization is framed as increasing access to high quality education and making government more accountable.[3] Given these claims, much more transparency is needed about these firms and their implications for public policy. In this book, I begin this project by mapping the financial and operational reach of some of largest for-profit firms in the K–12 education industry and in describing three cases of education privatization.

This book will not attempt to answer the question: Do for-profit firms in the education industry contribute to increases in student achievement? Neither is it a book that aims primarily to expose corporate greed. Both are questions in which readers may be interested, but they are beyond the scope of this work. Instead, my intention is to offer a close look at the activities and roles being transferred from the public to the private sector under new forms of education contracting and to begin to trace the implications of these trends. I hope the book will heighten public awareness of this topic, encourage us to think critically about the risks involved, and provide a basis for launching further empirical work.

In the next section, I begin with a discussion of the discourse that is propelling the new privatization. In the second half of the chapter, I describe the framework that I use to study these developments. In this framework, I draw on ideas from critical studies of education markets as well from the new institutionalism in organizational analysis.

Underlying Ideologies

The new privatization is harnessed to those broader ideological shifts in theories of economic and political regulation that are referred to as neoliberalism.[4]

Neoliberalism

Under neoliberalism we are expected to believe that the market can do everything better and that government should be *remade* in the market's image.[5] Private property rights, free trade, consumerism, performance audits, and entrepreneurs become the means for improving social welfare. Government becomes an extension of the market; it is expected to do its work and follow its principles.[6]

Neoliberalism was once a new idea and required justification. In the current decade, neoliberalism has achieved more legitimacy.[7] It is called a prudent and measured policy alternative, rather than being viewed as extremist. Neoliberalism has lodged in domestic policies and practices across the globe in part through the efforts of international organizations such as the World Trade Organization and the World Bank. Neoliberalism also has helped establish and extend the reach of multinational conglomerates doing business in the global economy. Like many movements, neoliberalism is viral in the sense that it attaches to expedient political concepts. Through these dynamics, neoliberalism spreads across policy under the cover of concepts such public–private partnership, privatization, and globalization.[8]

The privatization of government services represents an important chapter in the rise of neoliberalism in the United States. As Stephen Ball notes privatization is "not an end in and of itself but part of a mix of [neoliberal] strategies."[9] Privatization generally refers to the use of the private sector in the provision of goods and services. Arguments for privatization derive from standard market theory: As the theory goes, the higher the competition across suppliers, the higher the quality product and the lower the production costs. From this perspective, the outsourcing of functions previously performed by government creates a competitive market for public services, increases the quality of those services, and reduces costs for taxpayers.

Arguments for privatization also derive from public choice theory. Under public choice theory, government employees are motivated by self-interest as opposed to public service. They do things that will protect this self-interest; for example, by seeking funding increases for their particular department or unit. In the aggregate, the self-interested actions of government employees can build bureaucracy and make government unresponsive, claim the public choice theorists. Privatization is invoked as a means for reducing the control of bureaucracy over government services.[10]

Privatization has a long history in the United States; but in recent decades has achieved more political clout. Once called a radical idea by mainstream conservatives, privatization is seen now as a legitimate strategy for reforming government. Some policy activity has centered at the Federal level.[11] For example, the past four presidents, including Democratic President William Clinton, have promoted various forms of privatization. Congress has passed laws enabling private firms to access public funds to provide social services previously considered the domain of Federal agencies. Federal Research and Development Laboratories are being privatized. In local government, the privatization agenda also is spreading. In states such as Florida, South Carolina, Indiana, and Massachusetts, governors have privatized state transportation, prisons, and child welfare and adoption services. In Indianapolis and Chicago, mayors advocating privatization have outsourced much of the city's infrastructure including its bus fleets, parking fines, computer maintenance, and city record-keeping.

Privatization and Education

As in other areas of American social policy, privatization has become a buzzword in education circles. In education, the term covers a broad range of activities, initiatives, programs, and policies. This includes reform ideas such as charter schools, vouchers, and the contracting out of education services such as school management.[12]

Education privatization has a long history in the United States. However, before the 1990s and the era of the Educational Management Organizations, contracting for services in education tended to focus on what has been called noninstructional services or nonessentials. Noninstructional services have included things such as food service, vending, transportation, and custodial services.[13] Historically, the most commonly privatized services in K–12 education have tended to be transportation, cafeteria services, vending, and equipment maintenance.[14] There are reasons for this. First, the argument has been made that these services supplement rather than supplant the role of government in education. Second, those who support the contracting of noninstructional services do so on the grounds of cost efficiencies. By this logic, if an outside vendor can provide a service more cost efficiently than a government employee, and if the service is nonessential or represents a one-time need, then government contracting in education makes sense.[15]

However, education privatization entered a new chapter in the 1990s, with the rise of educational management organizations (EMOs). EMOs are comprehensive in nature and include companies that manage entire schools or school systems. These firms typically assume full responsibility for all aspects of school operations, including administration, teacher training, building maintenance, food service, and clerical support. Educational Alternatives was one of the first EMOs. In 1990, it contracted with Dade County Florida to manage several schools. Soon thereafter, other EMOs were established and competing for contracts with urban school districts. From 1999 to 2003, the number of private companies managing public schools (mostly charter schools) tripled.[16]

Edison Schools, the brainchild of entrepreneur Chris Whittle, is perhaps the best known of the EMOs. Whittle had built a media empire around businesses such as television marketing broadcast in the waiting rooms of doctors' offices. Through Channel One, Whittle entered the public school market. Channel One provides schools with free television equipment and in return guarantees advertisers a captive audience of students.

Whittle's next project, EMOs, gained traction, in part because it coincided with a push for public school vouchers by Republicans, under the administration of President George H.W. Bush.[17] Chris Whittle was part of what one political insider called the education privatization brain trust. This group included Lamar Alexander, former Governor of Tennessee and Secretary of Education under President Bush, David Kearns, the Chief Executive Officer of IBM, and William Sanders, Professor at the University of Tennessee among others.[18]

This was the post *Nation at Risk* era—a time when corporate models of school reform were touted as a means to turn around both schools and the nation's economy. Policy talk and action centered on decentralizing authority to the building level and holding schools more accountable for performance outcomes. Books such as *Politics, Markets and America's Schools* by John Chubb and Terry Moe argued that the democratic institutions by which America's schools had been governed for the past half century were incompatible with effective schooling.[19] It was in this political climate, that the private management of failing public schools gained a foothold.

In spite of mounting political support, in the 1990s, there were strong negative public reactions to EMOs. It was reported that Edison was inflating test score performance in its schools as a strategy for buoying public and investor support. There were rumors, later confirmed, that Edison also was in deep financial trouble; it was losing money and going into debt. Wall Street investors in Edison grew skittish after *Fortune* magazine published an article identifying the Edison project as a failure. In 2003, the company went private.

The Market Model and Federal Education Policy

The Edison experiment attracted much public and media attention. However, at the national level, another defining moment in the rise of privatization was the Improving America's Schools Act of 1994 (IASA) and Goals 2000. Under these policies, states were expected to "establish challenging content and performance standards, implement assessments that measured student performance against these standards, and hold school and school systems accountable for the achievement of all students."[20]

Several states had been experimenting with content standards when IASA and Goals 2000 were passed. States such as Michigan and California had adopted what became known as standards based reforms. Standards based reforms established goals for what students should know and be able to do at different grade levels. In the mid- to late 1990s, mayors of several large urban school districts, including Chicago, Seattle, and New York, attempted a high stakes version of standards based reforms with incentives for test score performance.

Following in the wake of these local efforts, the administration of President George W. Bush successfully pushed through Congress, even stronger Federal education legislation that had accountability, choice, and privatization as an organizing framework. As noted above, the administration called the legislation

The No Child Left Behind Act (NCLB). NCLB is commonly understood as a turning point in US Federal education policy because it significantly expands the Federal reach in state and local education programs through spending conditions linked to test score performance. The law mandates annual testing of children in grades 3-8 including children in non-Title I schools and two populations previously excluded from testing—special education students and English language learners. In addition, NCLB attaches progressive sanctions to test score performance. I discuss these sanctions in more detail below.

NCLB represents a significant departure in Federal education policy in terms of its reach and regulations. However, another defining characteristic of the law is its neoliberal and proprivatization stance. It is not just a Federal version of standards-based reform with the added twist of high stakes consequences. NCLB also is a free market Federal education policy of a scope that we have not seen before.

To be sure, NCLB is a complex law. It is a law of intense regulation and a law of deregulation. It is a law that includes serious attention to the poor, and a law that benefits large corporations. It should not be reduced to being viewed as one thing. But, in NCLB, one stream of thinking, market principles, has without qualification, become more dominant. To a much greater extent than we have seen in the past in education, NCLB invokes the need for private involvement in public education and secures public funds for use by private firms. Under NCLB, Federal education policy becomes a vehicle for stimulating and protecting the market.

In some areas, the connection between NCLB and the market model is very explicit. The obvious links include statutes that require schools to make test score targets under strict timelines. The market model also is explicit in NCLB choice provisions. After two years of not making test score targets, schools must offer parents the option of transferring to a nonfailing school in the district. After three years, the school must make after-school program vouchers available to families, paid for with NCLB funds. Over time, schools not making test score targets may be closed and their staff fired. They may be reopened as charter schools and taken over by for-profit private firms.

But there are other ways that NCLB advances the privatization agenda that are much harder to see. This more invisible aspect of the Federal privatization agenda appears in the language of statutes, in the regulations that fill in the blanks of the statutes and in the nonregulatory guidance where appropriate action is defined. Deborah Stone has called this category of policy "standing orders." Under standing orders, there are no specific sanctions attached but there is always the threat of noncompliance.[21]

One also can think of the language of regulations, guidance, and budgets as a second layer of policy. They lie beneath the laws that are the focus of popular debates. While difficult to see, these second layer policies are important windows on the current ideologies used to stabilize public policy—what I referred to earlier as policy's center of gravity. The mandates establish the rules, but the regulations, guidance, and budgets will bring the game into being. When one analyzes this second layer of policy in NCLB, it becomes quite clear how much the law's designers trust in the market. In what follows, I offer some examples of what I mean.

Second Layer Policies

First, NCLB redefines what we should expect from government in the administration of the Elementary and Secondary Education Act of 1965 (ESEA). Essentially, the law ties the roles of those who administer ESEA to the market principles of centralized data. Program managers responsible for the flow of this data now have much of their work defined by test scores.[22] There are rules about what percentage of students that must take the tests (95%) if districts and states are to avoid sanctions. There are rules about when data must be reported (how it must be analyzed, the comparisons that must be included in that analysis) and who must be mailed the data.

NCLB ties the role of government employees more tightly to data by means of a narrowing of existing procedures. The law's redefinition of technical assistance illustrates this strategy. For much of ESEA's history, state education agencies have been required to provide technical assistance linked to districts and schools. NCLB defines technical assistance in very precise terms tightly linked to the law's accountability mandates. In the language of the law, "technical assistance shall include assistance in analyzing the data from the assessments required under 111b3. It also must include technical assistance to select methods of instruction based on scientifically based research and that have proven effective in addressing the specific instructional issues that caused the school to be identified for school improvement."[23]

Budget changes can be another indicator of the shift in logic used to stabilize policy. According to figures compiled by the Committee for Education Funding, the President's proposed budget consistently has called for reductions in or the elimination of several programs historically used by states and districts to provide technical assistance to underperforming schools even as there was an increase in the number of schools not making test score targets. This includes Title V, which provides flexible funding to states, and has been used for professional development as well as Comprehensive School Reform, which provides grants to districts through states to provide technical assistance to the low performing schools.[24]

NCLB also redefines the roles of parents in ESEA programs and their rights under the law. Federal programs that originated under the War on Poverty, such as ESEA, historically have had strong requirements for parent participation in program planning at the school, district, state, and national level. Over the course of different authorizations (with the exception of the Reagan years) these provisions consistently have been strengthened.[25]

However, under NCLB, through budget changes and new spending regulations, the role of parents in contributing to policy making at the school and district level is deemphasized while the rights of parents as consumers are strengthened. For example, since the 1970s, ESEA has contained provisions requiring parent participation and representation in local decision making. The 1988 law further required that parental involvement activities be developed through meaningful consultation with parents of participating children.

Under NCLB, these parent involvement requirements were kept, but decentered. For example, in 2007, for the sixth year in a row, the Bush administration sought to eliminate funding for the Parental Assistance and Local Family Information Centers (PIRCs)—a program that provided grants for school-based resource centers to support parent involvement in schools, and the only source of funding for the parent involvement activities required under ESEA. The administration also proposed the Even Start program: Modeled after Head Start, Even Start has had some of the strongest requirements for parent involvement and parent education. Under the Bush administration, the funding for Even Start significantly has been reduced.

While the Bush administration moved to reduce funding for comprehensive approaches to parent involvement, it simultaneously increased parents' rights as individual consumers, primarily by enhancing their procedural rights. Under NCLB, parents of children in underperforming schools are given options to exit the school and to attend any other school in the district that has space and is not underperforming. Parents also have notice rights to test score data, data on school performance, and the qualifications of their child's teacher. These and other NCLB provisions linked to testing mandates all focus on the rights of parents as individual consumers over emphasis on parents' role in collective decision making.

NCLB also shifts ESEA closer to the logic of the market through the assurances that it affords to private providers of services and as discussed later, through limited regulation of these providers. Rather than simply making contracting for educational services an allowable expense (as we have seen in the past), NCLB *mandates* contracting under certain conditions. Under the supplemental education services provisions, schools that do not make test score targets for three years or more must make after-school programming available to students in that school, paid for by the district. Under certain conditions, the district may provide services. However, districts that do not make test score targets for three years or more are prohibited from providing these services themselves, although they still must pay for them.

In chapter 4, I will talk more about the SES program and its policies. For now, I offer two examples of how NCLB clearly signals through its regulations that the access of private firms to public funds deserves government protection. First, as part of its responsibilities under the law, the state education agency (SEA) is required to provide annual information to vendors about contracting possibilities. In other words, its responsibility as defined by law is to make sure that potential vendors are aware of the policy and as a result of the mandates of the policy, possible demand for their services (and therefore possible revenues). Local education agencies (LEA) also are required to provide notice to parents of eligible children about the availability of services.[26]

The law is very specific on this point. States must make this information available to vendors on an annual basis. The importance of making sure the private sector has the information that it needs is *not* a footnote in the policy; it is identified as one of the state's major responsibilities. Further, the law requires that districts that have schools with choice and supplemental education services (SES) must ensure that all eligible students participate in the program. Second, under the regulations, if the district has demonstrated that there is demand for services, and does not meet this demand (students are not enrolled, the money set aside for SES remains unspent) than the district is considered out of compliance and can face sanctions. The unspent money must be carried over to the next year and reserved again for SES.[27]

Further, as described in chapter 4, under SES, states are strongly encouraged to do everything possible to maintain conditions for an open market and to restrict taking any actions that may place constraints on that market. Specifically, while they might establish a range for what providers can charge districts under SES contracts; they are strongly encouraged to set ranges rather than absolute values on pricing for the explicit purpose of not "unduly restricting providers' service delivery options."[28] In response to comment, final regulations attempt to make more explicit the responsibility of LEAs and SEAs to ensure that ELL and students with disabilities recieve appropriate educational services.[29] In fact, as I argue in chapter 4, the nonregulatory guidance appears to takes pains to exempt private SES providers from the civil rights responsibilities required of government SES providers. The guidance states that SES private providers are in principle *not* required to follow civil rights statutes because these statutes only apply to direct recipients of Federal funds.

There is more. For most of ESEA's history, districts have contracted with private firms to provide services to eligible students in both private and parochial schools. The services for private school students must be developed in consultation with officials of the private schools. NCLB strengthened these requirements by, among other things, requiring meetings with private school officials and a written affirmation signed by private school officials that the required consultation has occurred.[30] In these and other ways, current ESEA policy clearly seeks to give private organizations more flexibility, greater access to public funds, while shielding private firms from responsibility for children's civil rights. Writing about privatization in the United Kingdom, Stephen Ball describes "the multi-layered and multi-leveled" dynamics whereby business and policy are linked.[31] Policy texts also have multiple layers, and in U.S. Federal education policy, this is where the privatization agenda is being inserted—in the dense web of rules and regulations that frame policy meaning.

In the first section, I discussed the economic and political ideologies that are the root of current forms of privatization. I ended with an argument for how NCLB introduces a new chapter in the rise of neoliberalism and how design of the law shifts the meaning of parent participation, good government, and private sector involvement toward market principles.

Understanding the New Privatization

Next, I introduce the ideas that have framed my own thinking about privatization in education. I first consider the work of those in the field of education that have probed, from somewhat different disciplinary perspectives, the relationship between markets and education policy. I conceive of this work as critical studies of education markets. By critical, I mean that the studies step outside of the immediacy of policy requirements and popular trends, and think hard about policy origins and assumptions. The studies also are critical in their concern with the policies' social justice implications. I make no claims to being exhaustive here. My intent is to highlight the lessons learned so far through a discussion of representative scholarship.

Following this, I introduce another dimension of my frame, drawing on ideas based in the new institutionalism. The new institutionalism in sociology offers a complementary lens on the role of broader cultural norms in influencing organizational behavior. In contrast to older varieties of institutionalism, it incorporates questions of agency and conflict and in this way I believe both complements and extends the perspectives of the critical studies discussed next.

Critical Studies of Education Markets

Critical studies of education markets consider the links between developments in education and broader trends in social policy. I discussed some of these trends at the beginning of this chapter. Critical studies treat education privatization as nested in larger theories and economic thinking. This kind of work always is important; it is particularly important now, because of the dominance of market thinking in public policy. One possible casualty from the rise of market ideology in education is a further narrowing of our research agenda. Rather than questioning the logic of the market, we start to take that logic as given and align our research somewhat unconsciously with quasi-market values: These questions would include, "Are resources being used efficiently? Are performance indicators being met? What are the constraints being placed on the autonomy of organizations, that can take precedence in our research design and in research funding?" The values of the market start to frame the research we conduct in public education.

Seeing the Bigger Picture

I am not suggesting that we stop asking questions about the effects of reforms on student achievement. Data under certain conditions can make more transparent inequitable and racist practices in education. But, we also need to ask the broader questions about ideology and policy. When we ask how education policy is connected to broader trends in public sector reform and when we leverage theory in this work, we are offered in the words of Stephen Ball "the possibility of a different language which is not caught up with the assumptions and inscriptions of policymakers and the immediacy of practice."[32] To do so does not mean that we remove ourselves from practice; it means that we take care to not assume, in the questions we ask, that the logic of policy is necessarily right. This broader lens is also what we need to bring to current forms of contracting in education. We need to ask, not just whether the contracts "work" in terms of saving money or increasing student outcomes, but why the rise of contracting now and what broader functions is the trend serving?

New Roles, Harmful Effects

The second issue concerns how the logic of the market moves in and through education practice. How if at all are market models changing how we are supposed to think about certain practices and the roles of different stakeholders? For example, Michael Apple talks about the remodeling of schooling under neoliberalism into a vast supermarket where all are expected to play the role of sellers or buyers:

> In effect, education is seen as simply one more product like bread, cars, and television. By turning it over to the market through vouchers and choice plans, education will be largely self-regulating. Thus, democracy is turned into consumption practices. In these plans, the ideal of the citizen is that of the purchaser. The ideological effects of this position

are momentous. Rather than democracy being a *political* concept, it is transformed into a wholly economic concept.[33]

Parents become consumers; students become human capital with their education calculated in rates of return; administrators are expected to act like managers and entrepreneurs. More than just an abstraction, this refashioning of roles makes its way into policy, examples of which I offered earlier in my discussion of NCLB.

The redefinition of roles under neoliberalism can have very harmful effects on communities. In her insightful analysis of the Chicago School Reform Act of 1995, Pauline Lipman demonstrates how the high stakes reform undermined community in schools, how it nurtured a culture of fear in some of these schools and tore apart what teachers had built.[34] Writing about education reforms in the United Kingdom, Stephen Ball describes the conflicts that emerge for classroom teachers when policy is modeled after the market. He refers to the recasting of teachers under neoliberalism as the "culture of performativity."[35] In performativity, the work of the teacher is organized around judgments, comparisons, and displays. These pressures as Ball notes can create profound professional dilemmas for teachers. In the aggregate, they can have the effect of redefining a profession in ways that are deprofessionalizing.

Gold and colleagues expand the frame by arguing that market based education services can have negative consequences on community organizations as well. In their analysis of Philadelphia's education contracting model, they posited that contracting relationships in the district made it "difficult for [neighborhood organizations and advocacy groups with limited resources]— so often important voices for equity and sustainability in a district—to take an independent stance from the district."[36]

As the model of consumerism rises, perceptions about the private sector can shift as well. I noted earlier how NCLB expounds the idea of private firms having a legitimate claim on public funds, using the 2003 regulations around supplemental educational services as one example. The law also requires that districts that do not make test score targets (which not incidentally tend to be districts that serve the poor) be eliminated from the market. As noted earlier, under NCLB, a district not making test score targets must cease being a provider of after-school programming although it must pay for this programming.

In a model that shrinks the role of parents to that of consumer, and narrows the idea of technical assistance to the management of data, there is much more room for profit-oriented firms to do work typically performed by government employees. In other words, policies of privatization create a vacuum by shrinking the role of the state to certain functions that private firms then can fill.

Political Dynamics and Market Models

Market models of policy do not simply descend onto education; they enter discourse and become lodged in policy through political work. Two strands of literature are particularly useful for understanding the political work linked to market-based education policy. One strand develops the argument that neoliberalism creates unlikely but powerful political alliances. For example, in their analysis of the charter school movement in California, Amy Stuart Wells and associates describe successful efforts by neoliberals to shoehorn a conservative charter school agenda into the broader movement for systemic reform and specifically how the Right used charter schools to gain financial support for home schooling.[37] In a similar vein, drawing on research conducted in England, the United States, and New Zealand, Michael Apple maps the ways in which the neoliberals have succeeded in bringing the interests of the new middle class (and concerns with efficiency, management, and accountability) under their wing.[38]

Another strand of literature, linked to a political perspective on education policy, employs regime theory for examining political activity in education privatization. Bulkley maps the insights of this work in the context of applying the frame to the Philadelphia contracting model. Among other insights, the work draws attention to the political dynamics whereby former district employees leave their positions and become contractors themselves.[39] Other work in regime theory has examined the political relationships that support education contracts. The relationships extend both horizontally (to not-for-profits subcontracting with for-profits) and vertically (up the ladder from district level politics to state level politics).[40]

This combined research helps us see the political strategy behind market based education policy. In my own work, I also pay close attention to the political activities that support the new privatization. I focus in particular on the work of individuals and organizations that are operating nationally. This includes former education officials now working in the private sector and using their government experience to stimulate investor interest in the education industry. It also includes large privately held for-profit firms whose business strategies are shaping the K–12 education industry. I also examine the rise of hybrid organizations that stitch together neoliberal education policy with the investment strategies of Silicon Valley social entrepreneurs.

In my analysis, I also consider how privatization's intermediaries as I call them push the movement forward through less direct political work. This includes activities such as the establishment of investment criteria for education ventures, the quiet authoring of promarket regulatory guidance, and report writing by market researchers that extols the industry's promise. I explore these and other examples in more depth in chapter 3.[41]

Present Dangers

Privatization proponents characterize the market as neutral in its effects. It may not solve all of the problems of society, but it will *not* make them worse. In critical studies of education markets, this assumption repeatedly has been challenged on the basis of empirical evidence. The heart of the critique is that market education reforms such as charter schools and vouchers can have the effect of reproducing inequalities. For example, in a review of school reforms in the United Kingdom under the governments of Thatcher and Major, Geoff Whitty argues that the weight of evidence shows that neoliberal policies reproduce race and class based hierarchies rather than replacing them.[42] Amy Stuart Wells reaches a similar conclusion in her meta-synthesis of school choice research, writing: "Whose interests are being served by this [the charter school reform]? The answer is, rarely the most disadvantaged students. And this clearly echoes research findings from the United States and abroad regarding the effect of school choice policies."[43]

The neutrality of markets also has been challenged on the ground that it serves to erode democratic processes in education. In his analyses of the choice movement in the United States, Jeffrey Henig states, that the "real danger in market-based choice proposals is not that students may attend private schools at public expense but that they will erode the public forums in which decisions with societal consequences may be resolved."[44] Henig is making a critical point about the importance of expanding our frame for thinking about the effects of privatization. Beyond the shifting of resources and authority (public to private), market-based education policies can have destabilizing effects on decision-making structures in education. This includes the basic premise that the complex nature of education necessitates collective decision making and collective input into policy design. Market based education governance is a different model of governance—based on consumerism and competition. When it is on the rise, decision-making processes anchored in principles of collaboration, collective input, and deliberation, struggle to maintain a foothold in schools. As neoliberal policies create more space for market principles, they can make less space for democratic processes in education policy and policies informed by public interest.[45]

From the perspective of an economist, Henry Levin also writes about these issues and has been doing so for many years. In the 1980s, at the outset of the current privatization movement,[46] Levin recognized the presence of a perceived dichotomy between public and private interests, but questioned its premise, writing, "a public choice approach could yield greater benefits, while not undermining the other ones."[47]

In sum, critical studies of education policy and markets raise serious questions about who benefits, who loses, and at what cost to democracy. The consensus in this literature is that the poor will bear the burden of market failures.[48] I carry these lessons into my work on new forms of privatization. My interest in the new privatization is tightly connected to my concerns for social justice, specifically whether and how the most economically disadvantaged students are faring under emerging forms of privatization. To what extent are they able to access the services and products that are intended for their benefit? What do patterns among the largest firms reveal about how much the market actually values low-income high need students? What if anything about local governance is evolving and at what cost to the democratic purposes of schooling?

What Does the New Institutionalism Have to Do With It?

In this section, I describe another set of ideas—work done largely outside of education—that further frames my analysis of the new privatization. This is the new institutionalism. Institutional theorists studying organizational behavior have been concerned with three central questions: Why is it that organizations located in diverse settings and that have little interaction nevertheless adopt policies and practices that are similar? Institutional theorists also have been concerned with the break between organizational design and actual practice. For example, why is it that, in education, there are many examples of reforms that have been faithfully implemented and yet very few examples of sustained improvements at the core of schooling? A third question concerns how broader cultural forces contribute to the stability of practices across organizations. For example, why are outdated practices—such as the one-size-fits-all approach to teacher staff development—so hard to change?

For several years, I have been thinking and writing about how ideas from the new institutionalism can be used in education studies.[49] A 2001 piece by Brian Rowan sketched the contours of a research agenda for examining the school improvement industry. This piece and Rowan's subsequent work further postioned my thinking about the new institutionalism as a frame for examining what has started to happen under NCLB.[50] Specifically, Rowan calls for more research on market processes in education and on private providers working in education as part of institutionalized processes. As noted by Rowan, much of the focus in education policy research has been on formal policies and regulation.[51] Drawing on ideas from institutionalism, Rowan makes an argument for more attention to the market and its transactions as a form of social and political regulation.

In other work, I have set out my own version of how ideas from institutionalism can be used as a framework for analyzing education policy. The thrust of this work is on how recent theorizing can be used as a lens for looking at the role of for-profit and not-for-profit firms in the design of policy, how the work of these organizations is embedded in broader cultural frames, and how the activity of these firms creates tensions and possibilities within education. Here, I offer a simple introduction to four ideas (processes of institutionalization, isomorphism, organizational fields, and field effects) and their relevance to the new privatization. In the book, I illustrate these concepts and return to the larger frame and its relevance in chapter 7.

Processes of Institutionalization

From an institutional perspective, the practices and policies adopted by schools and governing agencies reflect the rules and structures in wider society.[52] Ideas about what people should do, what the problem is, who has the expertise to solve it are the stuff of policies. Policies reflect these ideas and their broader social construction as opposed to somehow automatically solving them. Earlier in the chapter, I described how current forms of privatization are harnessed to neoliberal thinking. I develop these ideas further in the chapters that follow. Specifically, I point to the absence of empirical support for current forms of education privatization as further evidence of the institutionalizing processes at play. The market model of policy as any model of policy is based on a particular set of ideas about how the world works.

Isomorphism and For-Profit Firms

Structural isomorphism refers to the convergence in policies and practices among organizations operating in a similar environment or competing for the same goods. Organizations in that environment adopt practices that they think others view as exemplary or that are considered routine. These cues exist in the broader environment. For example, they may be reflected in public policy designs or laws; they may be visible through the practices of "model" organizations.

In education research, explanations of structural isomorphism generally have referred to the mimicking of processes across *public* entities, in particular schools, districts, and states. For example, Ogawa has argued that the popularity of school-based management as a reform strategy in the 1980s derived from institutional pressures (structural isomorphism) and schools' efforts to imitate other schools and to signal their commitment to decentralized authority.[53]

In this book, I view for-profit firms, not just public agencies, as embedded in institutionalized environments. Rather than necessarily challenging established practice and the status quo (as privatization proponents claim they will) the involvement of for-profit firms can reinforce the status quo. In their marketing materials, for-profit firms may highlight the innovative character of their products and services. Frequently, however, their influence preserves common, but outdated and ineffective practices. The firms perhaps are innovative in their forms of delivery but the content and form of educational activities also can be routine. For example, for-profit firms sell curriculum based on pedagogy that some researchers have identified as ineffective. To offer another example, for-profit firms can work in and with top-down forms of district management, rather than taking a more grassroots or decentralized approach.[54]

Policy Processes and Organizational Fields

Policy studies in K–12 education have tended to concentrate heavily on the governmental system—on interactions within and across state departments of education, school districts, and schools. Particularly, in an era in which there is a greater diversity of organizations involved in K–12 education, and in an era in which the role of private firms in aspects of policy is *mandated*, frames are needed that place nongovernmental organizations and their influence on the main stage in policy implementation.

Institutional theorists have introduced the field as a lens for examining how interactions across different organizations contribute to the building and dismantling of institutions. In this book, I use the frame of the organizational field to examine how the forces of policy and markets are converging and in the process creating a new organizational arena. In this arena, new kinds of governance arrangements are emerging where, for example, private firms make policy for public school teachers and where private firms regulate the use of public data through their own security systems.

Fields help use see dependencies across different kinds of organizations and how through these dependencies, reform ideas travel from the public to the private sector. The field frame also helps us look inside the K–12 education industry. To think of the K–12 education industry as one industry is a misconception. It is segmented into different kinds of enterprises, serves different age groups, and attracts firms with different cultures and rules of engagement. To fully understand what is happening in the industry, we need to look at different segments of the market within the field of K–12 education—an approach I take in the book in my analysis of different kinds of privatization. We can also think about the influences of the market and market-based education policy as rooted in place and time, rather than being atemporal. The processes and consequences will be different depending on the historical moment.

Field Effects

Recent scholarship in institutional theory also provides a wider lens for thinking about the effects of neoliberalism on K–12 education policy and practice. Field theorists view the settings for examining policy effects as broader than those typically presented in the policy literature, which tend to concentrate on policy effects inside of organizations and governing agencies.

In studies of policy implementation, researchers tend to ask, "Will this reform last?" "What effect has this reform had on schooling practices?" "Has the policy accomplished what it set out to accomplish?" These are important questions. However, in my research on the new educational privatization, I sought a frame that helped me account for other kinds of effects—those that lie outside of a single organization. How if at all is the new educational privatization helping to shift the policy space of local educational governance? What is the institutional debris being left behind?

In the book, I use the idea of field effects to examine what gets left behind when national for-profit firms get involved in the business of after-school tutoring for the poor, formative classroom assessment, and online curriculum. As a result of the new privatization, what kinds of firms are doing business with public schools? What new categories of organization such as venture capital philanthropies are emerging? How are the role of parent and the role of government employee being recast? It is my thesis that it is through these more institutional effects that the balance of power between the public and private sector shifts. As for-profit firms become more involved in the work of instructional reform, they change the environment for reform in ways that can linger long beyond any one policy, such as NCLB.

In sum, privatization is based on a circular logic as many powerful ideologies are. Under this ideology, markets provide the answer to the problems of government because they are markets. If the market fails, either the effects are not very important or somehow market mechanisms need to be strengthened. I sought a framework that would provide an alternative perspective to the market model and would help me ask a larger set of questions about the new privatization and its effects.

The market model assumes that markets somehow exist outside of policy and politics, and that firms operating in the market and contracting with government will be spared the institutional pressures that democratic organizations face. They will be free to innovate; they will have the flexibility to be responsive to parents' needs; they will be cost efficient and frugal all of the time. But, do the firms under the new privatization really exist in such a universe, one where information equals change and complex problems can be explained away? More to the point, does such as universe actually exist?

To come full circle, while helping me ask questions about the broader environment of the education industry, the new institutionalism provided a limited lens for looking at the social justice implications of the new privatization. Stated simply, institutional theory does not, on its own, invite questions concerning equity, access, and participation: Who benefits; who bears the burden of the cost; how are these patterns are deeply rooted in societal patterns? This is where the work of those who look critically at markets and education policy helped me enormously.

Thus, I knit together ideas and insights from these two bodies of work (critical studies on education markets *and* the new institutionalism) as a way of beginning to explore the hidden privatization occurring under NCLB and to trace its equity implications. Current forms of privatization have their origins in broader political and economic trends, and mirror dynamics in other sectors, such as health. While linked to broader dynamics, these institutional influences are not simply *done to* organizations and people, descending on them without agency. Individuals and organizations carry, reinterpret, reinforce, challenge, adapt, and submit to these trends.

While adopting aspects of the institutional lens, I stretch it in order to better "see and understand" the effects of institutionalizing processes on schooling inequalities. Metz's work helped position my thinking about the links between institutionalized processes and the reproduction of inequalities. I save mention of her work for last because it reflects the blending of the two frames that I have described. Metz' work, in particular, her argument about the common script of "real schools" provides an intellectual link between institutionalized processes and the reproduction of schooling inequalities. She argues that one function of the common script of schooling is the masking of deeply entrenched inequalities.[55]

Conclusion

The questions I ask do not have easy answers and the influences are many layered. Indeed, the more I look, the more complexity I see. For example, there are certainly places where the market can help education. In addition, there is a long tradition of institutional racism in public schools that has been sanctioned in part by government policy. Howard Fuller, who directs the Black Alliance for Educational Options in Milwaukee, frequently argues that the current public education system has run out of time. Too many children in communities of color are lost in government run schools. In some ways, Fuller's views on privatization are diametrically opposed to my own, but I agree with and fully support his conviction that radical change must happen. My worry is that in seeking this change, we settle for a system—the market system—whose costs far outweigh the benefits and which offers simplistic answers to complex questions.[56] This book represents my effort to continue thinking through these choices and issues.

In chapter 2, I lay the empirical groundwork for the trend that I am calling the new privatization. I identify the defining features of the new privatization. I look inside the market at the financial and operational activity of the largest of these firms and how they are drawing on the language of policy to do their work.

In chapter 3, I consider the political activities driving the new privatization. I pay particular attention to the activities of what I term privatization's intermediaries. These are individuals and organizations that straddle the worlds of policy and markets and who help drive the changes described.

Chapters 4, 5, and 6 each explore a different instance or case of the new privatization. Chapter 4 looks at changes in the market for supplemental programs, specifically the after-school tutoring market. Chapter 5 examines the growing market for virtual charter schools. Chapter 6 considers the rise in contracting for benchmark assessments tied to NCLB and other accountability mandates. These cases help illustrate the tensions that are emerging on the ground as the institutional landscape of education contracting evolves. But evolves how? In the next chapter, I describe and assess the shifts underway.

CHAPTER 2

Inside the Market

Education is rapidly becoming a $1 trillion industry, representing 10% of America's GNP and second in size only to the health care industry. Federal and State expenditures on education exceed $750 billion. Education companies, with over $80 billion in annual revenues, already constitute a large sector in the education arena. The education industry plays an increasingly important role in supporting public education by meeting the demand for products and services that both complement and supplement basic education services.[1]

Education Industry Association

The education industry defines itself as playing "an increasingly important role in supporting public education" with revenues nearing a trillion dollars. What is the industry selling? And, what are public school systems buying? In this chapter, I look inside the emerging education market at the rise of products and services linked to federal and local testing and accountability mandates, what I have termed the new privatization and also refer to as market-based education services.

There has been good work done already on particular segments of the K–12 industry. This includes studies of for-profit managers of charter schools, of supplemental education service providers, of educational management organizations, and test publishers.[2] However, in general, few studies have looked across different segments of the market. They have focused instead on case studies of individual companies or specific businesses.

I try to take a more integrated approach in this chapter. I look for patterns in the behaviors of firms selling to school districts as reflected in their financial and operational trends. Building on the frame I introduced in chapter 1, I conceive of firms selling in the market as part of a broader organizational field, which also includes public agencies and other kinds of organizations. I consider how different kinds of firms are approaching their work with school districts in similar ways, and begin in this chapter to identify some of the emerging issues. In addition, I examine the interactions within this field in the context of broader economic and political trends, for example the passage of NCLB and the rise of Internet trade.[3]

One could take the position that we should leave studying the business of public education to Wall Street and its financial analysts. However, I believe that the changes afoot and the level of revenue spent necessitates that we develop a better understanding of what the market is doing, based in part on the market's own reports. Thus, the arguments I make are based on comparative analysis of public legal documents—specifically statements filed with the Security and Exchange Commission and that the law requires of some companies. I also draw here on conversations that I have had with numerous representatives of the industry.[4]

From EMO to Specialty Provider

As I noted, education privatization has a long history in the United States. In the past two decades, much public and academic attention has been devoted to education management organizations or EMOs. These firms typically assume full responsibility for all aspects of school operations, including administration, teacher training, and noninstructional functions such as building maintenance, food service, and clerical support. However, education privatization has implications for public schooling far beyond what is evident in the efforts of today's EMOs. The current chapter of education privatization is being written by firms of a different kind, which have received less attention from the press but cannot be ignored. These are specialty service providers.[5] In contrast to other forms of privatization, such as vouchers to send children to private schools, under these new forms of specialty service privatization public school districts in theory maintain control of funds paid by putting out bids, writing contracts, and overseeing payment to vendors.

In the mid-1990s, district contracts with specialty service providers represented a small slice of the privatized sector in education and involved things like food service, transportation, and driver education. However, since 2003, specialty service providers have become vital players in the K–12 education market. By some reports, schools and local governments now spend approximately $48 billion per year to purchase products and services from the private sector.[6] While food service, transportation service, specialized instruction, and standardized tests account for a large part of that figure, in the past decade other sales linked to high stakes accountability reforms have become fast growing segments of the for-profit K–12 industry.[7]

Specialty services now include after-school tutoring, school improvement and management services, charter schools, alternative education and special education services, professional development for teachers and administrators and educational content providers. Some firms in the field are well-established players in the industry as textbook publishers and test publishers. This includes firms such as Houghton Mifflin, established in 1832, Kaplan, established in 1938, and Princeton Review, established in 1981. However, also represented are many new companies that were established since 1990 and even since 2002. This includes firms such as Educate (2003), K12 (1999), Blackboard (1997), and Connections Academy (2001). New privatization firms also represent a range of industries including home entertainment, Internet services, leisure products, and education services.

The K–12 education market, which was termed sluggish a decade ago by Wall Street analysts, is exploding through rapid influx of capital investments and public education revenue. Consider the direction of the trend presented in Figure 2.1. The figure tracks combined revenue levels in four market segments described next. The gradual incline (with a slight spike around the time NCLB was drafted) suggests steady growth with sales in the billions of dollars annually.

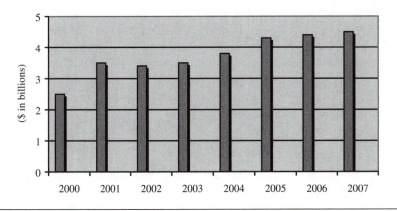

Figure 2.1 Growth of new privatization. *Source:* Estimated based on combined annual reported revenues of 18 companies representing after school tutoring, test development and preparation, data management, and analysis and on-line education content providers.

Table 2.1 Financial Data on Market Segments

Domain	Description of Services/Products	Annual Reported Revenue* (2006)	Gross Profits**	SG&A***
Test development/ preparation	Standardized test content/supplemental content	100–600	57%	35%
Data management/ analysis	Technology based assessment & school management software	70–90	60%	35%
Remedial services	Supplemental instruction after school to students who continue to attend classrooms during the day	14–100	40%	20%
On-line curricula	On-line courses & technical support	40–400	48%	37%

* Estimated annual reported revenue per company reported in millions
** Gross profits refers to how much of a profit firm is making after considering direct expenses or costs of goods sold – reported here as a percentage of revenue.
***SG&A (Selling General and Administrative) includes marketing expenses, corporate salaries and other fees not included in cost of goods sold.

Market Segments

Four functions are central to the new privatization: test development and preparation, data analysis and management, remedial services, and on-line curricula. Districts historically have contracted with outside vendors for services in each of these areas.[8] Table 2.1 estimates for each of the four domains, the range in annual reported revenue, gross profits relative to revenue, and the estimated percentage that firms spent on sales and administrative expenses annually between 2000 and 2006.

Test Development and Preparation

While districts historically have contracted with vendors to develop and administer standardized tests and to check the validity of test items, in recent years, the market for test development and preparation has exploded.[9] Key suppliers within this segment include test content and exam providers, standards alignment providers, and psychometric evaluators and providers of test-delivery services. Harcourt Education, Riverside Publishing, NCS Pearson, Houghton Mifflin, Kaplan, McGraw-Hill, and Princeton Review are examples of firms selling in this segment. In 2006, the top vendors reported annual sales in the range of 100–600 million. Firms show a pattern of increasing sales since the adoption of NCLB. Sales for 2006 were on average double the sales for 2000. By most industry standards, testing firms' gross profit margins also are high. After subtracting for test development and printing costs, firms reported gross profits of approximately 40–60 cents on every dollar earned.[10]

Historically, vendors' role in test development and preparation mainly involved creating the content of tests and materials designed to increase students' test performance. Since the late 1990s the role of vendors has expanded (discussed further in the next section). Firms are leveraging their experience in the testing market to sell more products to districts. There is software to allow district administrators to monitor teachers' use of standards and their alignment of content with standardized tests. For example, SchoolNet, a private firm established in 1998, designs and sells software and hardware to districts to manage and comply with the various accountability mandates of NCLB. As of 2007 to 2008, it had contracts with school districts in Atlanta, Chicago, Philadelphia, and Washington, DC. SchoolNet refers to its system of testing services and products as "a complete menu of Web-based instructional management modules."[11]

The modules are designed to work together but are sold separately, a characteristic of the field that I will explore in more detail later. Account is a "school performance monitoring system"; Align, a "curriculum management and instructional planning system; and assessment system." The company also sells Assign, a module to create, deliver, and evaluate standards-aligned assignments, exercises, and tutorials over the Web.[12]

Data Analysis and Management

Districts historically have contracted out aspects of data analysis and management, while keeping other elements of the work in-house.[13] However, as in the case of test development, new market segments are emerging. The top vendors specializing in data analysis and management each reported sales in 2006 of approximately $70 to $90 million. Here, as in the area of test development and preparation, the trend since the adoption of NCLB has been one of steadily increasing sales and gross profit margins.

In the 1980s and 1990s, data management products generally referred to test scanners and student information systems. Firms specializing in these products, such as Scantron and NCS Measurement Services generally operated under subcontract with large test publishers. However, in the past several years, large publishing houses, such as Houghton Mifflin and Pearson, have begun to acquire their suppliers.

Through these developments, test developers also have expanded their role. Instead of being merely designers of assessments, they are becoming designers of *systems* by which districts may pinpoint underperforming students. For-profit firms have arisen to offer such services as analyzing scores or designing computer-based information systems. In addition to compiling raw scores, most leading suppliers now offer data-interpretation services in which the district leases software to design assessments, administer them online, score them electronically, report the results, and analyze and disaggregate the test scores. Some of the software also includes preloaded curriculum whereby teachers are given suggestions for what and how to teach.

Mandated Remedial Services

The new privatization also has brought expanded opportunities for providers of mandated remedial services. Here, I refer to firms that contract with districts to offer supplemental instruction to students who perform poorly on standardized tests. Educate, Huntington Learning Centers, Club Z, and Kumon North America are examples of firms selling in this segment of the market. The top vendors in after-school programs reported annual sales in 2006 in the range of $80–100 million annually. As with other segments of the industry, the firms had high gross profit margins, although slightly lower than test development and data management segments.

In the past, districts contracted with outside firms to provide educational services for students whom the district believed it lacked the expertise to instruct.[14] For example, districts contracted with outside vendors to provide instruction for students with severe behavioral and emotional disabilities. They also contracted with vendors for foreign language instruction and driving school. Now, a growing number of districts are relying on outside for-profit vendors to provide remedial instruction to academically struggling students who continue to attend regular classrooms during the day. With services paid for by the district, the students attend after-school or summer-school programs located on or off school grounds and designed and staffed by outside firms. Through the development of this market segment, vendors are assuming central responsibility for the education of students who fail to make standardized test score targets. While new Federal policies define eligibility rules and mandate participation, outside vendors design the remedial curriculum as well as hire and train the tutors. I offer illustrations of this industry segment in chapter 4.

In 2003, for-profit tutoring companies took in $4 billion in revenue. By 2005, revenues exceeded $5 billion.[15] Sylvan Education Solutions, now a subsidiary of Educate Inc., is an example of a firm that has moved into the public school market. Before NCLB, Sylvan was the leading provider of private tutoring services. Since NCLB, its revenues have accelerated as reflected in financial statements filed with the Securities and Exchange Commission.

Online Content

Online content is the fourth area attracting industry attention.[16] Included here are sales of digitized curriculum, hardware on which the curriculum is loaded (for example laptops for children in the early grades), Internet-based technical support linked to the curriculum, and instructional materials that is used with the online curriculum (for example math blocks, or storybooks). Connections Academy, Renaissance Learning, K12, and eCollege, BlackBoard are examples of firms selling in this segment of the market.

Under the new privatization, districts are not simply buying textbooks "off the shelf" in hard copy. They also are buying and leasing software in core content areas. To get a feel for what is being sold, consider this product description by Renaissance Learning,

> Accelerated Reader is software for motivating and monitoring increased literature-based reading practice and for providing educators with student progress information to support and target instruction. A student selects a book at an appropriate reading level from a list of books for which the school has an Accelerated Reader quiz, reads the book, and then takes a multiple-choice quiz on a computer. For each book read, Accelerated Reader tracks the amount of reading practice achieved by calculating points based on the length and difficulty of the book and the student's performance on the quiz. The company has computerized book quizzes for Accelerated Reader on approximately 110,000 titles.[17]

The top vendors specializing in online content each reported annual sales between 2001 and 2007 in the range of $100 to $400 million, with all but one firm doubling sales during that time period.

Many suppliers of online content, also sell to individual teachers who pay to download and print instructional tools such as word cards, decodable stories, and student notebook pages.[18] More intensive packages offer teachers online trainer feedback and college credits possibly leading to recertification. Through these services, the vendor becomes a de facto district staff development office in providing not only instructional materials, but also ongoing technical assistance to teachers seeking to improve their practices.

To summarize so far, there is evidence to suggest that as policies based on testing, accountability, and consumer choice proliferate, the composition of the K–12 education field has shifted. Established segments of the market, such as test publishing and private tutoring are being reinvented to leverage shifts in Federal, state, and local policy. Industries other than test publishing, textbooks and educational management organizations are selling in the market. In their statements, for-profit firms explicitly frame education policy as supporting their revenue growth, as I explore next.

The Ties that Bind

There is a long history of government contracting with the private sector in public services, with much of this activity linked to the demands of social programs.[19] With NCLB, the ties between education contracting and Federal programs have been wound tighter. As I showed in chapter 1, these ties are evident in rule-making linked to the law's major provisions. Policy also is being written into the market in the context of market processes. Nowhere is this more apparent than in firms' statements to shareholders and potential investors. In these statements, firms explicitly name NCLB as establishing conditions for their growth.

Consider these examples, drawn from publicly filed financial statements. K12 is one of the leading providers of publicly financed virtual schooling. Founded in 1999, K12 leases web-based online learning supplies to schools, districts, and colleges. In 2001, K12 had annual revenues of $47 million. In 2002, (the year that the law was passed), that figure had increased to $69 million. By 2006, K12's annual revenues had reached $116 million, an increase of approximately 60% in five years. In a statement filed with the Security and Exchange Commission (SEC) in 2007, K–12 identifies NCLB as driving its growth.

> We were founded in 2000 to utilize the advances in technology to provide children access to a high quality public school education regardless of their geographic location or socio-economic background. Given the geographic flexibility of technology-based education, we believe the pursuit of the mission could help address the growing concerns regarding the regionalized disparity in the quality of public school education, both in the United States and abroad. These concerns were reflected in the passage of the No Child Left Behind Act in 2001 which implemented new standards and accountability requirements for K–12 public education.[20]

Educate is headquartered in Baltimore, Maryland and operates in a different market segment from K12. One of its primary businesses is after-school programming. Between 2002 and 2003, the firm's revenues increased 10%. By 2005, when a growing number of schools had begun to face consequences for not making test score targets, revenues had increased by 52%.[21] In its statements to shareholders, Educate Inc. attributes increased sales to the mandates of NCLB and also projects future financial growth based on the Act's mandates, writing,

> We believe the pre-K–12 education services industry is large, growing and fragmented and that the overall size of this industry has significant potential to grow as a result of a number of factors. These factors include favorable demographics, increasing parental dissatisfaction with the quality of public education, an increasingly competitive educational system and the heightened focus on school performance due to the continued failure of many students to achieve basic skills. We believe these trends will drive demand in both the public and private sectors for the types of supplemental education services that we provide.... While funding for our programs comes from a variety of sources, there are two federal government programs that are significant sources of funds for the services that we offer: Title I of the Elementary and Secondary Education Act and the Individuals with Disabilities Education Act (IDEA).[22]

These statements (and others like them compiled from an analysis of SEC documents across leading firms) offer telling illustrations of the education market's current view of education policy. Thus, in its statements to shareholders, K12 defines itself as on a mission to address "regionalized disparities created by income."[23] Educate appeals to the logic of American competitiveness by referencing "the failure of many students to achieve basic skills."[24]

In both cases, in the context of standard market procedures (reporting to the Security and Exchange Commission), Educate, K12, and numerous other firms further write public policy *into* the market by identifying it repeatedly as the driver behind their profits. My point here, in addition to showing the importance of NCLB in firms' explanations of their own profitability, is to illustrate how the market can participate in the definition and interpretation of policy. This is an example of the dynamic that Brian Rowan, in work noted earlier, references broadly when he talks about the role of market governance arrangements in public governance.[25]

My second point is that when firms shoehorn public policy into market processes, complex public issues of equity and access are reduced to economic concepts. Thus, K12 makes a passing reference to deeply rooted significant social problems such as disparities in educational opportunities linked to residential segregation. In the same paragraph, it assures its stockholders that their profits will grow. Not only is the reference to the social problem made in passing, but it also is framed as increasing the firm's rate of return. This is a troubling reflection of the idea that the growth of the education market depends on the perpetuation of the achievement gap.

Privatization and the Internet

It is impossible to talk about the new privatization without talking about the Internet. Nearly all of the products and services connect in one way or another to computers and information technology. To offer a few examples (which I discuss further in the case studies) private tutoring companies are creating online after-school programs. Rather than participating in tutoring at their school or at a community center, students attend online. The students log onto the site from their home computer and complete lessons and activities at home.

Other firms have incorporated technology into school management contracts. Firms selling virtual charter school products lease software to districts on a subscription bases (see chapter 5). Rather than purchasing the software outright, the district pays an upfront membership fee and then annual dues. As part of the contract, the firm has access to software that allows students to enroll online, access curriculum, and complete assignments, receive their grades online and communicate with teachers online.

There is work that examines the role of information technology in the rise of market-based education policy. This research usefully reframes the popularity of technology in education in terms of broader ideological and economic trends.[26] Clearly these dynamics also are at play in the new privatization. In the chapters that follow, I describe what these dynamics look like and some of their implications. Here, I introduce a point that cuts across the chapters that follow. It is simply this: The integration of technology into market-based education services offers firms clear financial gain and political advantages.

Here are a few examples of what I mean by this. Firms such as Powerschool, ecollege, CyberEd, and Edusoft automatically will be appealing to the public because their names signal something contemporary. But selling technology is appealing to firms for a different reason. It helps guarantee future contracts. In the world of technology, upgrades are always available and new products and services can be sold as necessary add-ons. Senior executives in the new privatization firms are very explicit about these benefits. To paraphrase one executive, if a contract includes some technology, there will be additional contracts for maintaining the technology. The firm usually can add on the cost of regular upgrades, which create the necessity for training, also provided by the firm to the district, but at an additional cost. In short, for the firm anyway, the technology "pays for itself and then some." It also contributes to a situation in which districts may be locked into buying more over time, from a single firm, in ways that are not always apparent to the district or to the general public. I look next at other aspects of the opacity of the new privatization.

Opaque Developments

While the education management organizations of the 1990s made national news, the activities of the new privatization firms are relatively opaque.[27] The firms have given subsidiaries a variety of independent names.[28] The public cannot easily see that a single for-profit firm is providing a large array of educationally central services to a district. Thus, while a district may establish various contracts of various lengths, with seemingly different businesses, they could all be subsidiaries of a single company.

Consider this example. As noted, in the 1990s Edison was a leading firm in the business of contract school management. It was a high profile firm, but then suffered financial losses and became privately held. In 2003, the firm announced a new business strategy aimed at expanding their customer base while keeping a much lower profile. In a 10-K form filed in 2003, Edison stated,

> We have historically focused on the direct management of public schools in the United States. Although we expect that school management will continue to be a major contributor of future business growth, we have developed strengths and capabilities through running schools that we believe can help students in other ways. We have begun to offer a variety of services in other areas such as summer and after-school programs and tutoring support.[29]

The firm sells these different products under various brand names. The Newton Learning division provides school districts with extended learning programs, including summer school, after-school, and supplemental education services. The Tungsten Learning Division provides school districts with consulting services, test preparation services, and assessments. Edison's original business—the full service management of schools—has been reorganized under a new division, which the firm calls its "district partnership division."

In its statements to shareholders, Edison specifically describes its growth strategy as "behind the scenes,"

> This business line [Tungsten Learning] developed over the past year, is built on the intellectual property developed in our directly managed schools. We are now offering these resources to entire school districts on a consultative, *behind-the-scenes* [italics mine] basis. The initial product offering is built around our Benchmark Assessment System that provides teachers and administrators real-time data on students' learning progress against year-end standards, thereby providing a powerful tool to help teachers adjust their teaching strategies to accelerate student achievement. Our service includes professional development and achievement support.[30]

The firm describes a business model in which it takes services formerly sold under its school management model, and sells them to districts à la carte on a behind the scenes basis.

Edison is not the only company taking this approach. It also is a strategy being employed to varying degrees by Plato, Educate, Princeton Review, Kaplan, and Pearson Education among other firms. As in the case of Edison, the products are being sold under different brand names, but they interlock in the sense that they are all tied to high stakes accountability mandates. Second, while sold under different subdivisions, the services are all part of the same company. They are driven by the same corporate management structure. While the revenue from various products and services flow to the same parent company, the full reach of that company is not immediately apparent to the public. As a testing executive explained, "each of the products are sold under different brand-names, but they are all part of a bigger business strategy that is engineered at high levels of our organization."[31] Another executive described how his company used contracts for after school tutoring (and NCLB mandates) to make inroads into districts that it might otherwise not have a reason for approaching, stating,

> We approach the district we have been working with in one area, and say listen, "We are already working in your buildings; we already are working with your educationally disadvantaged students, let's think about how we can approach these problems collaboratively and this is what we are selling." So our contract with the district in one area becomes the direct outgrowth of a sale in another. It gives us a reason to go back to them.[32]

From a business standpoint, this is a very smart strategy. When a firm sells a school district an assessment, it also gains entrée to selling the district a curriculum linked to those assessments. When a firm sells a school district after-school programming that is supposed to prepare students for doing better on tests, it gains entrée to selling the district classroom assessments to measure progress towards the tests. And as in the example just offered, when a firm such as Edison sells assessments, it already is planning for the next contract with the district. In this regard, the firm may call the strategy "behind the scenes," but the ultimate goal is the same: to become a major supplier of education services to a district.

Thus, as you look across firms, the trend is one of, over time, selling across different segments of the market, as opposed to concentrating more exclusively in one segment. Thus, rather than selling primarily textbooks, a firm will sell online curriculum as well as stand-alone assessments, management consulting, professional development, and after-school tutoring. Examples of firms already selling across different segments of the market include

Princeton Review, which sells tests, curriculum, after-school tutoring and school management services; K12, which sells online curriculum, application software, after-school tutoring, and school management, and Educate Inc., which sells after-school tutoring, teacher recruitment, and NCLB services for nonpublic schools.

The products sold under different brand names interlock and are designed in ways that will encourage consumers to purchase more than one product. To offer a few examples: Renaissance Place is a web-based tool that is aimed at enabling districts to centralize curriculum and assessment information on a single database. The web-based platform is designed to incorporate other Renaissance products, such as Standards Master, Accelerated Reader, and Accelerated Math. To offer another example, K12 sells technology-based services to virtual charter schools that work best when used in conjunction with K12's other products such as its online student enrollment and assessment system.

New Roles

As firms begin to sell districts more, their role within the district and the possibility of their influence expands. In the past, a municipality might contract with a vendor while maintaining its primary role as a policy setter and implementer. Now vendors are assuming responsibilities that give them more influence over critically important aspects of public school governance. Districts are paying outside vendors to assist them in the overall design and operation of accountability reforms. Firms that once simply developed tests now also play an important role in designing interventions for failing students and schools. Firms that once simply provided raw test score data make decisions that shape how schools and districts interpret the data.

An executive of a testing firm interviewed for the study noted,

> As you start to do this work [with the new assessment systems] you realize that you are getting well beyond the scope of the product per se, you are getting into as a company with curriculum development and teacher management. It's doing a lot of leading and guiding and creating a vision of what can be done.[33]

Similarly, an executive for a data management firm, described the strategy behind the firm's benchmark assessment division in this manner,

> We are not selling some districts a piece of software. We are selling a combination of things. They [our clients] are turning to us and saying, "I want to know about my kids, how to solve this problem." This is the trend, not turning to providers for one thing, but turning to providers for solutions. Saying to us, I have all these kids who are not

making the grade in mathematics, I have all this funding from Title I or wherever, I don't have any idea of how to reconcile the problem with the funding. I have all these racist issues. What can I do to customize the solution so Johnny coming from his particular environment will be able to read.[34]

In these statements, one hears executives claiming for their firm expertise that typically has been considered the domain of public policy.[35] This includes areas such a teacher management and leadership development, as in the case of the first example. In the second example, there are bigger promises. The executive expects her firm to help districts deal with racism in schools and the achievement gap, as suggested in the reference to "Johnny coming from his particular environment."

From one perspective, these activities simply represent efforts by districts to leverage the resources and infrastructure of the private sector in order to meet accountability. However, taken together, they add up to something much more. When school districts purchase products and services from firms such as SchoolNet, they are in essence hiring private firms to act as critical extensions of educationally central policy processes—to set preferences for what educational outcomes matter, to track educational outcomes, and to design interventions based on these outcomes.

To be sure, the district may continue to inform the design of these policies and systems; for example, through contract specifications. District staff may be the primary users of the systems. They may meet to discuss what the data means. However, important aspects of the design and production of education policy and direction become the domain of the firm with the contract. The firm designs the technology; it leases it to the district; it decides what to do when the system goes down; and it decides how to use or reinvest the profits generated in part through public revenues. In these dynamics, the traditional role of the public agency (as the enactor of public vision and values) is shifting, although not necessarily shrinking. Under new forms of education privatization, the district's role becomes highly technical, organized around the management of contracts and the need for greater efficiency, while substance is shaped by the contracting private entity.

To further illustrate, take the case of district-sponsored after-school tutoring. Before NCLB sponsored after-school programming, there was 21st Century Learning Grants. This is a Federal program of community learning centers that provide academic enrichment opportunities during nonschool hours, as well as during summer school, for students who attend high-poverty and low-performing schools. The theory of action behind the grants is explicitly one of power sharing between community and district.

The grants are competitive but priority goes to proposals in which schools or districts establish a partnership with a community-based organization. For example, a district might lead or collaborate with an organization such as the YMCA in designing an after-school program. In this scenario the district also hires and staffs program coordinators and, in some instances, may provide additional funding for the program.

Under the market-based version of after-school tutoring (supplemental education services), the role of the district shifts. Individual parents select an after-school tutoring firm from a list of vendors approved by the state. Vendors choose the curriculum; districts are by law not allowed to be involved in the choice of curriculum. The vendors hire tutors and have responsibility for training them and for communicating with parents about their children's academic progress. In districts that do not make test score targets, the district actually is forbidden to provide tutoring unless it receives a waiver from the U.S. Department of Education. In certain instances, vendors are incorporated into district-level rulemaking through the formation of influential advisory councils.

Money for Marketing

In many industries, firms typically spend quite a bit on advertising and marketing to build a brand name. Firms in the new privatization of public education are no exception. Typically, firms spend between 30–40 cents on every dollar earned on sales and administrative expenses as reflected in Table 2.1. Some spend much more. For example, between 2003 and 2007, Princeton Review consistently spent on average 63% of its revenue earned on sales and administrative expenses also known as SG&A.[36]

The amount of money that firms such as Princeton Review, are spending on SG&A is comparable or higher than that of firms such as Proctor and Gamble and Nike, retailers that sell consumer goods such as toothpaste and sneakers and are known to spend a considerable amount on advertising. Both Nike and Proctor and Gamble, reported spending less on sales and administrative expenses than did several new education privatization firms, including Princeton Review, Plato, and K12.

The companies in the new privatization are quite sure that investing in advertising is good business. By building their brand name through marketing, they expect to expand sales at a rate that exceeds costs and in this regard, increase their profits. For example, in 2003, Educate Inc reported spending approximately $32 million on SG&A. For 2006, it reported spending approximately $54 million. In March 2007, Educate described the rationale for its investment in television and Internet advertising:

We believe our multi-year investment in advertising has driven a high level of brand awareness and favorable consumer perceptions about our brand. Our marketing strategy relies primarily on direct response marketing using an integrated, multi-channel approach. We have found television advertising, such as our "We have a Tutor for that" campaign, to be effective at delivering a compelling message to consumers. Accordingly, we commit a majority of our advertising funds to television and Internet advertising.[37]

The sales managers of Educate described the model in a panel presentation at the Education Industry Association conference in July 2006. They reported that by investing in advertising, they stimulate parent inquiry and that one of three parent inquiries leads to a sale. Like other firms under the new privatization, Educate's business model pairs significant investments in advertising with cost reduction in other areas. In the presentation, staff referenced the benefits of a business model that could draw on a large supply of part-time instructors (on contract rather than salary).

It is not unexpected that companies are spending money on advertising in order to grow their business. However, the trend suggests broader, important issues of relevance to public education. The first issue, as suggested by the preceding example, is that money spent on advertising is money *not* spent by the firm on something else. The something else may be very important to educational quality and equity. Thus, what is more important over the long run, increasing sales or investing in full-time bilingual instructors that are experienced in providing remedial instruction to ELL students? What is more important, having a weekly full-page advertisement in an education newspaper, or investing in research on formative assessments for special education students? These are not hypothetical needs, as I will illustrate in the chapters that follow. I do not mean here to oversimplify the issue. However, ultimately we do need to ask where the money is going and where it is not going, particularly if one source of revenue is public dollars intended for economically disadvantaged children.

The second issue is an access to information issue. Plotting these basic and admittedly crude indicators of firms' use of public revenue requires digging and time. This is not information in other words that is easily accessible to the public, but shouldn't it be? Further, in order to "see" anything, one has to look at the statements of publicly traded firms. And yet, it would appear that at least half of the firms selling market-based education services are privately held. Once the money (via the contract) flows from the public agency to the privately held firm, it becomes very difficult for the public to assess whether funds are being used appropriately in relationship to public policy goals. Here is another way in which developments in the new privatization are unfolding outside of public view.

Future Risks

The final characteristic is one that I save for last because of its importance and because it offers some indications of the future. Up to this point, although in some segments of the market more than others, large textbook publishers are not dominating the new privatization. But, there are some indications that this pattern is changing.

Since 2003, merger and acquisition activity in the industry has intensified. The financial activity of Pearson Education illustrates this trend. Since 2002, Pearson has acquired six companies. This includes Chancery Software, Compass Learning, Powerschool, English Language Learning and Instruction System, ecollege, and Safari Books Online.[38] Although to a lesser degree, Houghton Mifflin, McGraw-Hill, and Plato also engaged in similar acquisition strategies during this period.

These trends suggest the possibility that the diversity of the industry, noted at the beginning of the chapter, may be relatively short-lived, particularly if revenues and competition for those revenues increase. If such is the case, and large multinational firms with extraordinary political and financial clout capture more of the market, two things are likely to happen. First, the power asymmetries that I have described may intensify. It can become easier for large firms to standardize curriculum, after-school tutoring, and benchmark assessments if they are not competing with smaller firms.

Second, the possibility for innovative, high quality products and services may decrease. I offer this assessment based in part on the descriptions and predictions of those within the industry itself. Corporate executives, particularly those on their way out of a firm, tended to be more forthcoming in interviews about what is going wrong with the industry than those individuals who write their annual reports. In conversations, several executives characterized the biggest firms in the industry as inefficient. Noted one executive,

> One thing you learn very quickly when you enter the business of education is that there are ways in which the industry does things that are highly inefficient. The big companies have been slow to change. The return of investment on this industry could be much better. A lot of work that is done is done wrong. Part of the problem, is that in the industry, there are not a lot of rewards for getting the job done well and there are not enough penalties for not doing it well. The same mistakes are made over and over again.[39]

Another executive described the acquisition of his firm by a textbook publisher as killing innovation in the firm. According to the executive, the founder of the firm believed that classroom teachers should have equal access to test score data and should not bear the burden of the cost. The founder had developed technology which he hoped would have a democratizing influence by making it easier for classroom teachers to access their students' data.

Propelled by this vision, the company did well financially. When a large publisher acquired the firm, much about the company, not unexpectedly, began to change. The big company hired more sales staff; it began to sell exclusively to large districts and it increased significantly the number of contracts. In fact, the company changed the pricing structure of the product, making the costs more prohibitive for the smaller districts with which the firm had once worked.

Through this example, I do not mean to suggest that *by definition* larger, more established firms in the industry are less innovative and less democratic than smaller firms. In several instances, in my field research, and as described in greater detail in later chapters, I encountered examples in which large firms offered families and districts alternatives to the status quo. But, according to those who have worked in the industry, big firms more than smaller firms have the tendency to adopt the kinds of bureaucratic practices for which school districts frequently are criticized.

Conclusion

In sum, it is clear that the business of education services is changing. There can be no doubt that in a number of ways, the forms of education contracting that are emerging *are* different from what has come before. Federal education policy has become an explicit driver; and its mandates surely have encouraged greater investment in testing and related products. Current forms of education privatization also come wrapped in new technologies. Furthermore, the composition of the field is changing as start-ups and firms representing industries other than textbook and test publishers converge on school districts.

That said, the new privatization is growing up in the shadow of a well-established industry that also is part of a highly institutionalized corporate culture in our nation. As in the case of other industries, much is being spent on marketing. Further, large firms are acquiring small firms as a means of maintaining their competitive advantage. In these ways, the new privatization firms carry forward the established rules of markets, and unfortunately some of the problems and false assumptions. In the next chapter, I examine the constellation of trade groups, research firms, and philanthropies that support the growth of the new education privatization.

CHAPTER 3

Privatization and Its Intermediaries

From an institutional perspective, education policy is composed of different kinds of governance structures, as noted in chapter 1. There is government with its formal policies of control, its regulations, and "moral" incentives. I introduced several dimensions of this aspect of the policy system in my earlier discussion of NCLB and its regulations that support education privatization. However, the policy environment for K–12 education also is comprised of market-oriented controls. I discussed several of these in chapter 2. One example is the use of advertising as a mechanism for spurring sales to school districts. Another example involves selling different kinds of products to districts as a means of capturing more of their revenue. These market dynamics, while not generally recognized as a form of education policy, are part of the broader governance structures in which schools and districts operate. They also are integral to the transformations underway in K–12 education contracting.

Next, I look at yet another component of the new privatization. My focus is on the actors that articulate, promote, and translate neoliberal ideas at wider levels. Here again I ask an institutional set of questions about these activities based on the framework that I discussed in chapter 1. In this chapter, I consider how formal organizations such as associations, research firms, and investors act as carriers of the new privatization and as intermediaries in the blurring of boundaries between markets and education policy.

As a means for framing my analysis of these dynamics, I next sketch the underlying assumptions of what has been a dominant model for understanding contracts between districts and private firms. This view frames the debate around district contracts in terms of economic rationality. Do contracts between districts and for-profit firms offering education services contribute to improvements in student achievement and if so, how or, if not, why not?

The premise of much of this work has been to justify the existence of education contracting based on measured contributions to school and district productivity.[1] Some of this work has focused on the inefficiencies of schools and districts themselves. It has considered the ways in which the governance arrangements of public education agencies are ill suited to improving instruction because of their bureaucracy and political self-interest.[2] More recent analyses have challenged this work by trying to show empirically that the basic arrangements of school districts (such as their size and centralization) do not explain differences in test scores.[3] Most of these studies fail to find a statistically significant relationship between bureaucracy and inefficiency and none can demonstrate any evidence of causality.[4]

There is related work that debates the efficiencies or lack thereof of firms that contract with districts to manage instruction. This research has sought to define with great precision the features of the for-profit contracting model and its impact on student achievement.[5] The underlying assumption is that if students exposed to the model are shown to have higher levels of achievement, then public policies that support education contracting can be justified. Perhaps one of the most consistent findings from this work is that more research on effects is needed.[6]

There have been other approaches to understanding the interactions between private firms and school districts, although this work has not been framed in terms of district contracts per se. For example, there has been very good work done on how districts learn or fail to learn through their interactions with outside organizations.[7] This research has addressed the ways in which district culture can establish conditions for effective work with community organizations or professional development organizations, for example. It has expanded the argument on the role of outside organizations in district reform to include a focus on growing district capacity. So far, however, the focus of much of this work has been on districts' interactions with *not for-profit* organizations.

Although building on these findings, I ask in this chapter a different set of questions about education contracting, linked to my interest in the institutional dynamics of for-profit firms. Who are the carriers of the new privatization? I refer to these individuals and groups as intermediaries because they work in between the worlds of markets and education policy. There are four types of intermediaries that I consider: former U.S. Department of Education officials, trade associations, investors, and market research firms.

Officials Turned Contractors

There long has been a widespread problem of the revolving door from Congress or agency staff positions into lobbying firms and also corporations selling services and products directly to government.[8] The move from Congress to K Street (where most of the lobbying groups still have offices) can be lucrative. Whereas a deputy undersecretary might earn $140,000, an oil lobbyist can make $400,000.[9]

There are rules about this. While in office, federal employees are restricted by law from using their public offices for personal gain to avoid financial conflicts of interest. They also are prohibited from having discussions related to their future employment in a firm. They have to disclose if they have any financial interest in prospective bidders for contracts. They are not supposed to participate in any discussions with firms in which they may have a financial interest.

While widespread in areas such as the Department of Defense, the revolving door dynamic is emerging in education. Until the current era of privatization, former Department of Education officials did not have many lucrative, private-sector job opportunities. Unlike their counterparts in Defense, they tended to move to foundations, universities, or think tanks. This still occurs. However, in the post NCLB era, the moves made by former department officials more closely resemble those of other regulatory agencies, such as Federal Drug Administration employees moving to drug companies, Department of Homeland Security employees moving to the security industry, or Pentagon employees moving to the defense industry. The outsourcing incentives embedded in NCLB have given former education officials much better options for profiting financially from their government experience.

One way to show the growing extent, influence, and high pay of the new education industry that NCLB has fostered is to itemize the movement of high officials who crafted NCLB rules that favored private providers and then moved into the employ of lobbying groups or private companies, often leading those companies to add or expand their efforts in the particular field that the person oversaw while at the Education Department.

The sources for this data are public records. The U.S. Department of Education archives information on the former employment of public officials. Documents available through the Security and Exchange Commission (examples of which I offered in chapter 2) identify current employees and provide information on their former positions, including those in positions in federal, state, and local government. Trade journals are another good source of information in the reporting of promotions and executive hires in the industry. While this information is in principle, all public, it is not very accessible. Thus, as in other aspects of the new education privatization, much of this is happening under the radar and out of public view.

From 2001 to 2007, 27 high U.S. Department of Education officials resigned, all of whom were involved in integral ways in the design, administration, and oversight of NCLB. Sixteen of the 27 assumed positions at for-profit firms selling consultative or other services and products to schools, districts, and states linked to the mandates of NCLB.[10] These private firms gained the experience and knowledge of senior education officials with deep understanding of the law and its loopholes and close political ties both to the U.S. Department of Education and to interest groups such as the Heritage Foundation with a strong promarket agenda. As employees of private nongovernmental firms, the officials possessed the freedom to lobby for policy that would protect the financial interests of the firm.

Consider these examples. Four senior officials in the U.S. Department of Education, including the former Secretary of Education, his Chief of Staff, a Deputy Secretary of Education, and an Assistant Secretary, moved from the Department to the Chartwell Education Group. Chartwell's Web site describes the firm's role as "providing strategic services to the private sector and…enhancing the philanthropic community's ability to link their investments to education needs."[11] Chartwell sells its services to governments and industry. Its U.S. clients, the names of which are undisclosed, include urban school districts that have not made test score targets, a commercially based television network which sells to schools and districts, an online curriculum company, and a firm described opaquely on Chartwell's Web site as "an educational information broker, empowering transactions between multiple government and business entities while retaining complete privacy, security and authentication as information is shared or as transactions are processed."[12]

Chartwell's niche is directly tied to the mandates of NCLB. It offers consulting services through two divisions: pre-K–12 Education Consulting and the Chartwell District Renewal Initiative (CDRI). The pre-K–12 division offers consulting services in areas including charter schools, educational outsourcing, curriculum restructuring and alignment, and educational technology. The district renewal division offers services and products specifically targeted to districts that have not made test score targets under NCLB. Districts can purchase services or products in the following areas: "school closures, unacceptably low student performance in reading or math, district operational issues like designing and implementing outsourcing strategies or compliance with state and Federal programs."[13]

Chartwell was founded by Rod Paige's former Chief of Staff John Danielson. Before becoming Chief of Staff, Danielson was a founding member and senior executive for a for-profit contractor hired by districts such as Atlanta,

Houston, New Orleans, and Philadelphia to run out-of-school programs for students who were expelled or dropped out of school. While in his position as Chief of Staff, Danielson was Rod Paige's chief advisor and the principal liaison for then Secretary Paige with the White House and Congress.

Dutko Worldwide is a management consulting and lobbying firm founded in 1981. *Fortune* magazine has identified Dutko as one of the top 10 most powerful lobbying firms in the country. One of the principals in the Dutko Group also served as a board member of K12, the virtual school provider, described earlier. The President of Dutko is Craig Pattee, who was a U.S. Department of Education official in the first Bush administration. Dutko Worldwide is described on its Web site as "offering a multi-disciplinary suite of professional services" in areas such as health care, homeland security, and telemarketing "to shape public policy outcomes."[14]

Eugene Hickock, former Undersecretary of Education, the number three position in the Department, who has long been an ardent supporter of privatization, heads Dutko's Education Group. While in government, Hickock was centrally involved in the both the design and administration of NCLB, and earned a reputation on the part of states for pushing a strict interpretation of the school choice provision within NCLB that would require schools to hire extra teachers or build new classrooms to make way for students transferring in from failing schools.[15] In a 2003 interview with *Education Week*, Joel Packer, a lobbyist for the National Education Association, described Hickock as "the force behind the department's strict interpretation of the legislation, and very strongly pushing school choice and extra academic help for students in failing schools."[16]

In 2005, Hickock joined Dutko Worldwide as part of its education group. In the press release announcing his appointment, the President of Dutko Worldwide identified Hickock as well prepared to help the firm secure a competitive advantage as a financial consultant to the education industry,

> Education is rapidly becoming a $1 trillion industry, representing 10% of America's GNP and second in size only to the health care industry. Federal and state expenditures on education exceed $750 billion while education companies generate $80 billion in annual revenues. Yet there remain few national experts in education business consulting. Dutko Worldwide is unique in this space. The firm's unique capabilities at the federal and state levels give Dutko a decisive advantage in assisting education clients and has enabled Dutko to help shape education policy at all levels of government.[17]

Thus, in addition to selling management consulting services to school districts and states, Dutko also sells management consulting services to private-equity investors in education. Hickock advises corporations in the industry on the markets generated by the laws and regulations that he helped craft.

Nina Rees is a former Director of the Office of Innovation and Improvement and one of NCLB's chief architects. While in this position, Rees directed the public school choice and supplemental education services provisions of NCLB. Prior to joining the U.S. Department of Education, she served as a Deputy Assistant for Domestic Policy to Vice President Dick Cheney, where she also worked on the passage of NCLB. Before this, Rees served as a Senior Education Analyst of the Heritage Foundation where she authored policy briefs related to its advocacy for charter schools and vouchers.

In 2006, Rees resigned from her government position to work as a Senior Vice President for Strategic Initiatives at Knowledge Universe, a private investment firm founded in 1996 by Michael Milliken. During Rees's appointment, the firm made several key investments in firms operating in the marketplace driven in part by NCLB. In 2003, it invested $20 million (the first round of funding) in K12, the provider of online curriculum and virtual charter schools. In 2004, the firm purchased EdSolutions, a supplemental education services provider. In 2006, it purchased Education Station (another supplemental education services provider) for an undisclosed amount.

Clearly, how the current contracting regime evolves and even whether it lasts depends in part on policies such as NCLB and their reauthorization. However, the future of education contracting also depends on the activities of the market-based education intermediaries of the likes of Ms. Rees, Mr. Dutko, and Mr. Danielson among others. In his work on neoliberal reforms in the United States, Stephen Ball describes the selling of education policy and how knowledge of education policy has become a trade.[18] In the United States, the move from federal education official to government contractor is part of this dynamic.

It also is part of the cross-pollination of ideas across sectors on which most institutions depend. Market-based education policy needs a revolving door because it is based on the idea that public policy should serve the interests of the market, as noted above. Individuals who move from the U.S. Department of Education to the private sector and possibly back again are important to these dynamics because they are both in and out of government and the market. These individuals have an intimate understanding of public policy, an understanding and experience that public dollars earned them. While working in the private sector, they are drawing on this knowledge and using it for the market while being freed from government regulations and the responsibilities of public office. They also are part the blurring of private and public sector roles that define the new privatization, as I described in chapter 2.

As privatization intermediaries move from positions in the public sector into positions in private firms, they take policy and their knowledge of policy with them. Concepts that former education officials/now contractors made much of while working for government, such as equity, access, and opportunity, for the time being are shelved. Instead, the value of policy is reframed without apology as financial; it becomes an economic concept. Thus, the Dutko Group is happy to have Eugene Hickock because he can help them leverage the trillion-dollar industry and take advantage of a niche in the market. A former government official is happy to be in the education industry because there "isn't much money to be made in government over the long run."[19] In these and other ways, education policy becomes more closely knitted to market activities. I look next at the role of trade groups as intermediaries in the new privatization.

Reinvented Associations

The voice for the growing K–12 education industry—in communicating with government on the one hand, and in networking with business on the other—is the Education Industry Association (EIA). Its members include local, midsized providers operating in one city or region as well as large conglomerates with national contracts. Founded in 1990 as the Association of Educators in Private Practice (AEPP), it was in the decade before NCLB a small and homogenous organization composed of small tutoring programs. In 2001, the AEPP was reorganized and renamed the Education Industry Association. In 2006, it moved its offices from Wisconsin to a suburb of Washington, DC as part of the Association's strategic plan to "build the EIA brand as an educational industry umbrella organization (beyond SES advocacy) with media and policymakers."[20]

This reorganization was in part motivated by the efforts of the EIA to increase its financial stability by diversifying its membership. Prior to 2006, the firm counted among its members several of the largest supplemental education services (SES) providers including Huntington Learning Centers, Kumon North America, and Catapult Learning. Beginning in 2006, it began to recruit membership among online organizations and EMOs. In the course of this transformation, many of the original members, the small tutoring programs, dropped out of the network or moved to the periphery as larger national firms stepped in and exerted their influence over the organization's agenda.

At the time of writing, the current director of the EIA was Steve Pines. Prior to joining EIA, Pines was the Vice President of Sylvan Learning Systems, a leading business in the after-school tutoring market. The Board of Directors has included representatives from Edison Schools, Knowledge Learning Corporation, Pearson Education, National Heritage Academies, Huntington

Learning Centers, and Houghton Mifflin. The Leadership Council pays a supplementary subscription fee beyond the association's regular dues. On the Council are represented publicly traded as well as privately held firms including Pearson Learning, Edison Schools, K12, Fairmont Schools, Kumon Learning, Huntington Learning Centers, and Knowledge Universe. Other organizations serve as corporate sponsors. This includes Eduventures, a firm I describe in more detail in the next section of the chapter.

EIA lobbied extensively to maintain the supplemental education services provisions of NCLB. In 2005, it launched a policy campaign to promote enrollment of students in supplemental education services programs because at that time demand was low. It formed a new task force to spearhead the campaign, the Campaign Executive Committee, which in 2005 consisted almost exclusively of national supplemental education services firms including Huntington Learning Centers, Catapult, Princeton Review, and Edison Schools.

In the early years of NCLB implementation, EIA concentrated its efforts on policy linked to supplemental education services. One of the group's goals was to lobby states to introduce policies that would increase and protect revenue streams for its members. In 2005, EIA lobbied for and obtained legislation in Florida that made it harder for districts to use set aside funds for supplemental education services for nontutoring purposes and to give providers more time after signing a contract before they must start delivering services. "The big providers in Florida bonded together and got the legislation passed," said Michael Maloney of Educate Inc, speaking to a July 2006 EIA conference.[21]

In February 2008, the EIA hosted its 8th annual legislative forum in Washington, DC. The session was advertised as providing members with inside information on federal policy developments, as noted in promotional materials for the 2008 meeting,

> If your education business is affected by Federal action, or if you want to make new business connections with your peers in the industry, then you must attend the Education Industry Association's Education Industry Days legislative forum. The breaking news from the Senate is that both Senators Kennedy and Enzi, are nearing completion on a bi-partisan bill to reauthorize No Child Left Behind and that this bill will be unveiled just in time for E.I. Days![22]

The February 2008 event also included an invitation only luncheon for the EIA Leadership Board. The luncheon featured Secretary Spelling's Deputy Chief of Staff, Holly Kuzmich. In January 2008, EIA prepared a white paper, broadly addressed to future presidential candidates. The paper identified core concerns in the reauthorization of NCLB. As part of its platform the group urged future presidential candidates "to set high academic standards and related academic systems to document student achievement with input from business and higher education" and to increase funding for "new techniques, approaches and methodologies" defined as including "such innovative approaches such as charter schools, diverse provider models, supplemental education services and online instruction."[23]

Even as it actively pressed for further ratification of NCLB's core design, EIA watched closely for small changes in laws or policies viewed as adversely affecting their member companies' profits. For example, in October 2007, EIA alerted its 900 members to a House Committee proposal that would limit the eligibility of for-profit firms to obtain government contracts funded by federal education dollars. The coauthors of the letter included The Software Industry Association, Knowledge Alliance, and the National Council of Education Providers (NCEP), a smaller industry lobbying group. The NCEP draws much of its membership from firms in the home schooling and virtual schools industry, including K12, Mosaica Education, Connections Academy, and Charter Schools USA. The Software Industry Association and the Knowledge Alliance, meanwhile, represent technology companies that have benefited financially from the testing and reporting mandates. An October 2007 letter highlighted both the importance of NCLB to the industry and the close efforts of groups such as EIA to protect these interests:

> Across America, non-profit and for-profit entities provide a rich array of education services, technology, professional development, assessment services and instructional materials to public schools. It is a system based on market place competition and local control over education-twin pillars of our society. Our organizations—representing both for-profit and non-profit providers of educational products and services—are concerned that language in the Committee's discussion draft for the reauthorization of the Elementary and Secondary Education Act (ESEA) will deny state and local education leaders this flexibility in making certain procurement and partnership decisions. With the distinction between for-profit and non-profit organizations becoming increasingly irrelevant, we encourage you to continue your long tradition of seeking the very best for the nation's schools. We ask that you permit a diverse array of providers, including for-profit and non-profit entities, to compete in the marketplace, and let local and state officials have final control over whom they choose as partners.[24]

This statement illustrates the ways in which the EIA seeks to influence the standards of debate in discussions of education privatization. The EIA challenges a proposal to limit the access of for-profit firms to ESEA revenues by arguing that the distinction between for-profit and not-for-profit firms is becoming irrelevant. Through these activities, posted on its Web site, the EIA further recasts public policy in terms of the rights of private firms. In the EIA statement, "market place competition and local control over education are twin pillars of society." Through this logic, when making education policy, Congress has responsibility to protect both the market and the principle of local control.

And in this and other work, the EIA has been relatively successful. It has pushed changes in policy that in essence grant after-school providers more revenue. It has formed alliances with large software firms that have credibility with investors. Thus, the EIA represents yet another bridge between the ideas of the market and policy processes in education. As in the case of the policy intermediaries described in the previous section, EIA through the lobbying activities of its members operates in between government and the market.

But, as a trade group, EIA serves another purpose. Through conferences, newsletters, and political work, EIA is redefining the organizational field of K–12 education and has established a forum for different kinds of firms to coidentify as having a shared interest in that market. As I discuss further at the end of the chapter, this creates political resources for the new privatization that may extend beyond the life of NCLB. Other aspects of the conversation are being driven by the activities of organizations whose agenda is more ideologically complex than the EIA. I examine one such organization next.

Hybrid Forms and Funds

A new breed of hybrid organization, a cross between an investment firm and traditional philanthropy, represents another important supporting organization for the new privatization. John Doerr, a venture capitalist from Silicon Valley, started the NewSchools Venture Fund. He is a partner in the venture capital firm Kleiner, Perkins, Doerr, and Caufield (KPDC). Doerr's first education investment was KPDC's funding in 1999 of Lightspan, a for-profit venture started in 1995 that sold digital content and interactive data management media to schools and districts.

The NewSchools Venture Fund identifies itself "as a cross between a philanthropy and an investment firm."[25] The fund invests in both for-profit and nonprofit firms that specialize in market themes of competition, choice, and accountability in public education. It has concentrated its investments in firms that run charter schools and in those that sell content focused curriculum. Its charter school investments have included LearnNow, Great Schools.net, and University Public Schools. Its investments in curricula include the Success for All Foundation and Carnegie Learning, Inc.

As suggested by its name, the NewSchools Venture Fund identifies as part of the next decade of school reform. However, its approach embodies elements of earlier corporate models of education reform. In the 1980s and 1990s, as noted in chapter 1, the idea gained credence that educational reform should follow a corporate model. The vision was not necessarily one of selling to districts, but transporting business models into education reform. In some of its work, NewSchools takes a similar approach. Examples of this business model are documented in a comprehensive case study of the organization published by the *Harvard Business Review* and that included interviews with senior staff. The case study identified NewSchools' typical investments as in the range of $200,000 to $5 million. These investments are structured in the form of equity, loans, or grants. The authors of the case study described the core eligibility requirements, of successful proposals in the following terms. [They should]:

> be scalable (able to expand its reach over time), with the potential to impact thousands, hundreds of thousands, or millions of students; it should be sustainable (self perpetuating and lasting), so that its impact will intensify with time. Sustainablility should be demonstrated through a sound revenue model and/or clear and credible funding plans; be led by passionate entrepreneurs who have expertise in education and business management, and the wherewithal to execute the venture's vision.[26]

The statement stitches together a mix of ideas circulating within different sectors. There is reference to the importance of leadership and opportunity, themes that have been central in education policy debates. However, there also is reference to the market principles of business management, sound revenue, measurable outcomes, and scale. In order to be considered a good investment by NewSchools, the venture or reform must reflect these standards of practice—which also reflect the logic of the new education privatization and its neoliberal underpinnings.

Traditional philanthropies typically fund proposals but remain somewhat at arms' length from operations of the funding recipients. In contrast, after it makes the decision to fund a project, NewSchools invites one of its investors to sit on the board of the company. This business model borrows directly from the venture capital approach used in Silicon Valley during the dot. com rush—a time in which investors took a hands-on approach, assuming management positions on a start-up's board of directors, and influencing operations in such areas as product design. One board member interviewed by the case study authors, said, "To get a deal done in the venture capital model, several partners have to sponsor it and at least one has to go on the board. Committing a board seat injects discipline into the process. It avoids the process of simply sprinkling money across some projects and hoping something will happen."[27]

Ted Mitchell, one of the partners in NewSchools, described the theory that shaped the firm's strategy as follows,

> There were a couple of founding principles behind NewSchools. First, we believed the spirit of energy and entrepreneurship was missing from public education and yet could have tremendous potential for changing schools. Second, we felt that the new economy approach of identifying areas for investment and then capitalizing on them was missing from public education and then capitalizing on them in a rapid way through redesign and experimentation wasn't being done in education and again could have enormous potential. We wanted to make sure that NewSchools just didn't become another foundation, so it was extremely important to us to stay linked to the intellectual discipline of the venture capital approach used in the new economy.[28]

The NewSchools Venture Fund sees lobbying as critical to its agenda. Like the EIA, it has formed powerful alliances with the software industry, although given Doerr's background these alliances were seeded from the outset. Doerr teamed with the cofounder of the Technology Network, TechNet, to push for changes in California's charter school legislation including a bill that increased the cap on California's charter schools from 100 to 250 in 1999 and 100 additional schools thereafter. Doerr described the campaign as a success:

> Influencing public policy can be a very high leverage way to create change. We spent $4 million on a campaign to put our charter school ballot on the initiative before the legislature agreed to include it in a spending bill. If you think about it from a return standpoint, over a ten year period, we will have 1,000 new charter schools in the state of California which will each receive an average of $3 million in state funding a year. So that's a $3 billion annum return on a $4 million investment campaign—an outstanding return—worth the time, worth the money.[29]

Here again, as in the examples from the Dutko Group and the EIA noted earlier, lobbying for policy change is viewed as a highly effective strategy for securing more attractive conditions for the market. If a firm invests this much in lobbying, it can expect in return to secure that much more in public revenue.

However, the vision of the NewSchools Venture Fund goes deeper than lobbying policymakers on behalf of the market. It also embodies a broader political agenda to generate empirical evidence on the effectiveness of charter schools including both nonprofit and for-profit schools. The founder of NewSchools believes that nonprofit organizations that serve economically disadvantaged students can team successfully with more powerful economic and political interests in ways that improve social outcomes for the poor. These ideas are direct reflections of the broader trend toward neoliberalism that I described in chapter 1.

The example of the NewSchools Venture Fund points to the complexity of ideologies that lie under the surface of the new privatization. NewSchools funds nonprofit charter schools that are located in economically disadvantaged communities. To offer another example, the EIA includes among its membership small nonprofit tutoring firms that are locally run and locally staffed. Seeing the ideological and political diversity forming under the umbrella of the new privatization is important.[30]

However, underneath this ideological umbrella are some of the very same ideas identified in chapter 1 as prominent in the nascence of the privatization movement. One of the partners in NewSchools, who runs the firm NetFlix, recently described public education in an interview with the *Wall Street Journal*, as the "last big government monopoly."[31] The idea that the central problem in public education is *public* governance remains very alive even though there is new money and different organizations involved.

Research Retail

I conclude my discussion of the new privatization intermediaries with a shorter example, similar in kind in some ways to the EIA, but different in others: the market research firm. Potentially as the form evolves, it is likely to become a very powerful mechanism for the new education privatization. The basic model of the market research firm would be an organization such as Eduventures, which was established in 1993 and is based in Boston.

Many of the leading firms in the testing industry are or have been subscribers to Eduventures. This includes Pearson, Edison, McGraw-Hill, Scantron, and SchoolNet. Its program of research includes formative assessment, virtual schools, and supplemental education services among other areas. Recent publications have included: "Testing in Flux: Future Directions in the Pre-K–12 Assessment Market"; "Staying Ahead of the Curve: A Value-Chain Analysis of the K–12 Assessment Market"; "Digital Content Adoption in the Pre-K–12 Publishing Market"; and "What Can Virtual Learning Do for Your School?"[32]

The firm identifies its role as "providing research and strategic analysis designed to improve the performance of organizations operating in the K–12, post-secondary, and learning markets"[33] Its role is in part one of cheerleader. To illustrate, one Eduventure's report has a section titled, "Investor Activity Indicates Continued Optimism about Education Industry Growth." These reports help signal to investors that the education industry is turning a corner and should remain the focus of their investment.

Eduventures also hosts conferences, at cost, for senior executives and senior managers. In an appropriate bit of symbolism, in 2004, the conference was located across from one of the Edison Schools. Chris Whittle, CEO of Edison Schools, referred to by some as the "granddaddy of the industry" is a regular keynote speaker at the conference, along with proindustry scholars such as Paul Peterson of Harvard University.

The Eduventures conference has tended to be part trade show, part networking forum, part policy update. The two-day conference typically includes morning and afternoon sessions that involve a panel of executives representing leading firms along with officials representing state or local education agencies that have contracted with one or more of the firms. At the 2006 conference, 100 of the 200 conference participants were district and state employees that were recruited to attend the conference and compensated for their participation through a financial voucher. Breakfast networking sessions created opportunities for the school board members, superintendents, and classroom teachers attending to "share" information about their district's reforms, also giving vendors (with interests in selling to the districts) the opportunity of passing out their business cards. Like the EIA, Eduventures plays an advocacy role for an industry in transition. It also serves the function of hosting conferences where representatives from different firms network on a routine basis and in this way, further defines membership in the field.

In the current era of blogs and Web sites, the organizational forms of market research also may be evolving. Increasingly, one finds Web sites such as edbizz in which information on market opportunities in education policy is posted and regularly updated online. On his resume, the author of the edbizz Web site, Marc Dean Millot, identifies his "personal mission" as one of "harnessing business concepts to social purpose to achieve quality, scale and sustainability in public education via market-oriented solutions."[34] In venues such as edbizz, market-based education policy and its ideas are carried to the public through new channels. These Web sites in fact may increase the transparency of what is happening in the market and the access of the general public to this information.

Conclusion

In this chapter, I have considered the constellation of individuals, trade groups, investment firms, philanthropies, and market research firms that serve as supporting players behind the new privatization. As revenues for government education contracts have mounted, many of the original architects of NCLB have traded their jobs as senior officials in the U.S. Department of Education for lucrative positions as executives within lobbying firms or firms involved in the direct sale of NCLB related products. Trade associations such as the Education Industry Association have created a networking forum for companies selling market-based education services. They have taken political action to lobby against changes in federal and local policy that limit regulation of for-profit firms selling education services and products. Market-oriented philanthropies provide money for start-ups organized around the reform principles of competition, choice, and contracting. Market research groups such as Eduventures have supported growth in the industry by forecasting what products and services are likely to sell, given consumer demand and policy action.

In summary, the new privatization has emerged and will continue to emerge through the effort, actions, and ideologies of an organizational field composed of disparate characters and interests. This includes multinational corporations representing different industries, state and national regulating agencies and legislators, venture capitalists, market research firms, and lobbying associations. Individuals working within these organizations carry ideas back and forth across the worlds of public agencies and private firms. These individuals and their organizations represent and reflect the changing landscape of K–12 education in that they are simultaneously of the private sector and the public sector. At one level, the kinds of organizations that I have profiled here would seem to be doing different things and working on very different kinds of enterprises. In fact, while separate entities, arrayed on different sides of the public–private continuum (the U.S. Department of Education on the one hand, the entity responsible for oversight of the nation's education policies, and Knowledge Universe on the other, a large for-profit firm investing billions of dollars in for-profit education companies), these entities and the individuals who work in them are part of a common organizational field. By looking at their efforts as a single field, policy researchers can better see the connections and tensions between apparently separate entities (public/private; philanthropy/investment firm; local nonprofit and multinational) whose interactions are critical to what happens in K–12 education.

CHAPTER 4

Shadow Privatization
Local Experiences with Supplemental Education Services

The tutoring industry has been transformed since the late 1990s. Multinational corporations see there is much money to be made in tutoring students after school, and are competing for business.[1] In the United States, the No Child Left Behind Act (NCLB) has helped drive these transformations through mandates that I identified in earlier chapters. Specifically, districts with schools that have not made test score targets under NCLB must set aside a percentage of their Title I funds for after-school programming also known as supplemental education services (SES).[2] Parents of eligible children select an SES vendor from a list approved by the state. SES providers may include for-profit firms, nonprofit firms, and school districts. The district pays the firms directly from Title I funds. As the number of schools failing to make test score targets increases, so does the level of funding allocated for this purpose. The funds set aside for SES increased from $1.75 billion in fiscal year 2001 to approximately $2.55 billion in FY 2005.[3]

A small but growing body of literature has examined these developments and offered policymakers a useful framework for thinking about the implementation challenges of SES and its effects on student achievement.[4] However, so far this work has examined the dynamics and effects of SES independently from its market based origins: neoliberalism. This chapter begins to address the silence in the discourse by examining SES as an instance of the broader trend toward market-based education services, described in chapter 1.

My focus is on how district administrators, tutors, school staff, and parents experience the shift toward more market-based models of after-school tutoring. The themes I discuss are based on qualitative methods; specifically, interviewing and participant observation, conducted between 2006 and 2008 as part of an in-depth study of SES in one district, which I call Riverview.[5] As part of my larger project on the new privatization, I also had the opportunity to talk with a dozen senior executives and middle managers of for-profit and nonprofit tutoring firms located throughout the United States. The latter helped frame my understanding of developments in policy and markets at the national level.

In my analysis, I explore SES as a shadow form of education contracting.[6] By shadow, I mean several things. SES represents a form of market-based education services that occurs in the shadows of the regular school day and in this regard generally has escaped notice. By shadow, I also am referencing a key concept that surfaces continually in the new privatization. This is the idea that rather than bringing something new to public education, market based education services imitate standard practices of public schooling. As I describe in more detail later in the chapter, in SES, this shadowing is manifested in the use of worksheets and teacher-centered instruction.

I also argue in this chapter that there is a fundamental issue within SES that is linked to a larger problem in market-based education services.[7] The underlying intent of the law appears directed toward not placing undue costs or barriers on providers rather than ensuring an adequate supply of services and accommodations for special needs students and English Language Learners (ELL). Federal requirements offer little in the way of adequate protection to these students.[8] The next section of the chapter describes the national context of SES and its characteristics of a strong market and weak state. This discussion, which further develops themes introduced in chapter 1, provides a framework for understanding and interpreting local experiences and effects.

Emerging Market

Since the 1980s, political support both in the United States and abroad has grown for the idea that government contracts with the private sector are the key to improved public sector performance.[9] Such market-based reforms are consistent with and part of the larger neoliberal trends in economic and political discourse, which have promoted the reforms at a rate outpacing evidence of their effectiveness. As noted in chapter 1, political arguments for outsourcing are based on the idea that market strategies of choice and competition are a necessary and sufficient condition for improving the quality of services while reducing costs.

In public statements, federal education officials have characterized SES as an open market that can support a wide range of providers, from small faith-based organizations to large national firms.[10] Current trends, however, suggest an industry that is starting to bear little resemblance to the open market that federal officials describe. In the analysis that follows, I explore several indices of increasing consolidation in the SES market whereby large national firms are uniquely positioned to capture market share and exert a significant influence on industry practices.[11]

Large Firms Benefit

While the overall number of providers is expanding, a small percentage of participating firms are positioned to capture market share by providing services across several states. Among the 1,859 providers approved nationally in 2005 and 2006, 2% were approved in at least 10 states. That large SES firms are enjoying a hospitable climate for growth also is reflected in the size of their revenue increases. Four of the five publicly traded firms approved in at least 10 states in 2005 and 2006 experienced increasing revenues since the implementation of the SES provision. Educate On-line, the on-line segment of Educate after-school tutoring saw revenues increase by 402% from 2003 to 2004. Princeton Review's K–12 Services division, responsible for delivering supplemental services, saw revenues increase by 152% from 2006–2007. Kaplan's Supplemental Education Division experienced revenue increases of 47% from 2004–2006. While revenue measures are not available for privately traded firms, increases in reported number of contracts among these firms also suggest substantial revenue growth. For example, in 2002, Huntington Learning Systems had SES contracts in 10 districts mainly in the New York and New Jersey region. By 2005, that number had increased to 126 districts, including contracts within large urban districts in other regions of the United States with high levels of SES revenue, such as Florida and New Mexico.

Mergers and Acquisitions

Tutoring companies have positioned themselves to gain an even greater share of the market. For example, in 2002, Educate launched Education Station, a business specifically targeting students eligible for SES, leveraging the "willingness of school districts…to utilize third parties to provide supplemental education and specialized support services to students," matched with "increases in Title I spending."[12] Furthermore, beginning in 2002, companies began leveraging and integrating existing businesses to compete for market share and the increased revenue potential created by the SES market. For example, in 2003, Princeton Review's Test Preparation Services division teamed with its K–12 Services division to provide supplemental services and gain traction in the SES market. The K–12 division developed content and the Test Preparation Services division provided human resources in the form of teaching techniques and personnel.

Other companies exercised an acquisition strategy. Between 2000 and 2003, for example, Plato Learning acquired six companies specializing in online instructional content: CyberEd, Inc., a provider of science courseware; Wasatch Interactive Learning; TeachMaster Technologies, a standards-based curriculum company; NetSchools Corporation, a leading provider of internet-based e-learning software and services; Learning Elements, the developer of the Focus reading and language programs for K-3 readers; and Lightspan, Inc., a provider of curriculum-based educational software as well as online products and services used in elementary and secondary schools, at home and in community colleges. The acquisition of these companies enabled Plato to provide services across grade levels through proprietary online content while also positioning the company to compete nationally in the SES market.

Targeting States with the Greatest Revenues

The largest SES providers also use their size and national scope to identify states with the greatest available SES funds and are targeting their services to these states. The largest providers gravitate to the states with highest available revenue while avoiding states with lower levels of available revenue.[13] On average, the largest providers were approved in approximately 7 of the 10 states with the greatest available SES funds. In contrast, the average participation rate among the 33 providers in the smallest states was 28.9 %, indicating that, on average, each provider was approved in approximately 3 of the 10 states with the least available SES funds.

The fact that SES companies with national scope are concentrating marketing and services in states that have the most potential in terms of revenue is not surprising. However, these trends and practices point again to the potential for increased consolidation in the market. National firms are targeting states with the greatest available SES funds while limiting their participation in states that offer less in terms of possible SES revenues. As I will describe further later in the chapter, these patterns have consequences for the ability of smaller local vendors to provide services alongside of large firms, as suggested by trends in one district.

Barriers to Entry for Small Firms

Locally owned firms have a hard time competing with large, national brand names, especially when the national brands are willing to sacrifice some short-term profits to further build market share. As argued in chapter 2, firms in the new education privatization business showed a pattern of rising sales and advertising expenses. For example, in 2002, Princeton Review's K–12 Services division spent approximately $7 million to advertise and administer its SES program; in 2005, the company spent approximately $8 million. Princeton Review's SG&A expenses for its K–12 Services during 2002 represented approximately 73% of its total revenues from SES; in 2004, this ratio of SG&A expenses to total SES revenues increased to 94%. So, while the company's revenues increased by 178% from 2002 to 2004, the amount of money spent to advertise and administer the SES program increased by 184% over the same period.

Thus, as the SES market matures, a handful of large providers are uniquely positioned to capture market share in those regions of the United States projected to have the greatest Title I revenue. There is nothing inherently surprising or unique about the dynamics unfolding in the SES industry. We have seen them many times before in other industries. Motivated by the promise of revenue, large firms are acquiring smaller firms, reaping significant revenues, and attempting to establish a competitive edge by capturing market share. Scholarship on the privatization of government services suggests that anticompetitive forces are typical in new markets created by privatization. The analysis provided above suggests that the SES market has started down this road.[14]

The Limits on Government

As noted, under neoliberalism, local government is expected to play less of a role in service delivery and more of a role in contract management. The design of SES reflects this model. For example, NCLB requires states to solicit applications from providers at least once a year. States also are charged with monitoring the performance of vendors, reporting results, and removing from the state list any vendor that has not helped students improve their achievement for two or more years. The law also places considerable responsibility on districts to manage and administer the program, but does not provide additional funds to do this.[15]

Yet there is a severe disconnect between the responsibilities and requirements of public agencies and those of SES vendors. The use of standardized tests as a measure of providers' performance is optional. In lieu of standardized tests, providers may rely on measures such as parent satisfaction surveys. In short, there are no benchmarks or standardized evaluation measures to determine the effect of the impact of an SES vendor on student achievement. This lack of parity is important particularly given the amount of revenues being spent on the provision, and it is just one example of the difference in how public agencies, compared with private vendors, are treated under the current system.

Policy Handcuffs

Under NCLB, public school systems are held directly accountable for the performance of all students. However, the law vests little power in states or districts to influence the design of the tutoring program. For example, regulatory guidance forbids states or local school districts from requiring providers to hire highly qualified teachers as defined under NCLB. It forbids local school districts from influencing the curriculum or pedagogy of the providers. It forbids states from setting absolute limits on what providers can charge per hour.[16] These regulations can have a significant effect on the character of instruction because providers are reimbursed at a fixed, per-pupil rate. The higher a provider's hourly rates, the fewer instructional hours it can provide.

Schools, districts and states are accountable for the academic performance of English language learners and students with disabilities and will be sanctioned if student performance does not improve. However, under the design of the law, state education agencies and local education agencies cannot require SES providers to make services available to students with disabilities and English language learners.[17] Instead, responsibility for ensuring that English language learners and students with disabilities have access to these services rests with local school districts. Regulations require that the design of tutoring for students with disabilities be consistent with the child's individualized education plan required under the Individuals with Disabilities Act (IDEA). However, the wording of the law also includes important loopholes that could undermine the legal force of IDEA. After-school tutoring does not have to be integrated into children's Individualized Education Plan (IEP); requirements simply encourage that it be consistent. The original legislation specified that providers were only responsible for including students with disabilities in SES programming if this can be done "with minor adjustments," although final regulations eliminated the minor adjustment standard. And in many instances, these students require more resources, in essence making them more costly and less profitable for firms.

The flexibility given to SES vendors regarding students with disabilities stands in stark contrast to the explicit civil rights laws that govern how public education agencies serve students with disabilities during the school day. Schools, districts and states must develop individualized education plans (IEP). The IEP contains approximately 300 legally required components that school staff, parents, and districts must manage and track. Teachers and administrators face lawsuits if they cannot support claims of student progress, appropriate service delivery, or due process. These safeguards are noticeably absent in the rules that apply to the publicly funded, private SES firms.

As in the case of students with disabilities, in instances where none of the SES vendors choose to provide tutoring services appropriate for English language learners, the district must provide these services itself. Further, there is no specific guidance in the SES provisions for how tutoring services might be structured to strengthen achievement among English language learners. Here again, there appears to be a lack of parity between what is required of public educators and what is required of private educators working with the same population.

Gray Areas

Under NCLB, states must give English language learners a yearly English proficiency test and must meet annual objectives to improve the scores of the students in five areas, explicitly outlined in the law: speaking, reading, writing, listening, and comprehension. If after-school tutoring is to contribute to these objectives, it needs to be aligned with and anchored in instruction in language issues and acquisition. However, there are neither requirements nor guidance specifying the need for after-school tutoring that addresses the skill areas specified for effective in-school curriculum for English language learners.

The law is explicit about the obligations of government entities to ensure the provision of supplemental education services to eligible ELL. An LEA or SEA cannot require a provider to offer SES to ELL students. However, if no provider is willing to provide such services including necessary language assistance to an eligible ELL student, the LEA must provide these services, either directly or through a contract. In other words, the LEA must serve as the provider to ELL students or find a provider that will provide these services. The law establishes general criteria for ensuring that parents of English language learners are aware of services. The wording of regulations states that the letter to parents informing them of the option must be in an understandable format; states and districts have the option of providing materials in families' native languages, but are not required to do so. Yet NCLB is explicit that local education authorities and state education authorities cannot require that teaching staff hired by SES vendors have preparation in language issues and acquisition.

Guidance prepared by the U.S. Department of Education takes pains to protect private SES vendors from the full legal responsibilities for meeting applicable federal, state, and local civil rights laws (as well as health and safety laws). As recipients of federal monies, districts and states are required to document compliance with these laws. However, for-profit vendors are buffered from these responsibilities through federal guidelines that identify them as indirect rather than direct recipients of federal assistance. As indirect recipients of funds (the district pays the vendor), the guidelines suggest that vendors are not to be held directly responsible for complying with civil rights laws as well as health and safety laws.[18]

As noted above, some good work has been done on the implementation of SES. From this work, we have learned about some of the halting efforts of local and state education authorities to provide information to parents on SES options and choices, and on the part of some states to institute minimum reporting requirements in monitoring firm performance.[19] In information that I compiled with collaborators, we found few states requiring that SES firms provide concrete evidence to back up their claims of effects. Further, at the time of our work, few states required that firms identified as having services accessible for students with disabilities or for English language learners provide evidence of doing so.[20] I will examine in more detail later in the chapter the consequences of these choices for access and availability of programming for these populations.

The trends that I have described provide another example of how neo-liberal ideas of weak government and strong market have been imprinted in federal education policy in the United States. As rights of private firms revenues expand, governments are assigned new responsibility for alerting firms to contracting possibilities. Simultaneously, the SES policy places new limits on government authority to monitor the activity of private firms and to ensure highly vulnerable populations basic rights. One example of the latter concerns restrictions on districts and states to set price limits on what vendors charge districts.

Up to this point in the chapter, I have traced some of the ways in which these dynamics play out in the context of NCLB. In the next section of the chapter, I focus on the effects of these dynamics in one district. While the action around SES is framed in and through wider level dynamics between markets and policy, its meaning is refracted and negotiated through local interactions. In the next section of the chapter, I begin to show what these dynamics look like and to trace their implications.

The Ground View: SES in Local Context

What follows is a close examination of SES practices in a large urban district based on a two-year qualitative study. I find evidence of growing market influence in local decision making around SES. I also find that while there are exceptions to the rule, there is much about SES that resembles some of the most uninspired and inequitable practices of schooling. For those children and youth who have been poorly served by public schools, the increased activity of for-profit firms has, in an unfortunate sense, brought more of the same. Much tutoring shadows the very practices that one is told contributed to the problem in the first place. The theory of government contracting is that competition and choice bring innovation and change. Based on my analysis, however, the changes that may matter most for students have not occurred, at least not yet.

Background on the District

I call the district, Riverview. It shares many of the same characteristics of other large urban districts in terms of the demographics of its student population, patterns in student achievement, and levels of Title I funding. It is one of the largest school districts in the United States. Like other districts of its size, its student population is largely minority and poor. In 2002, more than half of the students enrolled in the district were African American. Nearly 59% of schools in the district have 75% or more students eligible for free and reduced cost lunch. As in other large urban districts, Title I under NCLB thus represents an important funding stream for the district. According to statistics provided by the district in 2006, over 40% of Riverview's 4th and 8th grade students could not read at grade level; by grade 10, over 50% of its 10th graders could not read at grade level. Less than 40% of Riverview students graduated from high school.

District Steps Back, Large Providers Move In

As in other districts, Riverview students who attend schools designated as in need of improvement (i.e., those that did not make test score targets for two years or more) are eligible for SES. During 2003 and 2004, there were 43 state-approved providers in Riverview, one of which was the Riverview Public Schools (RPS). Twenty-three schools in the district were required to offer SES. Approximately 4,000 students were registered in the program. RPS served approximately 3,100 of these students, or 70%. In addition to being the main provider of SES services that year, RPS also was responsible for administering the SES program. This included establishing contracts with vendors, paying them, providing information to parents, and monitoring program quality.

By many accounts, that first year—the year in which the district provided SES services alongside private providers—the district made many mistakes. "It did not go well," said the Title I services director of RPS's efforts to be a SES provider. The problems of the first year convinced RPS staff that the district should no longer be a direct service provider. "We wanted to get out of being the direct provider and focus more on administering and supporting the other programs approved by the state," she said. The shift by the district from service provider to contract manager reflects the redefinition of government roles defined as central to the new privatization.

The district's withdrawal as a provider created more space for private providers. The following school year, the number of local SES providers nearly doubled. During 2004 and 2005, 23 schools in Riverview were required to offer SES. Seventy-nine providers reported serving at least one student in the district, up from 46 providers the previous year. Seventy-one of the SES providers were local in that they were headquartered in Riverview or the surrounding suburbs. Eight of the active providers were national firms that had contracts in multiple states and districts and had their headquarters in other parts of the country.

Since SES providers are not competing against one another on the basis of price—they are paid the same total per student allocation—larger firms enjoy a competitive advantage because they can spend more to gain access, crowding out smaller companies that do not have the economic strength to sell and advertise their programs or to do so while sustaining other hidden costs of being an SES provider, such as insurance and administrative costs. These dynamics can create important contradictions in the market assumptions underlying SES and its goals of expanded choice and improved quality of services.

Additionally, in Riverview the market for SES was not as "open" as NCLB designers claim. During the 2004 to 2005 school years, 9 of the 79 providers served a total of 2,981 students, 86% of the total number of students receiving services. Five of the firms were locally owned firms, headquartered within the community. The directors of these organizations resided in the city and all were active in local civic affairs. Three of the nine firms were national for-profit firms with SES contracts in dozens of districts across the United States. These firms had local staff; but they were employees that reported to a regional office, which reported to a national office.

In 2004 to 2005, the four national for-profit firms collectively served 37% of all eligible students as reflected in Table 4.1. By the following year, the four national for-profit firms had increased their market share to 45%. Two of the four national firms served 39% of all students served. These two firms also reported that 36% or less of the students enrolled in their programs during the 2004 to 2005 school years made academic progress. In contrast, the market share of the locally owned firms represented among the top eight

Table 4.1 Patterns in SES Provider Activity: Riverview School District 2004–2006

	Percentage of all students served (04/05)	Percentage of all students served (05/06)	Percentage change in number of students served (04/05 to 05–06)	Student-teacher ratio	ELL services	Special education services
LOCAL						
Merit	9%	3%	(−67%)	5:1	N	Y
Ballard	14%	0%	(−362%)	15:1	N	Y
Learn Group	14%	15%	3%	6:1	N	Y
Step Up	12%	7%	(−39%)	5:1	Y	Y
Urban	8%	16%	81%	5:1	N	N
NATIONAL						
Academic	4%	1%	(−158%)	1:1		
On-line	N	N				
Arise	7%	30%	300%	8:1	N	N
Norfolk	14%	5%	(−62%)	10:1	Y	N
Kingdom	12%	9%	70%	3:1	N	N

decreased over the same time period from 57% to 41%. In contrast, one local firm that experienced significant *decreases* in enrollment reported that 71% of students enrolled in their program made academic progress during the 2004 to 2005 school years.

One might interpret the dominance of national firms in the Riverview market as reflective of parents' preferences for these firms. However, this assumption is not born out by the data. In Riverview, during the 2005 to 2006 school years, 4,219 parents selected an SES provider of choice from the list of 185 approved providers in the state. 2,478 parents (58%) selected a local provider headquartered either in the same city in which their student attended school or a nearby suburb; 1,741 (42%) selected a national provider headquartered in another state. Although a higher percentage of parents selected a local provider as their SES provider of choice, the percentage of students served by national providers exceeded that of local providers.

Mirroring patterns nationwide, demand for SES in Riverview is growing slowly. For example, the number of students receiving SES from 2004 to 2006 in Riverview rose only slightly, from 3,438 students to 3,462 students.

Thus, in districts such as Riverview, when a handful of firms capture greater market share in local communities, other firms may experience a reduction in revenues. In Riverview, during the 2005 to 2006 school years, two firms achieved percentage increases in the number of students served of 300% and 70%, respectively. That same year, five of the top eight firms experienced significant declines in the number of students served, from 39 to 362%. Three of the five were locally owned.

Markets and Local Discourse

As large firms gained greater prominence in the local market, the policy discourse in Riverview also shifted perceptibly.[21] There were several indications of market logic becoming more important to how after-school tutoring was talked about, thought about, and debated in district decision making. During the 2005 to 2006 school years, the largest vendors in the district began to complain about low levels of student enrollment in the program. In response, RPS created an SES advisory council composed of representatives from large, for-profit firms. The explicit purpose of the council, as described by the district itself, was to create a forum for SES vendors to influence district policy. "We needed the advisory council to give vendors input relative to supplemental education services," the Title I director explained. The reason was low enrollment in SES. "We are not filling our seats, so if no other reason than politics, we had to create a way for vendors to feel like they had an opportunity to really weigh in and provide suggestions to the district relative to what our district role was as intermediary." Note how the district administrator described the role of the districts as a middle man between the market and schools. In a climate in which revenues flow from the district to vendors, the district felt as though they needed to give vendors more voice in district policy. Here is an example of the multidirectional influences between education markets and policy described in chapter 1. Through its mandates, NCLB created increased demand for after-school tutoring. Large firms moved to capture more of the market and public revenue. This helped trigger a response on the part of districts—in this instance the refitting of policy to market needs.

The district also hired a new full-time SES coordinator with Title I funds. She had over 20 years of experience in the district as a teacher and district administrator working in the area of community recreation. Among other responsibilities, she organized and ran the monthly SES advisory council meetings, just described. Each approved vendor in the district was invited to send a representative to the SES Advisory Council meetings. A group of approximately 10 to 20 vendors, a mix of both national and local, regularly attended the meetings. The SES director referred to local vendors as the "home-grown" groups and to the larger providers as "the nationals."

The district used an online system designed and leased from a software application vendor to process the invoices of SES vendors; this was a new system, specifically purchased to streamline payment and help the district manage increased administrative demands due to the increased number of contracts under SES. Here is another example of policy decisions cast under the logic of market-based education services. All vendors had access to the system, which they used to input data and view relevant information such as the absolute numbers of students enrolled in their program or registered with other SES vendors in the district. Through the database, vendors had access to up-to-the-minute records of eligible students and relevant student record data. Significantly, access rights were not extended to school staff. School principals and classroom teachers did not have access to the database.

When it became apparent that a few providers were serving the bulk of the students, tensions across vendors mounted. Smaller, local vendors charged that the district was not doing enough to ensure a free market; there were rumors of vendors stealing students from other vendors by luring children with gifts such as free computers. Recalling that period, the SES director commented, "We had people who were giving kids iPods for signing up or giving them $100 if they completed their 26 hours. There was all of this stuff going on. So then vendors' kids were transferring from vendor to vendor to get the different incentives they could get." The smaller vendors argued that as "home grown" vendors, they didn't have the same networks or resources that big vendors did, putting them at a competitive disadvantage when it came to offering incentives. By many reports, the incentive issues came to absorb more time in district policy discussions.

The incentive issue became a flashpoint for rising tensions between local and national providers and was raised at the advisory council meetings. Some vendors lobbied for the district to place a dollar limit on the kinds of incentives that could be offered to better level the playing field. Others argued that there should not be any incentives at all. Alerted to the problem by the district, the state department of education eventually issued new regulations in August of 2006 that ruled that vendors could only distribute educational incentives for attendance or achievement. Incentives for signing up with a particular provider were prohibited. The list of acceptable incentives included educational software, magazines, highlighters, books, or museum field trips, but not gift cards, pizza parties, or movie passes, for example. Noneducational incentives only could be distributed if they were donated to the provider and not purchased with federal dollars.

Rather than resolving the issue or diminishing the tensions, the state's restrictions on incentives appeared to incite new tensions. There were charges that some vendors were finding ways to get around the regulations through loose interpretation of the term *educational*—for instance, applying the term to free magazine subscriptions offered as prizes. Some vendors viewed the state's regulatory definition of educational incentives as out of touch with reality. "What student would enroll in after-school tutoring for a highlighter?" scoffed a vendor at an April 2007 meeting. By the end of the 2007 school year, little about the incentive issue had been resolved and the district remained in search of a solution.

In sum, as large national firms gained market share in the district, they sought more of a voice in local policy. New governance structures (the advisory council) and structural arrangements (a system for alerting vendors to schools with eligible students) were established, and were explicitly designed to serve the financial interests of firms. In Riverview, the advisory council became an important vehicle through which larger firms could voice and lobby for their interests. It became a shadow policy structure that mirrored power differentials between large and small vendors.

The council established a new arena where the interests of large national providers would prevail. The community in the form of local providers, also served on the council, but as newcomers to the business of education, their concerns received less play. In contrast, the national providers could exert considerable influence on district policy. This was in part because they served the majority of students in the district. However, it also was because when it came to SES, they "governed" a bigger jurisdiction. They were direct providers of Title I services in multiple states and, on several occasions, used their national influence to change local policy in their favor. Smaller vendors might find it difficult to compete with large vendors around the incentive issue; when they complained, their protests were blocked by larger firms who used their greater organization and institutional capacity to protect their financial interests. In these and other ways, the logic of the market and the pressure of capital inserted themselves into the local policy dynamics and decisions of SES.[22]

More of the Same

One of the criticisms of public education is that curriculum is pulled from many different sources, with the end result being little bits of information with little attention to building in-depth understanding.[23] If such is the case, then much of the tutoring offered by SES vendors in Riverview took the form of more of the same. Providers pulled curriculum from a wide range of sources. Some vendors used commercially prepared curriculum; others drew loosely on worksheets and homework assignments that students brought with them. Another designed its own curriculum specifically for SES. Depending on the provider, students could expect to participate in one hour of tutoring two to three times a week to two hours of tutoring one to two times a week. There was also variation between the planned curriculum and the in-use curriculum by vendors.

We recorded the following field note in observing one tutoring session:[24]

> We all sat down at a round table and the instructor went through each of the three students' general ability level in reading. She handed out a worksheet on Jackie Robinson. They went through the worksheet in a very structured way with lots of direct Q and A between students and the instructor.[25]

Another vendor was observed offering instruction to larger groups of students, sometimes greater than 1:10. From another field note:

> The instructor demonstrated a problem on the board to a group of 6 students at the front of the room, asking questions, and students would practice with their worksheet. While this was going on, 2–3 students were working independently on their own math worksheets and a group of 3 students pretty much just worked on homework the whole time at the back of the classroom.[26]

The time actually spent on tutoring also varied considerably. Some vendors spent the entire tutoring session on academic content; others spent only 30% of the session on academics, with the remainder dedicated to socializing, meals, and logistics. Depending on the vendor, students could also expect differences in the qualifications of tutoring staff. For example, one vendor required that all tutors be certified teachers in the subject matter that they were teaching; a second vendor only required that their tutors have a bachelor's degree.

Both for-profit and nonprofit firms relied heavily on practices prevalent in students' regular day curriculum: worksheets, packets, deskwork, homework, and so on. Specifically, there were a lot of worksheets photocopied from textbooks where students answered multiple-choice questions. In our visits to tutoring sessions, we also saw considerable evidence of deskwork. Students were seated at desks for the entire tutoring session and could only leave their desk with permission from the instructor.

On occasion, we saw evidence of differentiated instruction that took students out of the classroom and provided opportunities for students to work on interesting problems linked to the things that they were doing during the school day. For example, one provider took students on academic field trips: the zoo (and had them design exhibits and explain why certain animals should be included) and a local children's science museum. Upon their return, the students did a follow-up activity that involved physical movement, group collaboration, literacy skills, and an element of differentiation. There were these and other exceptions to the pattern of more school, but again, they were exceptions.

Limited Information for Parents

Market-based education policies are based in part on the assumption that local education agencies are not responsive to the needs of parents, particularly low-income parents. In public school bureaucracies, it is claimed, someone is always leaving early so the phone rings and is never answered; it is hard to get good information, and if one complains about services, typically nothing happens.[27] However, as described by parents, private firms, like large public school bureaucracies, also can be hard for parents to access when they need information or have complaints.[28] One parent who had initially received information from the school had difficulty reaching the provider she selected after the enrollment period. She commented, "I had to call them [the provider] several times and they started late...I don't know what the problem was but everybody else started the month before." Reflecting the experiences of the other parents at the school, the parent found the provider "hard to reach" and was left in the dark about critical information such as the program start date.

Other parents felt that they received erroneous information from the provider when they did receive contact. A parent who was active in her foster sons' schooling through the PTA and the School Council, cited her experience with one provider in particular. She recalled: "I was mad because they said they would get a computer and all they got was a hundred dollars. They were absent, see, like from school that day, and that counted against them. I felt cheated on that note." In this way, respondents frequently stated that it was not an issue of quantity of information but of quality of information. Parents felt that the information made available by providers was nebulous at best.

A guardian whose teenage granddaughter was enrolled in tutoring, stated,

> There are so many [providers] that you end up getting information on but not enough information...if you complete this class and show up then you have an opportunity to get a computer. That's one of the reasons that influenced some of the kids because there was some incentive at the end of this but yet...what happen with that computer thing? Didn't that get lost out there? I don't know that didn't anybody get one from one of the companies. I never got a lot of good information.

These comments reveal how the challenges of being a recipient of government services can be exacerbated when multiple private firms are involved in the design and delivery of those services. There is a lot of information sent to parents at once; it is hard to process or even to know from whom it is coming. A parent who was President of the school PTA and who was extremely involved in her son's schooling both in and out of the building, noted that the glut of materials may have contributed to what she saw as some parents' lack of awareness of SES. Stated the parent, "There's brochures that come out mailed to all of their homes. So you really can't say that the information wasn't made available, it's just that you didn't pick it up. [They] saw that there was [the district's name] on it, thought it was just another piece of junk mail. I'm just going to tell you that's how it is." In this way, there was some variation among parents around their perspectives on the availability of information. Some of this variation could be explained by the powerful influence of factors such as parents' ability to sift through materials in addition to fulfilling a variety of other work and family responsibilities.

Parents based their evaluations of the success of tutoring by the grades that their child received at the end of the school year. However, all respondents stated that they had little idea of what instruction was going on during tutoring sessions. As one parent stated, "I was assuming that she was getting what she needed. She got good grades, don't get me wrong, but I don't know was it because of the tutoring or because she just really understood what was going on." In the absence of any clear information about how their children were being taught, parents were understandably suspicious about how much SES was actually responsible for grade improvements. Commented another parent, "I was seeing a difference in my son with some of his work, and the last marking period, he got a 3.7, but you know, a lot of it is the parent." Parents also frequently raised the question of how tutoring services were being assessed. A parent whose son had arguably had the most positive experience with tutoring out of the children in the sample, still felt that a serious shortcoming of the tutoring program was the lack of assessment. She stated, "There needs to be better outlines as to what will be happening in the tutoring. Because I don't really recall…I think that they do evaluations on the kids but I really don't think that they do an assessment of the child. They really need to set guidelines as to the outcomes of it, what do you expect the child to get out of this, should there be an exit test, what kind of improvement they've had." Her comment points not only to the need for assessment of the children, but also accountability for the providers who, in the eyes of the parents, may or may not be meeting expectations.

Power Asymmetries

Several of the parents quoted above did not feel that they had appreciable control over the quality of the structure of the tutoring program beyond removing their child from the program or confronting individual SES instructors. Even a parent who said that she felt that she had a handle on how to make her son's needs clear to his instructor did not attempt to raise structural concerns with providers, noting,

> No, I don't feel that parents have control over the tutoring program because it's already established. So, you know, all I can do is snatch my kid out of the program, or you know, that's my right. Where I can go up there and talk to the teachers, that's my right as a parent on any given day.

Ultimately, parents felt that the tutoring services had the potential to be positive influences on their children's educational experience. Still, they felt that there were a number of glitches that needed to be worked out before the programs could have their desired effect. Parents did not, however, feel that their input would necessarily lead to changes. As a whole, the parents felt that their interventions could only be made on the part of their individual children and would not have an appreciable effect on the overall structure of the program.

At the same time, all of the respondents felt that tutoring services had great potential to enrich their children's schooling. Although they identified areas of the policy in need of improvement, the parents saw something of potential value in the SES program. As a whole, they felt that additional instruction outside of school could only benefit their children and welcomed an effective intervention with that purpose.

These patterns suggest that when for-profit firms become the primary deliverers of after school tutoring, parents do not necessarily gain any more control over insights into instructional programming. Rather, they continue to be left in the dark about curriculum and instruction. These dynamics are made more troubling by the fact some parents believe emphatically in the goals of SES and its potential to have a meaningful impact on their children's education. However, in general, they did not feel that there were opportunities to voice their concerns. These dynamics further reflect how some of the practices of public schools are carried forward in the market. Parents of color who are low-income are likely to find that their perspectives and needs for in-depth information may be easily ignored.

Who Gets Left Behind?

It is clear that under SES, for-profit firms operate with considerable autonomy in terms of how they hire, how they organize instruction, and how much or how little information is provided to parents. In these ways, for-profit firms can sometimes resemble and reproduce some of the inequitable practices of public schools. Under market based education policies, there may be fewer safeguards for ensuring access and participation for students with disabilities and English language learners.

Consider the following. During the 2005 to 2006 school year approximately 33% of 9,173 eligible SES students were registered for SES, and 19% of eligible students attended at least one tutoring session. The law required that districts ensure that SES services were made available to students with special needs. However, the regulations indicated that compliance could involve simply making sure that at least one vendor, or if not the vendor then the district, offered services that were appropriate for English language learners and special education students. The state simply required that in their end-of-year reports, vendors indicate whether they had services accessible to these populations by checking a box. The vendors responded to this flexibility in general by deciding not to make their services available to English language learners or special education students.

In some respects, large national providers are well positioned to provide supplemental education services that are individualized. First, they have other educational divisions and in this way have the capacity to integrate SES with other services and products. For example, large multidivisional firms also contract with districts for regular-day special education services, curriculum, test score analysis, and professional development. They already have the technology and staff to diagnose students' needs and to pair students with special services. As explored earlier, they also have sizeable and multiple revenue streams that they might potentially invest in developing innovative approaches to making supplemental education services accessible to English language learners and special needs students.

However, on this principle as in others, the claims of a market-based approach to supplemental education instruction have yet to materialize. In the district, as revenues for large providers accelerated, products and services for serving disadvantaged students, particularly English language learners and special education students remained flat. Among the top eight providers serving 86% of the market in 2004 to 2005, only one provider reported having Spanish-speaking staff and none reported staff or materials available for non-Spanish speaking English language learner students—a critical condition if services are to be accessible to students with limited English proficiency. None of the national firms represented among the top eight providers in 2004 to 2005 reported offering services appropriate to students with special needs. This contributed to a situation in which students with special needs could be denied access to SES services.

An SES administrative assistant for the program had considerable contact with parents. In that position, she also witnessed how the market could leave students with disabilities and their parents out in the dark.

> You know there are only certain vendors in RPS that handle special needs kids and you know, they don't tell the parents [if they aren't],

because a lot of these parents are signing up for these groups that don't offer special needs tutoring at all and they then have to find another group and then the parents are kind of left out in the dark so to speak. We had an issue this year with a child at one of the middle schools. His primary problem was that he was physically disabled so he had to have accommodations somewhere for his wheelchair and some academic stuff. I think it was going to be at his home or something but anyway the tutoring provider dropped the kid because he was special needs because of the wheelchair and also he had some learning disabilities. The tutoring group called here to have us find another group for the parent. And then I talked to the mother, and she seemed quite over-whelmed, you know and so I told the schools to help this parent out and nobody helped this parent out.

Similarly, school administrators were concerned about both their special education and ELL students having access to the same level of choice and quality in SES services as other eligible students:

With us, we don't really have [providers] that can meet the needs of our English Language Learners, our special education students, okay? So, and that's a large population and right now with the whole testing and accountability, and now they're adding language as another "got you" to the schools, and if you don't make progress in acquiring English skills, now you're zapped too as not meeting AYP.

In addition to a lack of administrative services, none of the providers had evidence of curriculum materials specifically targeted to English language learner students and only one tutor was observed formatting instruction for English language learner students (lessons were conducted in Spanish). A tutor talked about a student with whom she had a difficult time communicat-ing and therefore was showing little progress. She explained her frustration: "Those students…they have learned to speak a different language first. I feel that if I had the teaching tools of teaching English as a second language they would be far more accepted than the tools that I may have to work with." The tutor, who was not bilingual, described ways in which she compensated for the lack of an English language learner curriculum or instructional tools:

It is an issue because the very first time I was in High School I was in a room with 16 students, 2 of which spoke some English, the rest of them only spoke Spanish. How effective can that be? You know? So since then we worked into a pattern which is helpful and there are students that do know the English language well enough and are compassionate personality-wise that they step up and help each other.

Although this compromise may have been "good enough" to get though the tutoring sessions, it is certain that these students were not getting the same quality of tutoring services available to English proficient students. This represents a significant access barrier for a critical population of students eligible for SES services.

Conclusion

The idea of supplemental education services has many promising features. It is a good idea to provide economically disadvantaged students with expanded opportunities for academic after-school tutoring to help level the playing field. As designed, however, I believe SES has little promise for ensuring that after-school programming adds value for the students for whom it was intended.

In the first part of the chapter, I discussed the transformations underway in the United States in the tutoring market, the increasing activity of large corporate firms paired with controls on government. In SES, the idea is that the market will govern itself with minimal oversight from government (as reflected in the legal constraints on state and district authority). The second part of the chapter described how these ideas (the assumption that the market will do the work of government so government should help the market do its work) made the journey through a school district in the early years of enacting the SES mandates. I offered several examples of how the design of SES policy (strong market/weak state) was mirrored in local dynamics—what issues were afforded the most attention (incentives) and what issues were not (access by students with disabilities and ELL students). These dynamics contributed to a situation in which those for whom NCLB funds in part were intended faced continued inequities. Parents were left in the dark about programming; some students were restricted from programming all together.

Working under very difficult circumstances, some instructors and program directors found ways to provide students with enriched curriculum (connected to what they were learning during the school day but differentiated in terms of format) and with some opportunity for personalized learning. Vendors of online curriculum created alternatives for older students who wanted to participate in tutoring but had responsibility for younger siblings. However, these innovations were exceptions to the rule. What generally emerged as firms' standard tutoring practices took the form of "more of the same"—more worksheets, more large groups, little communication across instructors. The problems of the school day curriculum were replicated and reinforced in a setting in which for-profit private firms were afforded more resources and as I have argued more influence. If SES is to make a significant difference in the lives of students, the tendency of even private, for-profit firms to drift toward uninspired practices must be acknowledged and addressed.

Thus, what the experience of Riverview helps reveal is how deeply entangled the market is with the institutionalized practices of schooling. More often than not, privately designed, publicly funded tutoring provided students with more of the same. The case of Riverview also shows the relevance of the organizational field as a frame for examining market/policy dynamics. It is inaccurate to think about the implementation of SES as a top-down relationship that starts with federal policy and works its way in a somewhat linear fashion, down and through state and district context and into schools. This view is reflected in literature and statements that identify states' and districts' weak implementation as the reason why demand for SES has remained low. Particularly in the policy environment described in chapter 1, how students experience current education initiatives involves a complex interface that includes private firms, public agencies, and their respective policies. In the case of SES, these dynamics, which can have very important consequences for children and families over time, operate in the shadows of the regular day curriculum. What are the risks and possibilities of these more hidden forms of privatization? How do the dynamics contribute to shifts in who participates in policy discussions and who is marginalized? I continue asking these and other questions in the discussion of virtual schooling that follows.

CHAPTER 5

Invisible Influences

For-Profit Firms and Virtual Charter Schools

Virtual schooling is a fast growing segment of the education market. The first virtual K–12 school was opened in the mid-1990s. According to a recent estimate, virtual schools in the United States enroll over 139,000 students and growth continues at an annual rate of over 30% per year.[1] More than 36% of all U.S. school districts offer an online class. Two of the oldest virtual schools in the country, Utah's Electronic High and Florida's Virtual School, each doubled their enrollment since 2002 and now serve approximately 15,000 to 35,000 students each.[2] K12 Inc., established in 1999, currently enrolls approximately 27,000 students.[3] Between 2004 and 2007, it increased its enrollment at an annual rate of 35% and nearly doubled its revenue, from $71.4 million in 2004 to $140 million in 2007.

One touted aspect of virtual schools is the fact that teaching and class work happen online through the Internet and the Web. Freed from the constraints of an actual school building, virtual schools are advertised as providing learning anytime and anywhere. A student logs onto a computer and onto a server. At the computer, the student completes and submits assignments. Teachers in virtual schools grade online, communicate with students and parents online and on occasion, teach a "live" class by means of interactive technology.[4]

Some virtual schools are private schools supported through private tuition. But, increasingly, virtual schools also can be public schools. They are paid for with public revenue; they have a public school identification number; they hire public school teachers and administrators. Whereas in the past, the district might choose to offer one or two courses online, virtual charter schools are designed to provide students with a full day's curriculum. In completing a sequence of classes, students also can advance across grade levels. When students graduate from the school, they receive public school high school diplomas. In virtual charter schools, students also can live hundreds of miles way from the district in which the school is "located."

The school districts contract with private companies for the technology (curriculum, management services, and technical support) and pay firms with local, state, and sometimes federal funds. Depending on the scope of service, a firm can charge the district up to the full per pupil amount allocated by the state. By some estimates, online learning costs an average of $3,000 to $5,000 per student a year.[5]

As the number of virtual schools increase, proponents are making broad claims about their benefits. Virtual schools are described as closing the achievement gap between students living in poverty and those living in more economically advantaged communities. Virtual schools, it is argued, create alternatives for students with severe emotional and behavioral problems, for whom attending schools in regular classrooms may prove difficult. In addition, and as described in more detail in the next section, federal officials also identify virtual schools as potentially expanding choice and opportunity for low-income students and as addressing the shortage of qualified teachers in low-income communities.[6]

Much of the market discourse emphasizes the public and private benefits of virtual schools. By investing in virtual schools, it is argued that taxpayers and policymakers can address poverty and also can save money. Consider the statement of one of the largest virtual charter school companies,

> Many states have embraced virtual public schools as a means to provide families with a publicly funded alternative to a traditional classroom-based education. For parents who believe that their child is not thriving and for whom relocating or private schools is not an option, virtual public schools can provide a compelling choice. This widespread availability makes them the "most public of schools." From an educational policy standpoint, virtual public schools often represent a savings to the taxpayers when compared with traditional public schools because they are generally funded at a lower per-pupil state average reported by the U.S. Department of Education. Finally, because parents are not required to pay tuition, virtual public schools make our learning system available to the broadest range of students.[7]

In these and other statements, firms frame virtual schools as having both economic and social benefits. They make (passing) reference to the inequities of schooling linked to residential segregation and the importance of providing choices to low-income parents who cannot afford private schools. At the same time, indeed in the same paragraph, virtual schooling is framed in very economic terms as offering taxpayers a cheaper form of public schooling.

While the number of students enrolled in virtual schools increases, the literature on virtual schools is limited. As of 2007, there were only a handful of published studies examining the trends. This includes a meta-synthesis of quantitative studies conducted between 1993 and 1997 that examined the academic effects of online learning,[8] a one year evaluation of the Virtual High School,[9] and several policy briefs published by federally funded regional laboratories which included some descriptive survey data.[10]

This work is useful in mapping the scope of the developments and in providing a framework for considering achievement effects. However, with a few exceptions, the literature does not consider how virtual schooling is linked to broader trends in the K–12 education industry and to neoliberal policies. Further, where the literature treats policy issues, it focuses on state or federal level developments, and does not look critically at some of the assumptions behind the trends.[11]

In this chapter, I argue that virtual schooling further illustrates the rise of market based public education, its relatively invisible influences on local policy, and its reproduction of inequities. I will spend time in the chapter describing what contracts between virtual school firms and K–12 public districts involve in practice—the decisions and players involved and the tensions that erupt. My focus is two districts: one rural and one semiurban. Each district contracts with one or more for-profit firms selling products and services in the virtual school market. By focusing on local practice as framed by wider dynamics, I continue the work I began in chapter 4 in my parallel analysis of supplemental education services.

Double Drivers: Technology and Federal Policy

Before turning to the two districts and their experiences, I look first at wider policy and market dynamics that frame what is happening locally. I focus on two aspects of this broader context: developments in technology that have increased profit margins for firms selling virtual schooling and federal actions that have recast virtual schools as closely linked to the goals of federal education programs. Here again, as I will show, federal policy is being used to lay the ideological and political groundwork for local education contracts.[12]

The Financial Benefits of Technology

In the past, distance learning involved correspondence by mail and the use of tapes, CDs, and videoconferencing. In virtual education, the primary tools are the Internet and the Web. The student can access curriculum and complete courses online. She communicates with teachers via e-mail and instant messaging. Teachers assign work and grade it online. School administrators send updates and instructions to teachers via the school server. In short, nearly everything involved in the organization of schooling happens online. From the perspective of companies in the education business, the technology serves another purpose. It provides a rationale for approaching districts with an offer.

As noted earlier, in the past, districts have been more likely to contract for noninstructional services, such as payroll, than for instruction. For a district to contract with a firm for instruction, it needs a compelling reason. In the case of supplemental education services as described in the previous chapter, the reason is a federal mandate. Federal policy requires districts to contract with outside firms for after-school tutoring. Virtual schools present a somewhat different case. There are no laws that require districts to contract. However, hundreds of school districts across the United States *are* struggling with revenue shortfalls.

Now, virtual school companies can argue that by contracting with for-profit firms for instruction, the district can increase revenue. How is this possible? The arrangement looks something like this: The district obtains authorization to open a charter school. It contracts with one or more firms for the technology to enroll students from other districts. When students from other districts enroll, they continue to reside in the same district. However, the state per student revenue flows to the district that has the virtual school. The big virtual school companies have sales staff that scout out potential districts and use this argument as part of their pitch.

The technology also allows for-profit firms to expand sales without increases in capital costs. The firm can expand its enrollment in one year without having to purchase or lease a school facility. The firm also can expand its enrollment without necessarily having to hire more staff. In virtual schools, one instructor can be assigned to 40 to 60 students without attracting very much attention. The public cannot readily see the classroom and the overflow. Further, in some states, the instructors hired do not need to be certified and they do not need to be full time. This allows the firm to keep personnel costs down and increase profits.

Also key to growth in the virtual school industry is something I mentioned in chapter 3—the importance of private financial investment. As I have demonstrated, the new privatization is part of a larger movement that includes former senior education officials, investment firms, market research firms, and trade groups. Among other functions, these actors provide financial support through their investments. Since 2002, Apollo Management, Sterling Ventures, and Knowledge Universe—some the largest investors in the education industry—have poured millions of dollars into virtual school companies. For example, in 2003, Constellation Ventures invested $20 million in K12. In 2004, Apollo Management acquired Connections Academy, identified as a close competitor of K12, for an undisclosed amount.

Thus, part of what is driving virtual charter schools is the technology and the market's investments in these technologies. The firms are selling districts solutions based squarely in market logic. By this logic, districts need to compete with other districts in order to survive. If firms can convince families from neighboring districts to enroll in *their* district, the district can in principle increase their revenue and maintain their autonomy. What happens to the district losing student enrollment, and to the community, is not a central consideration. Thus, current developments in education contracting inject market principles into governance arrangements—in this instance the relationships between districts in one state.

Federal Policy Support

While the market provides one rationale, current federal policy provides another. The federal government has moved deliberately to reinvent virtual schools as a public good that contributes to the broader policy goals of increasing access to high quality curriculum for economically disadvantaged students. Federal officials have pursued three central policy strategies in this agenda: (1) using guidance to include virtual schools as a legal option for meeting the mandates of No Child Left Behind (NCLB) or for applying or using Federal monies for other purposes, such as technology grants; (2) expanding the level of funding available for charter schools; and (3) encouraging the dissemination of information about virtual schools through sponsorship of white papers and conferences.

As noted, under the choice mandates of NCLB, schools that do not make test score targets for two years or more must provide parents with transfer options. In 2004, federal officials released guidance that allowed districts to use virtual schooling as a legal option for creating additional capacity for students wishing to transfer under the choice option. Students can transfer to a virtual school even if the school is not in their same district.[13] The guidance also permits schools and districts to use virtual schools as a means for meeting the high quality teacher provisions. Under current regulations, schools or districts may use an online instructor in lieu of a teacher who is physically present if the online instructor meets the highly qualified provisions for the state.[14]

In addition, the U.S. Department of Education has created new revenue sources for virtual schools. For example, NCLB established the Enhancing

Education Through Technology (Ed Tech) Program, which consolidates the current Technology Literacy Challenge Fund (TLCF) Program and the Technology Innovative Challenge Grant Program into a single state formula grant program (ESEA Title II, Part D, Subpart 1).[15] The primary goal of the Ed Tech program is "to improve student academic achievement through the use of technology in schools." In addition, the initiative encourages the establishment of initiatives (including those involving public–private partnerships) that are designed to increase access to technology, particularly in schools served by "high-need local educational agencies." According to the law, an eligible partnership is one that includes at least one high-need LEA and may include a "for-profit business or organization that develops, designs, manufactures, or produces technology products or services or has substantial expertise in the application of technology in instruction."[16] Here again, we see the rights of for-profit businesses being written into ESEA policy, as I also illustrated in chapters 1 and 4.

In 1995, the federal government launched a competitive grant program to provide federal financial assistance for the development and operation of publicly funded charter schools. In 1998, the Charter School Expansion Act was changed so that private individuals and organizations could operate charter schools. NCLB amended the definition of "eligible applicant" to eliminate the requirement that a charter school developer enter into a partnership with an authorized public chartering agency in order to qualify for a start-up grant. The change had the effect of increasing access to federal charter funds by for-profit companies selling goods and services for virtual schools. Between 1995 and 2005, the level of federal funds authorized for charter schools increased by a factor of three dozen from $6 million to $217 million.[17]

Finally, by channeling funds to conferences that promote virtual schooling for evaluation, the federal government has sought to increase public support for virtual schools and to link it to ESEA goals. Between 2003 and 2004, the Office of Innovation and Improvement sponsored two conferences organized around the theme of using online learning as part of NCLB. The 2004 conference, was titled "Increasing Options Through eLearning," which, in the words of an agency press release, "brought together local, state, and national education leaders…to explore the concept of virtual education and its potential to expand the opportunities for learning any time, any place in support of the No Child Left Behind Act."[18] As part of the conference, the DOE commissioned a number of white papers paid for with public funds such as "How Can Virtual Schools Be a Vibrant Part of Meeting the Choice Provisions of the No Child Left Behind Act?"[19] The department also has directed $56 million toward studies of educational technology at the K–12 level including the use of online curriculum to support student achievement.[20]

Up to this point, I have argued that markets and federal policy are converging and creating a new segment in K–12 education contracting. In this market segment, for-profit firms can increase their revenue exponentially while keeping costs down. As districts struggle with budget shortfalls, they are looking for ways to increase revenue. This makes district contracting with an outside firm for instruction more financially attractive. The technology provides a means for the district to increase revenue by increasing enrollment without the costs of having to build a new facility.

Federal policy is assisting the market through incentive grants and by funding research that aims to provide the intellectual and political argumentation for more virtual schools. In white papers and conferences, virtual schooling is framed as in close alignment with the goals of NCLB and its focus on low-income students. Under the logic presented in federal discourse, by supporting virtual schools, we also can expand options for economically disadvantaged students. Here again is the idea that markets can succeed where government has failed and the role of policy is to cheerlead and stimulate demand.

Emerging Tensions

In analyzing the interplay of markets and policy, we need to pay attention not simply to the constraining effects of these dynamics, but also to the possibilities for agency. Even as the discourse of policy shifts, "actors are making meaning, being influential, constructing responses, dealing with contradictions, attempting representations of policy."[21] I will take up this point in depth later in the chapter when I describe local encounters with virtual schools. But, here, let me offer two brief examples of how the blending of markets and policy stimulates contention.

From the beginning, Christian conservatives have leveraged virtual charter schools as a funding mechanism for home schooling. The point is made clearly by Apple:

> [A] growing number of Christian conservative parents have become quite adept at taking advantage of government resources for their own benefit. By taking advantage of home school charter programs that connect independent families to the use of the Internet and the Web, they are able to use public funding to support schooling that they previously had to pay for privately.[22]

Seeing the financial possibilities in the home schooling market, virtual charter school providers have focused their advertising campaigns in home schooling communities. For example, in 2002, K12 scheduled one of its annual meetings near one of the largest residential populations of home schoolers in California. It then sent out a direct mass mailing to families in the area offering them an opportunity to attend the conference for free. And, as noted earlier, the U.S. Department of Education has played a very proactive role in representing home-based Internet schooling and choice policies as aligned.

Although clearly Apple is right that conservative home schoolers have leveraged charter school policy, the union is not without its detractors. In a 2003 statement, the Home Schooling Legal Defense Association urged home schoolers to see virtual charter schools as a direct threat to their movement's principles:

> Charter schools are a new phenomenon rapidly gaining popularity across the country. All charter schools are created or "chartered" by public school boards, which establish a mission, educational program, and methods of assessment. Most charter schools are classroom based. However, some charter schools are home based. When parents enroll their child in a full-time, classroom-based charter school, it is obvious that they are signing away much of their parental right to direct their child's education. Home-based charter schools gloss over this surrender by giving parents a wide variety of "free" benefits, all for use at home: computer and Internet access, books, school supplies, support from certified teachers, and a diploma, etc. In reality, parents who accept government money through home-based charter schools are still signing over ultimate educational control of their children to the state. Enrolling in a home-based charter school creates a little public school in your home.[23]

What the Home Schooling Legal Defense Association (HSLDA) is saying is that its constituency needs to beware of how the market and policy are colluding. They see these developments as threatening to the ideals of their movement. Part of what HSLDA is challenging is not just more government reach but more government reach via the hand of the market, through the "wide variety of 'free' benefits, all for use at home: computer and Internet access, books, school supplies, support from certified teachers, and a diploma."[24]

The rise of virtual schooling is triggering other political tensions and inviting new questions. In the past several years, a number of states including Minnesota, Wisconsin, and Florida have filed lawsuits against school districts that have contracts with for-profit firms to operate virtual charter schools.[25] One issue that has emerged in the debates accompanying the lawsuits is how virtual schooling confuses the meaning of local. Under federal guidelines in ESEA, districts are responsible for students as long as they live in the district. In at least one instance where lawsuits have been brought against charter school operators on behalf of the state, virtual charter school operators have argued that they "are located" in many different places, making "geography-based conceptions like location meaningless." In at least one case, the local court rejected this claim on the basis that "location remains a meaningful and often indispensable concept, particularly when it comes to relationships between governmental units."[26]

I use these two brief examples to draw attention to the importance and the possibility of agency in the rise of the new privatization. In focusing on the general drift in policy, we can overlook how people in it path, resist, reinterpret, disassociate, or reassert nonmarket principles, such as the importance of public governance. In the example offered above, the courts are saying at some level that the idea of place and the idea of a local school district linked to place remains relevant in policy, even if it may seem irrelevant to the market.

Thus, while understanding the new privatization certainly requires attention to its constraining effects, as it unfolds in practice, the trends described also can stimulate renewed discussion and reflection around important questions. These questions include what is public and what is private, and what is public policy and what is market practice.

For-Profit Firms and Virtual Schools in Local Context

In this next section, I begin to look further at the interactions between local school districts and national for-profit organizations and at the conflicts and power dynamics at the heart of these interactions. The context for the analysis is two virtual charter schools, located in different regions of the same state and established approximately the same year. Each school operates under a charter from the local school board under the state's chartering laws. Each school is managed and operated by a different national for-profit firm. The study is based on qualitative research, in particular in-depth interviews. The work was conducted over a one-year period, from October 2006 to October 2007 (see appendix A for an in-depth explanation of the research design and data collection methods).

Einstein Academy

Einstein is a virtual high school that enrolls somewhere in the range of 500 to 800 students. Since the opening, the school population has been almost exclusively White and representing middle and high-income families.[27] Children of color, children eligible for free and reduced lunch, and immigrant children have as subgroups made up less than 5% of the student population, according to enrollment data provided by the state. Data on the percentage of special education students was not available. Approximately 95% of the students enrolled in the school reside in other districts, attending school via a home computer. In 2005 and 2006, students enrolled in the virtual charter school represented well over 100 different districts throughout the state. The school is financed largely by per-pupil revenues allocated for these students by the state, which can be in the range of $8,000 to $9,000 dollars per year. Thus, the school district receives per-pupil revenues from over 100 districts based on the student's place of residence that would otherwise be counted as revenue within that district.

While the students enrolling in the virtual charter school are largely White, they come from districts that, relative to state averages, are disproportionately populated by minority students and students coming from economically disadvantaged backgrounds. Einstein Academy has 10 full-time teachers and 11 part-time teachers. Approximately half of the teachers are male and half are female; all are White. Under the terms of the contract, the school district is responsible for the hiring and training of Einstein's teachers and has adopted an informal policy that all teachers employed must be "local"; that is, they must live in the area and have some teaching experience in the district itself. All of the teachers are members of the teachers' union. There are two primary school administrators, Dan Donovan, the school principal or director, and Jane D'Angelo, the school manager. Donovan is a former director of technology for the district and is paid with funds from the district. D'Angelo is an employee of Elearn , the national for-profit company, which has a contract with the district to assist in the management of the virtual school.

Palermo has long been a politically conservative city, many of whose oldest residents came to the region to work in the nearby foundries. Currently the district is part of the outer ring of communities that surround a large metropolitan city and is part of the commuting route from the suburbs to the city. The last two referenda for raising property taxes in the district have been soundly defeated. Since the late 1990s, the district has had to eliminate most of its librarians, increase class sizes in all grade levels, and reduce the number of guidance counselors and art and music programs.

In contrast to the sociodemographics of Einstein Academy, a significant percentage of students residing in Palermo and attending bricks-and-mortar schools in the district are eligible for free and reduced lunch. The number of Latino/a students in the district is nearly twice the state average. Thus, not only is Einstein Academy more White and more economically advantaged in its student population than the districts that are sending the students, but its student population also is much more White and much more economically advantaged as compared to students enrolled in bricks-and-mortar schools in Palermo.

In 2004, Davies sent two district staff to the state's annual charter school convention with the explicit purpose of making contacts with an external provider that had the expertise to help them run and manage a virtual charter school. Davies and his staff in the district were concerned about the rising costs of educating students in the district and the limited funds to support these costs. There was some indication that district residents were taking advantage of the state's open enrollment policies to enroll their children in virtual schools in other districts, contributing to fears of declining enrollment and declining revenues in the district. "Rather than whine like other districts losing students to the virtual schools," Davies recalled, "we decided to compete." There were a number of virtual school providers at the conference. Based on contacts made at the conference, Palermo initiated preliminary contract negotiations with Elearn. The school board had been clear that if a virtual school were to open in Palermo, the provider would need to be flexible and responsive to local concerns. "We wanted to maintain local control of our curriculum." Donovan explained. "We had heard from other districts that larger firms tended to come in with a prepackaged and standardized curriculum. We didn't want that."

Blind Spots in the Contracting Process

The district signed a contract with Elearn. In addition to managing virtual schools, the firm had proprietary rights to an online curriculum, which it licensed to school districts as part of its contracts. Under the terms of the contract, Elearn had responsibility for the management and operation of the school and under a separate contract, licensing agreements for the Elearn curriculum. The firm charged the district per curriculum unit and per pupil enrolled in the class. In retrospect, Davies believes that the district's inexperience in virtual schooling, relative to the experience of the firm, put it at a significant disadvantage. Specifically, according to Davies, because it had contracts in other districts, the firm knew that state course requirements guaranteed them certain levels of revenue. For some required courses, the firm could bill the district up to $3,000 per student.

The firm was careful to establish contract terms that protected it from potential losses due to student transfers. Under the terms, the district was charged for students even if they transferred to another school several weeks into the school year. Where the firm was guaranteed the revenue, state policy only reimbursed the district for the number of days that the student was enrolled. Therefore, the district would be charged for per-student costs by the firm but could not count on the revenue for the student from the state. This element of the contract ended up costing the district huge sums of money. In the first year, nearly 50% of the students enrolled in the school had transferred back to their own district by the third week of September. Elearn billed the district for the curriculum costs for these students, although they were no longer enrolled in the program and the district would not be receiving the expected per-pupil allotment for them.

There were other aspects of the contract that proved problematic for Palermo. In principle, the school board was the chartering agency and had the authority to review and approve its curriculum. In practice, according to several teachers and an administrator, Elearn exercised considerable influence over the curriculum used by the school. Donovan acknowledged that, "I would be lying to you if I told you we didn't look at this [Elearn's] curriculum first. It was made clear that this was the expectation and strongly encouraged by Elearn." The district did end up selecting the curriculum owned by Elearn, which stood to gain financially from the choice under a separate contract. Still, while teachers felt pressured to use Elearn's curriculum, several also said they considered it a better product than a competing curriculum from another firm that the program had originally planned to use.

Some Students Need not Apply

During the first year of operation, Elearn administrators and Palermo district staff met to discuss strategies for retaining students. Both parties were concerned about the financial costs of students transferring early in the school year. The strategy they adopted focused mainly on the application process and the admissions office. Students who were perceived as at risk of dropping out were counseled out in a process that had several layers. First, the school introduced a required "assessment interview" of parents intending to enroll their child in the program. Second, a rubric was developed to assess parents' "readiness" for the program in particular their ability to guide their child in coverage of the curriculum and the extent to which they would be present with the student at home during the school day. Students who did not appear to be a good "fit" with this profile were encouraged not to apply. Third, in the application process, school staff also discouraged enrollment by students with mild learning disabilities who did not qualify for supplementary services under the mandates of the Individuals with Disabilities Education Act (IDEA).

School administrators characterized these students as a poor fit with the school because of expected difficulty in mastering the regular curriculum. By one administrator's report,

> We learned the hard way. Each year, we have a few of these students. They are unable to follow and access the regular curriculum and do not qualify for support services from their residing district. In those instances, we were forced to really have a teacher work one on one to tailor the curriculum to the students' level, which was extraordinarily expensive.

Invisible Work

The teachers and administrators I spoke with acknowledged that each year and in every class, a handful of students struggled academically. Several teachers had many years of experience in regular bricks-and-mortar schools. One of them was Peter Ahearn, the biology teacher. In the interview, he also expressed concern and frustration over his inability to reach students that appeared to be struggling academically,

> In a face to face class, there is always that student who sits in the back of the class, who hates science, but you can see him and you can be in his face and talk to him, and sometimes it doesn't work, but by March, you usually have some kind of breakthrough and he will say, Hey, Mr. Ahearn, I love your class. In a virtual school, it is easier for that student to remain invisible for longer.

The approaches Ahearn and other Einstein teachers take to serving students who are struggling academically suggest ways in which large national firms in the virtual schooling industry are forcing the costs of differentiated instruction onto school staff, rather than making systemic and institutional change that support greater student diversity and strengthen student retention. Ahearn is frustrated by the limitations in his ability to identify these students, make a personal connection with them, and develop curriculum in response to their learning styles. Under the present policies of the firm, students are not required to participate in any "live" classroom sessions. According to school administrators, corporate executives worry that if live sessions are required, they might lose an important customer base, namely home schoolers, who bristle at state curriculum mandates. In contrast Ahearn and other teachers view live virtual classrooms as settings where students struggling academically become more visible and where personal connections between teacher and student may be forged. Here is one of the places where there is clearly a clash between the corporate agendas of the company and the public service mission of classroom teachers.

Fiscal arrangements impose additional obstacles to designing and implementing intervention strategies for struggling students, and teachers end up paying some of the hidden costs of virtual schools. In the absence of any specific financial support from the firm, teachers have had to devise their own strategies on their own time. In several instances, Ahearn has developed supplementary curriculum for individual students— activities that are not included in the purchased curriculum but that he believes the students need in order to master the regular curriculum. On occasion, he has been discouraged from doing so "because if the school board hears about teachers developing their own curriculum, they may wonder what we are paying for."

He and other teachers reported that they continue to invest and spend time developing these materials anyway.

In summary, the claims of virtual school providers and their supporters is that students enrolled in virtual schools will receive both differentiated curriculum and personal support. However, classroom teachers such as Ahearn, who work inside of virtual schools and with its technology, see things somewhat differently. Particularly when they are discouraged from doing more for these students (because of cost considerations) these claims can seem like empty promises. These pressures do not come exclusively from the corporate headquarters; they also emanate from the district because of its cost concerns.

The experience of Einstein Academy also points to the power asymmetries between small school districts and large virtual school providers. From the outset, Palermo school district acted intentionally to maintain some control and autonomy from the firm. For example, the district would only consider providers who would hire local unionized teachers. It sought a provider that did not come with "a prepackaged curriculum." In spite of these efforts, the large firm clearly had the power advantage, reflected both in the terms of the contract (described above) and in the firm's influence on the school's adopted curriculum.

Learning Point Academy

Like Einstein Academy, Learning Point Academy is a virtual charter school. The chartering school district for Learning Point is a very small rural district, Shriver. In 2006 and 2007, Shriver's combined student enrollment was approximately 1,600 students. Close to half of all students enrolled in Shriver are enrolled in the virtual charter school and reside in other districts in the state, some as many as 300 miles away. All together the school enrolls students from approximately 200 districts. Of the approximately 1,000 students who attend the school, 95% are White and 96% do not qualify for free and reduced price lunch. During the 2005 to 2006 school years, approximately 7% of the students at the school were identified as having disabilities under IDEA. None of the students were identified as having limited English proficiency.

The demographics of the school district with the charter for Learning Point mirror that of the school population. During the 2005 to 2006 school year, less than 4% of students enrolled in the district qualified for free and reduced price lunch and 96% were White. However, as in the case of Einstein, the students enrolling in Learning Point reside in districts with much higher levels of student diversity, both in race and ethnicity and in socioeconomic status. They are districts where close to 20% of the student population qualifies for free and reduced price lunch and where the population of both

African-American but particularly Latino/a students is increasing. Taken together, enrollment patterns in the both Einstein and Learning Point, relative to student population in the home districts of their students and in the state as a whole, are Whiter and more economically advantaged. This two-tiered system of White and economically advantaged students enrolled in a virtual charter school while students of color or from economically disadvantaged backgrounds are enrolled in noncharter, bricks and mortar schools, reflects broader patterns in charter school enrollment nationally.[28]

The superintendent of Shriver school district was instrumental in the establishment of the school as a means of increasing enrollment and revenues in the district. He also wanted to increase the use of instructional technology in the bricks-and-mortar schools in the district. He envisioned Learning Point as a testing ground for technology-based reforms that could be offered to students in the district itself. The superintendent began a series of conversations with a former colleague from another district who was working as a consultant for a national virtual school company. When the district established a contract with that company to open a virtual school in the district, the consultant was hired by the firm to manage that contract.

The administrative offices for Learning Point are housed in a suite of rooms in the district offices. The district offices are housed in the same building as the district's elementary school; the district's middle and high schools are in nearby buildings. The administrative offices for Learning Point are cramped with little space for administrators to congregate. When administrators meet they "borrow" a multipurpose room that functions as a school board meeting room and a time-out room for children during school hours.

Since its inception, Learning Point has contracted with a national virtual school provider, Ackroyd Learning, to manage and operate the school. Under the terms of the contract with Ackroyd, the Shriver school district pays the firm both up-front and annual licensing fees for proprietary curriculum developed and owned by the firm and for fees related to the marketing of the school, enrollment, teacher recruitment, hiring and evaluation; costs related to the lease of computers to each student, and mailing supplies for instructional materials that supplement the online curriculum. The company specializes in online content and the management and operation of virtual charter schools. Its online curriculum also includes an online school platform, which is a Web-based software application that provides access to its online lessons, lesson planning and scheduling tools and a progress tracking tool, and a student information management system.

Virtual Curriculum

Learning Point uses a comprehensive curriculum sequenced from one grade to the next. The role of the teacher in the virtual school is to help students move through the lessons in the proper sequence and on occasion to conduct "live lessons" through interactive media. For example, the Kindergarten Language Arts Lesson emphasizes classic literature—fairy tales, fables, folktales, and poems. Parents are instructed to read their children these tales and, through a variety of scripted games, to discuss character action and conflict in the text.

Thus, the role of teachers and parents in this curriculum is both central and scripted. In the early grades, parents essentially act as coteachers, reading directions, checking assignments and answering questions. Teachers are expected to review assignments, grade them, troubleshoot when students and parents are stuck on particular assignments, and conduct the occasional live lesson. Although the curriculum appears by design to be highly packaged and standardized, in the majority of interviews teachers raved about the curriculum and consistently used words like *powerful, rich, challenging,* and *engaging* in describing its content. A school administrator who was somewhat critical of the firm's corporate mentality nevertheless described the curriculum as "designed for 7th graders who want to do great things with their lives." He used the example of a geology lesson that enables students to look at three-dimensional pictures of the earth and peel away layers at the core of the earth. Some teachers we spoke with talked about the effective organization of the curriculum, the care taken to build background for students so that each stage of the curriculum offers "both new challenges and new rewards."

The curriculum is the most visible part of Learning Point and those I interviewed spent considerable time talking about it. However, as in the case of Einstein Academy, there were other elements of the work that were as important but much harder to see. These activities did not emanate from corporate headquarters; in fact in describing this work, teachers and administrators suggested that the firm might not even be aware of them. This local work included the design of a series of parent workshops. Teachers conducted these workshops live and then archived them for parents. Administrators talked about breaking down the walls between school administration, parents, and teachers through strategies such as text messaging and e-mail. "The school is open 24 hours a day. It is a community school," reported one administrator and as evidence to support this claim, he shared e-mails sent to and received from others the prior evening. "Look, here's a 1 am message from Kathy H, the kindergarten teacher to me, and here's my message back to her." In the content of the message, he responds thoughtfully to a concern she has about the organization of the language arts curriculum, a multiparagraph e-mail, signing off, "Great question. Go to sleep Kathy." Learning Point teachers also described how they initiated virtual bimonthly meetings with grade level teams. They described these "unofficial staff development" meetings (the firm also had an annual staff development day at its headquarters) as very helpful to them in their teaching.

Winnowing Process

Like regular schools, all charter schools in the state are required to test students under the mandates of No Child Left Behind. Learning Point has consistently made adequate yearly progress (AYP). Under the present regulations, districts are not required to report AYP for populations under a particular cell size. In interviews, Learning Point administrators described increasing pressure from the firm to continue to make AYP. This pressure took two forms. Company executives pressed school administrators to make sure that the school had at least a 95% test participation rate, because a school can be identified as not making AYP if participation falls below a certain threshold. Testing under NCLB in a virtual school can be a logistical nightmare. State law permits students to attend virtual schools while residing as far as 200 miles away. Under federal regulations, however, they must test in person rather than online. Thus, every year schools such as Einstein and Learning Point must rent space throughout the state for test administration. Parents pay for transportation to the test site for students.

The test pressures also create indirect incentives for school administrators to discourage admission of students who might endanger AYP. If the school has few students of color or from low-income backgrounds, it does not have to report separate scores for these students, nor does it risk failing to make AYP solely because of their scores. These pressures were reflected in the school's admissions practices. The school principal explained, "To the parent who can't make the time investment, we sometimes say, 'Are there other options that you can pursue?'" Administrators adopted practices that seemed aimed at discouraging low-income students in particular from enrolling in the program. References to "parents who are a good fit for this program" barely disguised the stigma and discriminatory practices against families of limited economic means. One administrator stated baldly, "There are parents that are not able to do this [put in the time required]. I have to say this school is not for their child. What I am really saying is that you can't do this."

Thus, claims in marketing materials that Learning Point contributed to more equitable treatment of students and offered increased responsiveness of the curriculum to diverse learning needs appeared disconnected from the approaches and processes in use. Interviews with parents were used to ensure a homogenous student body. In addition, Ackroyd Learning provided little in the way of institutional supports for helping the school enroll and maintain a diverse student population. The firm did not cover the costs of the Internet connection, only providing a very small monthly stipend to offset the costs. Although investing millions of dollars in the development of the curriculum, in advertising—and later, in rights to an online test preparation program—the firm offered nothing in the way of curriculum appropriate for English language learners. Concurrently, the firm's aggressive strategy for making sure that students enrolled in the school would make test score targets, such as its pressure on the school district to ensure test participation, had the effect of winnowing out applicants perceived as likely to do poorly on the tests.

As in the case of Einstein, the teachers and administrators we spoke with appeared genuinely concerned about the experiences of academically struggling students enrolled in their program. At the same time, they acknowledged being stymied with how to develop effective interventions in an online environment. Commented one administrator,

> In regular public schools, we sometimes use repeated absence from school as a marker or warning sign that a student is struggling academically or not engaged in school, or there are problems at home. We have no way and no idea of how to keep track of this or what might be a comparable warning sign in a virtual school. By design, our program is supposed to be flexible. It is OK for students not to attend school on a regular basis. In the case of a struggling student, we miss the opportunity for these early warning signs.

The Corporate Line

The experiences of Eleanor Matthews provide a good example of the tensions that emerge for teachers and administrators working for virtual charter schools. In their work, these individuals straddle the public and the private sector. Matthew's formal job title at Learning Point is educational consultant. Ackroyd pays her salary, but she is based locally and grew up in a neighboring school district.

Matthews is considered part of the school's management team alongside of the principal and technology director. She commutes to the district at least once a week for these meetings. Matthews describes a very personal commitment to the people that she works with on a day-to-day basis in the school district. However, as she is the first to acknowledge, she also works for Ackroyd Learning, which pays her salary. She is expected by the firm to make sure that the interests of Ackroyd are represented in school meetings. Where she thinks the financial interests of the firm are at risk of being compromised, she is expected to intervene, and suggest policy alternatives that might be more amenable to the firm. One school administrator reported being very uncomfortable with Matthew's functions in the school. In private he called her, "Ackroyd's resident mole." He does not like the idea that someone can be privy to the district's internal policy conversations, while at the same time acting on behalf of a large for-profit firm.

Based on teachers' accounts, Matthews has played a critical role in broker-ing communication between the school and corporate headquarters. They offer examples of how Matthews repeatedly has sought to help the firm's national business office understand the educational costs of rapid expan-sion and increased student–teacher ratios. Matthews herself explains the conflicts in her work as based on a "clash of institutional priorities rather than individual differences." For example, on one occasion, she was asked by senior executives at Ackroyd to propose increasing student–teacher load in classrooms, from one teacher to 30 students to 1 teacher to 50 students. As a former public school teacher and principal, Matthews had conflicting emotions about the firm's press to increase class size. She understood the rationale from a business perspective but questioned its wisdom from an educational standpoint. "Recently and increasingly," she remarked in an interview, "I have struggled with the question, 'Who am I loyal to? Am I loyal to the district or am I loyal to Ackroyd Learning?' In the meetings with district staff, when I find myself arguing against things namely because they will cost the firm money, I wonder, is this my own professional judgment or is this the corporate line?"

Thus, Matthew's role at Learning Point involves a balancing act. As a member of the district community, she must form and maintain relationships with other administrators and with teachers. But, when she participates in administrative meetings, she also is expected to act on the firm's behalf. Mat-thews' work in the district becomes a mechanism for a firm with headquarters based in another state to be part of and influence local policy decisions.

Conclusion

In this chapter, I have described another instance of how the activities and the consequences of the new privatization are not readily apparent. Like supple-mental education services, much of the activity of virtual charter schools is invisible as are some of its most important consequences. Looking across the two schools, I next discuss several aspects of this invisibility.[29]

First, in a literal sense the relationships between school districts and virtual for-profit firms are hard to see because the organization of these relationships happens online, on the Internet and on the Web. Even though the schools are public schools, they have a public identification number and they are supported with public funds, ordinary access is limited. Any of us can in principle walk up to our local neighborhood school, explain ourselves, and get to see what the children in our community are learning, the character of instruction, and the safety of the facilities.

This is not as possible when the public school is a virtual charter school. In order to see the school in any descriptive detail (to see what is being taught and how instruction is organized), one needs to have a password. In order to get a password, one generally needs to have approval from the district. If the district is contracting with a for-profit firm, the district must first get approval from the firm before doing so. Of course, there also are restrictions in place when one visits a bricks-and-mortar school, but to a much lesser degree I believe. Thus, as in the case of supplemental education services, the assumption is that for-profit firms will increase the transparency of information about schools. But, here again the assumption does not appear to hold. When for-profit firms are providing the services, there can be as many if not more administrative layers as when the service providers are public agencies.

Second, in virtual schools, even with all of the technology, teachers and administrators still conduct much of the work. As in the case of regular schools, teachers can work long days and into the wee hours of the night and few will take notice. Much of the work that these administrators and teachers do is very personal as opposed to technical. As in the examples noted above, it involves establishing routines (exchanges about curriculum, teacher grade level teams, parent workshops) that are critical to building community. In the case of teachers, this work also involves reaching out to students who are struggling academically and developing curriculum that supplements what the firm has made available. The underlying premise of this work seems very different from the market-based logic of competition. There is much more that needs to be understood about the nature of teachers' and administrators' work in virtual schools. My intent in this description is to bring this more invisible, local work, into view.

Third, in virtual charter schools, for-profit firms can exert subtle but powerful influences on certain kinds of district policy decisions, and do so in ways that again, are not very apparent. The firm hires a local consultant to assist the district, but part of the work involves making sure that corporate interests are represented in local staff meetings. To offer another example, the firm exerts subtle pressure on the district to lease the firm's own curriculum, rather than considering other curriculum. The firm presses the district on the importance of making AYP, at any cost, and turns its head when schools develop admissions procedures that are exclusionary. The nature of this influence may not be very visible to those of us on the outside looking in. However, the economic and political power of the firm presses very hard on school staff.

Fourth, in contrast to the highly public debates about charter schools and parent choice, the rise of virtual schools as alternatives to regular bricks-and-mortar schooling remains quite hidden from view. It is obscured by the fact that most states do not keep comprehensive records on virtual school enrollment or on patterns in transfers of students under state open enrollment. It also is obscured by the rhetoric of proponents and owners of virtual school operations, who like other firms in the K–12 education industry have become masterful at employing the language of civil rights in marketing their services. The approaches adopted by the two virtual schools suggest the importance of very close attention to the access of students of color and students from disadvantaged backgrounds to virtual schools. Both virtual schools enrolled a significantly lower percentage of minority students and low-income students than the districts where the majority of the students lived and from which they were sent. Parents of White and higher income students are leveraging their social capital to enroll them in virtual charter schools more likely to have a homogenous population—more White and higher income.

Finally, as in the case of supplemental education services, the emerging forms and practices of these new virtual schools do not simply descend silently on local communities. They stimulate debate, reaction, excitement, and resistance. Local school districts are seeking ways to establish contracts that allow them to retain some dimension of local control. For example, Palermo would only contract with a firm that allowed the district to hire its own teachers. It insisted that these teachers be certified by the state. Classroom teachers in both schools worried aloud about what students the virtual environment was leaving behind. Meanwhile, other employees, specifically, the Learning Point consultant, asked hard questions about whose interests come first when a large for-profit firm powers the school. Thus, the cases further suggest that while for-profit firms are deeply involved in contracting, there may be changes underway that limit the power of their discourses and practices, especially those driving toward profit at the expense of educational quality.

CHAPTER 6

In the Interstices

Benchmark Assessments,
District Contracts, and NCLB[1]

For over a century, districts have contracted with outside vendors for functions such as test preparation and score reporting. They have purchased off the shelf tests from publishers and contracted with vendors to administer the tests, score them, and generate reports. Much of the activity has focused on summative standardized tests. Since the late 1990s, however, as I discussed in chapter 2, the institutional landscape of K–12 testing contracts has shifted. Current contracts between public school districts and testing firms encompass a broad range of activities. They also are closely linked to the mandates of NCLB, specifically its requirements that all students be tested, that test scores be analyzed and reported differently, and that schools and systems that fail to make test score targets face sanctions. The emphasis on data and measurement also is a central strand of neoliberal policy, as noted.

This chapter asks several central questions. First, how, if at all, is contracting activity in K–12 testing different from what we have had previously in the test-publishing industry? Here, I look at the firms entering the K–12 education testing market and the strategies that they are employing. In this analysis, I draw on interviews with senior executives and analysis of the financial and operational statements of publicly traded firms. Second, how, if at all, are districts responding to institutional pressures of high-stakes testing? Specifically, based on a small-scale survey of district practice, I ask what districts are buying, how much they are spending, and what policies are driving these purchases. Third, what tensions and possibilities are emerging as districts contract with vendors and seek ways of putting new technology to use? How are current testing contracts shaped by local settings? What are the commonalities and differences in how school districts approach their work with vendors? This portion of the chapter draws on in-depth interviews and some participant observation in three districts.[2]

I focus on contracts for what have come to be called benchmark assessment systems. As defined by Hayes,[3] benchmark assessment systems are the services and products that districts and states employ to gauge student performance on standardized tests prior to the annual state level exams that are used to measure AYP under NCLB. Over the course of studying benchmark assessment contracts, I have come to think of them as operating in the interstices of school district practice.

The image of the interstice is apt for several reasons. First, in benchmark assessment systems, *what* is being contracted is software that is aimed at helping districts see the achievement gaps—it is software that is designed to be used between the start of the school year and the end of the school year, when students in most states take the summative exam. Contracts for benchmark assessments also manifest how adept the market has become at finding a niche—a small space where something new can be sold. The something new here is a form of assessment that is designed to precede the summative assessment, which many firms already are selling. What is being sold is not quite instruction, but as I will show, it is not just a test either. It is something in between and therefore, perhaps not likely to garner much attention. In this way, as in others, benchmark assessment contracting is consistent with the trends of new privatization described in the book.

In my analysis, I will argue the following. First, while benchmark assessment systems have clear merits, they also represent a partial and costly solution to a complex set of problems. Those working inside of districts note for example, that having access to data does not automatically mean that one knows how to use the data, interpret it, or have the will to do so. Establishing benchmarks and having data is a far distance from making substantive improvements in teaching and learning. In this regard, and by designing products that skim the surface, for-profit private firms replicate the problems of public school reform. Second, even though the benchmark assessment systems sold by different firms share many of the same features (and I describe these below), how the contracts unfold in practice (their strengths and weaknesses) depends on a range of factors as suggested by the experiences of the districts I studied.

Benchmark Assessment Systems

To begin, I will identify the core characteristics of benchmark assessments. In spite of the range of firms doing the selling, the products sold look very similar in their design.[4] Firms look to other firms for what a benchmark assessment should be; in other words, there is evidence of isomorphism. Benchmark assessment systems produce, score, and store assessment data; they also analyze test score data and produce a variety of reports for different levels of stakeholders. A system may include assessments designed by the manufacturer or it may be a content-free database shell to which administrators can add their own exams. The systems are intended to allow teachers to generate additional classroom-level assessments tailored to their specific needs. The assessments may be administered online if schools have the computing capacity, or by using paper and pencil on an answer sheet generated by the system.

Benchmark assessment systems can aggregate data from the individual student level all the way up through the district level. The data can be aggregated and disaggregated in a number of ways, so that administrators can monitor student performance across categories which extend beyond grade levels, including those of race, gender, educational program type (e.g., English language learning, special education), or even by curriculum intervention type if they so choose.[5] Some vendors also sell separately a function that is aimed to help the district with reporting to the state.

Benchmark assessment systems typically have different permission levels so that only certain users have access to the broader data sets. These levels are usually set by the manufacturer, at the behest of the district. Typically, teachers will only have permission to view their own classroom data, while principals may view whole-school records and district officials can compare data from across schools.

In principle, test scores are not meant for comparison to other students or against an existing scale, but to help both student and teacher see where the individual student has made progress and where there is a lack of understanding.[6] In the current institutional context, however, these tools assume a particular meaning. They are being marketed as necessary purchases for helping the district meet the high stakes mandates of NCLB. Beneath the sophisticated technology, what firms are primarily selling is compliance with federal mandates. Terms such as *performance goals*, *benchmarks*, *efficiency*, and *reporting capabilities* appear frequently in the companies' descriptions of the new software. As one provider states in its marketing materials:

> There's a gap we can help you close. It is the distance between assessment and instruction. Edusoft's Paper to Web solution gives you the power to use your data to improve student achievement immediately. Are your assessments working intelligently and efficiently to improve instruction and achievement? To close the performance gap, it's essential to use

data to rigorously pinpoint student needs. Yet we hear from districts every day about the practical barriers that stand in the way. Edusoft solves these key assessment challenges. Our landmark Paper to Web technology helps you close the gap between assessment and instruction so you can help all of your students reach their potential. [7]

Alongside the emphasis on time efficiency is a parallel emphasis on cost reduction. One marketing testimonial reads,

For years, the district struggled with the reporting capabilities that are required by Federal, state and local agencies. Their business processes were based on a paper system that was slow and inefficient for current needs. They were losing revenue because the systems were not able to gather and report needed data. [8]

The emphasis on helping districts keep up with the relentless demands of the law is further reflected in the ubiquity of statements such as "the data is intended to help plan individualized instruction so districts can keep pace with performance goals." It also is manifested in materials that promise "implementation processes that can have districts up and running in time for the next benchmark."

It may well be that these tools help districts comply with mandates. But as to the more complex challenges at the root of improving instruction in the classroom, there is a deafening silence. Among the unanswered—indeed, unasked—questions: Once districts have the data and have analyzed it, how will they know what to do with it? Will they even be willing to consider and invest in what is needed?

Instead, the emphasis is on the individualized preferences and "customer ease." Educators and administrators purportedly will have the ability to "analyze complex data with a few simple keystrokes—Get statewide or individual student achievement information with just a few clicks on your keyboard. The [system] gives you instant reporting capabilities on any and all national, state, and local test results right at your desktop computer."[9]

These products are often open to purchase by individual schools, yet their Web sites reveal that they are marketed at the district level. Organizations will pay an annual licensing fee to the manufacturer for use of the system, and this fee is often represented as a "per student per year" cost. The annual fee for a system typically ranges anywhere from $5 to $20 per student, so the manufacturers' profit margins increase exponentially when the purchasing agency is a school district rather than one individual school. School districts may pay for these systems in a variety of ways: with district general funds, funds allocated by the state if available, or federal funds given to districts that will purchase technology to employ in meeting their AYP goals.[10] Greater enrollment size and funding sources therefore make school districts a much more likely client than schools for the manufacturers of benchmark assessment systems.

The vice president of one firm termed the large, urban school districts, "our big strategic districts." He described a scenario in which the firm bent over backwards to meet the needs of urban school districts and segmented their products for this target group:

> So, for example, in a large urban school district, you could spend all of your work day listening to presentations by possible vendors. What we have done is create a strategic sales team for that district. So, while we have lots of different products and services, each with different staff of sales representatives, in the big strategic districts, we have arranged it so that the district management has to deal with only one team composed of representatives from the different divisions.[11]

Smaller school districts, the vendor explained could purchase a "customization kit, we don't provide it for free; they purchase it." Although districts and states are required to serve all their students, the firms selling "solutions" to these districts and states can decide to target particular states and districts, and decide against entering particular regional markets because they are not cost-effective.

In the past, assessment data in paper form would be housed in the district offices—typically under the jurisdiction and lock and key of such offices as research and evaluation. In the current structure, data can be housed on a server managed and operated by external providers. Firms that sell assessment software offer these services at an additional charge. The security of these data is the responsibility of the firm, although the confidentiality of the data is governed in part by local and federal policy.

Typically districts lease the system for one to three years. The basic contract is for the database shell—the application that allows the district to store test results and generate and disaggregate data. The district will sign up for a software license and an initial year of support and services to implement the system. Firms typically charge about 20% of the license for the support services, which include telephone support and updates for the product, at a cost of $5 to $15 annually per student. In addition to the basic contract, districts may decide to purchase additional supplementary components such as professional development, kits for customizing analysis of data in ways that are aligned with state or local policies, and software for generating different kinds of reports.

As current subscribers, districts may receive free software updates from the contractor as they become available. However, these updates tend to be automatic, and every district contracting with the firm receives them. New software typically is loaded onto the district server whether the district desires it or not.

The cost structure of the system has implications for public access and ownership of the data. When districts purchase textbooks, they may not have control over the design of the content; yet through the contract, they acquire a physical asset—the textbook itself, which they keep even if they decide to adopt a different textbook series from a different publisher. In contrast, when they contract with private firms for software, districts do not own the software used to manage the requirements of NCLB and its instructional goals; they lease the shell or software program that allows them to manipulate the test score data. If they terminate the contract, they no longer have access to the shell and may not have access to the data as described in a subsequent section of the chapter where I describe the experience of three districts in the contracting process.

These combined developments reflect fundamental shifts in the institutional logic of K–12 testing. Triggered by high stakes policies, firms have introduced products and services that elevate the importance of standardized tests and technologies. The demands of policy and the response of firms also have introduced new pricing strategies with the potential to lock districts into contracts over time and contribute to situations in which data is housed in multiple locations—but powered and controlled through an off-site server managed by the private firm. Greater enrollment size and funding sources have made school districts a marketing target.

Overall, very little is known about the demand for and proliferation of benchmark assessment systems, particularly among large urban school districts. The manufacturers' websites indicate that these systems are used in a large number of schools and districts, yet there are few sources that can independently verify these claims. Information on the sales of the systems is notoriously hard to come by because they are mostly produced by private, for-profit firms who are under no obligation to publicize specific financial information or disclose their clientele.

This opacity in the industry is problematic because it may conceal conflicts of interest or thwart consumer attempts to regulate the costs and quality of the products, which are ultimately financed by taxpayer dollars. For example, some of these companies, such as McGraw-Hill and Pearson, hold contracts with one or more states to produce, administer, and score the tests used to measure AYP. In addition, some produce curriculum materials and offer professional development. This makes situations in which one company bears responsibility for curriculum, benchmark assessments, teacher training, and annual state testing not only possible, but also perhaps even likely.

What Districts Are Buying

In the last section, I noted evidence of a standard template emerging in the industry for what benchmark assessments should include. This pattern, I suggested reflects the kind of isomorphic or mimicking processes that have been described as prevalent in public schooling.[12] In the market, as in the public sector, organizations involved in the work of public schooling look to each other for cues about what they should be selling.

In this next section, I describe another dimension of this trend. We surveyed a small sample of districts to see what they were buying from the testing industry. Districts across the United Sates are purchasing benchmark assessments even though as suggested by the survey, little agreement exists in districts about their usage. Among other issues, these patterns point to the strong pull on districts and other education agencies to signal that they are complying with NCLB. The signaling occurs through the purchase of new testing products and services promoted by the market as addressing the achievement gap.[13]

Pressures to Buy

Large urban districts are purchasing testing technology and doing so in part to meet the mandates of NCLB. Over 82% of the responding districts indicated that their district currently invested in the testing technology commonly known as a benchmark assessment system that was intended to allow them to administer periodic assessments and score, disaggregate, and report the results to stakeholders in the district. Sixty-nine percent of these districts stated that they had purchased their system since the passage of NCLB. Five districts purchased their systems before NCLB. Two districts were unaware of when the system was purchased.

While NCLB is an important factor, district officials reported that the pressure to purchase these systems is coming from multiple directions. This includes pressure from school boards and superintendents (74%) and state mandates (52%). A much smaller percentage identified the pressure to purchase the system as emanating from pressures within lower levels of the system, including other district staff (13%), school administrators (9%), and teachers (22%).

Many Suppliers, No Monopoly Yet

Interestingly, although many of the large vendors of this technology claim to be working with hundreds of school districts, they were a very small presence among this group of large, urban districts. The most frequently mentioned products were Edusoft, a product of Riverside Publishing (a Houghton Mifflin subsidiary), and The Princeton Review, which is a public company specializing in standardized test preparation and since the passage of NCLB, supplemental education services. However, Edusoft is currently in place in only three out of the 23 districts. Princeton Review was mentioned by only four districts. Additionally, 50 to 75% of those districts that mentioned either Edusoft or Princeton Review also indicated other systems. Slightly more than one in 10 of officials indicated that the district chose a particular provider mainly because of a prior relationship with the firm. Therefore, although familiarity with a provider appeared to have no effect on a district's decision to buy a benchmark assessment system in the first place, it did give some companies a slight advantage over others once the district had made the choice to buy.

Cost of Systems

District officials across role groups appeared to have limited information about the costs of the systems. However, as reflected in Figure 6.1, of the 15 districts able to answer this question, all of them paid under $15 per student per year, and the majority (80%) paid under $10 per student per year. If these estimates were to apply to all the districts in the sample, the base annual cost of a system (without add-ons) would vary within the approximate ranges of $200,000 to $500,000 for the smallest district, and $1.4 million to $4 million for the largest.

The full costs of these services and products may be much higher given that 24 of the 28 districts reported purchasing additional components from vendors and that in interviews executives described setting up software licenses in ways that required customers to make additional purchases over

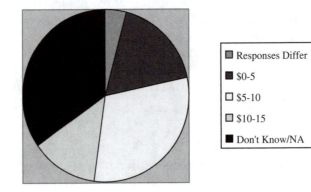

Legend:
- Responses Differ
- $0-5
- $5-10
- $10-15
- Don't Know/NA

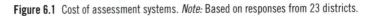

Figure 6.1 Cost of assessment systems. *Note:* Based on responses from 23 districts.

time as part of the contract. More than 43% of districts purchased services marketed as helping them customize assessments, while 30% of districts reported that they purchased additional question item banks. More than 20% of districts bought professional development and more than 25% bought a service contract. Only four districts did not buy any additional components, either because they were still investigating options or because they built their own systems and therefore did not have to purchase.

The districts in our sample spent $6,000 to $11,000 per student on total education costs each year. Thus, benchmark systems represent approximately 1% of what the districts spent on students every year. The district case studies that follow suggest additional indirect and hidden costs to districts that purchase these services. These additional costs include the significant expenses for development and administration of the Request for Proposal process, and the training and capacity-building of firms with little experience in school districts or in the education market generally. Data from the case studies further indicate that at least some of the costs are passed on to the district by the private sector.

While districts identify external forces—policy pressures from outside the district—as the principal drivers of purchases of these technological tools, they continue to rely heavily on their own general funds to cover those costs. In the survey, 61% reported drawing on district general funds. However, only six (26%) districts listed funds from ESEA as having helped to pay for their system, and a mere 13% drew on state funds (see Figure 6.2). In short, the policy impetus for buying the system is disconnected from the funding source.

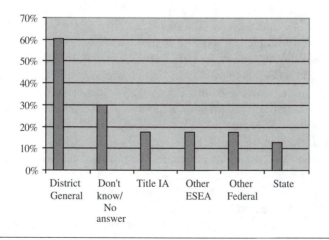

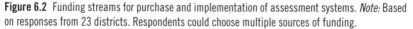

Figure 6.2 Funding streams for purchase and implementation of assessment systems. *Note:* Based on responses from 23 districts. Respondents could choose multiple sources of funding.

Information Gap

In the survey, we also asked district officials for their estimate of what percentage of teachers, school administrators, and district officials were active users of the benchmark assessment systems. The primary conclusion that the data on usage support is that (1) there is often not one prevailing perception of teacher, school administrator, or district usage within or across districts and (2) these perceptions are rough estimates. When disaggregated by district instead of by official, the responses also show that perceptions differ not only among districts but also within them. Within very few districts did respondents agree on what percentage of teachers, school administrators, and district administrators were active users. In slightly less than a third of the districts (31%) no one had any idea of how many school and district administrators were active users. There was only slightly less uncertainty when it came to perceptions of teacher usage. A full 27% of respondents had no idea how many employees in any role group were active users of the system.

The survey data also appear to contradict the reports of executives that they require school districts to purchase professional development as part of the sale. In our sample, less than 30% of those districts that purchased the system also purchased professional development or service contracts. In addition, school district officials responsible for overseeing the implementation of these systems appear to possess either conflicting or limited knowledge about critical aspects of the systems. While the systems are designed for use across multiple district departments, individual officials within districts appear to have limited and contradictory information about usage and cost.

These preliminary patterns suggest the following. First, the survey data provides further evidence of the role of NCLB in the selling of K–12 assessment services and goods. The pressure to buy in the wake of NCLB is coming from multiple levels of the system, such as superintendent/school board (72%) and state mandates (50%). Despite assertions that districts' decisions to contract emanate from or are based primarily on internal needs or capacity, a more nuanced examination suggests that, as in other aspects of the education market, the pressure to contract is inextricably linked to the external policy environment.

Second, there is a significant amount of money being spent on these systems. The 5 to 10% of an individual district's budget, when multiplied by hundreds of districts, yields a considerable amount in public funds for education being spent on software technology and being spent on tools that appear primarily geared toward helping districts comply with NCLB mandates. The result leads to a problematic circular policy dynamic. The federal government has created a policy with extensive mandates and stakes attached to compliance and in response; firms create products and services that will help districts comply with that policy. Districts spend money on these tools thereby forgoing spending elsewhere. While the survey data do not indicate how districts might otherwise choose to spend these funds, research on how schools and districts change offers numerous examples of alternative investments that certainly have a more established research base than the benchmark assessments systems. As the following cases indicate, benchmark assessments systems have some very positive features and can help draw attention to problems that districts would rather hide. At the same time, however, they represent a very partial solution to a complex problem.

Further, the conflicting or limited knowledge about usage and cost that school district officials responsible for overseeing the implementation of these systems display is important because districts may actually need more support than they are getting. The difficulty that district officials have in even agreeing on usage figures calls into question their ability to judge whether the implementation has been successful or whether the system has really helped improve instruction.

Benchmark Assessment Systems in a Local Context

I next consider the locally situated meanings and significance of the trends through three case studies of district practice. While the firms are selling similarly designed products, how these products are used in practice ultimately can look very different depending on the local setting. The first district, which I call Beachside, was a very large, decentralized urban school district with over 200,000 students.[14] The second district, which I call Westview, was a much smaller urban school district with a student enrollment in the range of 40,000 to 50,000 students. The third district, which I call Chesterville, also was urban. It fell between Beachside and Westview in terms of student enrollment, with just over 100,000 students. During the school year in which data were collected, Westview was not yet in program improvement. In contrast, Beachside and Chesterville have both been in need of improvement since the 2004 to 2005 school years.

In each district, we conducted extended interviews with several district officials across different departments from January 2007 to August 2007.[15] Data collection in each site included repeated semistructured interviews with district officials and extensive document review. In one district (Westview) we supplemented interviews and document review with shadowing of district officials and observations of school-level usage of benchmark assessment systems. In our primary case (Westview), we interviewed three staff members in the Department of Curriculum and Instruction, two staff in the Office of Technology and Instruction, and the Director of Assessment and Accountability. In Beachside, we interviewed the Director of Technology Instruction, the Director of Evaluation and Research, and the Director of Curriculum and Instruction. In Chesterville, we spoke with the current Chief Academic Officer and Executive Director of Technology Instruction, and the former Director of Middle School Programs.

Westview School District: Data Access and Test Exclusion

The school district of the city of Westview enrolls approximately 40,000 to 50,000 students and is located in the western United States. Approximately 6,000 to 7,000 of the students in the district are English language learners and 4,000 have individualized education plans. Close to half the students enrolled in Westview identify as Hispanic or Latino/a, approximately 30% are African American, and 10% are Asian. Approximately 16% of Westview's population lives below the poverty line. The school district was placed under court-ordered desegregation in the mid-1960s. Most of the city's poverty and crime are concentrated in one area of the city, which also is largely African American and Latino/a. This neighborhood also has the highest unemployment rate in the district and lowest educational rate as measured in terms of number of adults over 18 with high school diplomas.

In 2002, the district purchased a benchmark assessment system called Test Whiz. According to several district officials, Test Whiz offered many positive features. Before Test Whiz, teachers would score common assessments by hand. Staff would then get together at each school and with pencil and paper attempt to identify problem areas. There was little capacity for item analysis based on skill strands and little capacity for the district to develop a picture of student performance district-wide. District staff found Test Whiz to be a useful tool for making more informed decisions about where to invest resources. On one occasion, for example, the Curriculum Developer would analyze the test scores of students in schools and classrooms in which her staff had done intensive staff development. In other instances, district officials used Test Whiz to analyze the efficacy and equity of particular items on district level assessments. They would then use these data to assess students' difficulty with those items in relation to other items on a district-wide basis, again to help gauge where to focus staff development.

Test Whiz was identified by several staff developers as helping decentralize access to data within the district. Before the district began using Test Whiz, if staff in Curriculum and Instruction were interested in comparing the performance of certain schools to others in the district (for example, schools with higher proportions of White students to schools with higher proportions of English language learner and African-American students) they would have to go through the Office of Research and Accountability, a four-person department that occupied a small room on the second floor of the district offices. It could be weeks or even months before they could expect an answer. With Test Whiz, there was less paper and staff developers could simply conduct the analyses themselves.

While the district had a long history of collecting data—and like most districts, it had an entire department devoted to this purpose—according to several of those interviewed, it rarely did anything with the data. The data might show that there were significant differences in the academic performance of subgroups in the district by race or socioeconomic status, but from the perspective of two employees (who combined had over 30 years of experience working in the district and were the only African Americans in a largely White district office), the district rarely felt compelled to do anything about the gaps. Although time-consuming to obtain, the data were available, but even after being analyzed "they just sat there." One curriculum developer referred to her district's approach to data before NCLB and Test Whiz as "living on the average." The district paid attention to the kids in the middle and ignored the sharp differentials between the scores of children at the high and low ends of the scale. In a district that one employee characterized as largely indifferent to the needs of students of color, Test Whiz made available to the district for the first time periodic, rather than annual, data of student performance by race and income level.

In other ways Test Whiz was disconnected from the core issues of equity and access in the district. One core issue involved equal access and participation in the tests by students with disabilities. In a workshop on the use of Test Whiz, the presence of data did not diminish the practice of excluding special education students from testing:

> Item from Field Notes, May, 2007. There are about 50 teachers sitting at tables when Sharon and I enter the room where Sharon is to give the workshop. I sit at an empty table near the group that turns out to be the special education teachers. White female special education teacher in her mid-30s with a tan, speaking to me during break in the workshop, "I don't really understand why special education teachers have to be here, most of our kids come from Centerville [poorest part of town] and probably won't even graduate from high school. They let us leave early at the last workshop because there were lots of items that your average kid got that our kids didn't."

One of the premises of NCLB is that testing children with special needs alongside of other children will contribute to improving the quality of education the children receive. If the teachers who work with these students are excused from workshops where test scores are analyzed—in other words, nothing is done with the data—then the added value of the five-times-a-year testing and Test Whiz becomes questionable.

Westview's experience points to some of the possibilities of, but also the considerable limitations on, private sector test-analysis solutions. The software did help the district begin to collect and more efficiently process and manage standardized test score data. Potentially, this tool could be part of a solution for making more transparent the ways in which the district has shortchanged children of color. Yet Westview demonstrates again that the so-called achievement gap is inextricably linked to broader structural inequalities. More data in itself may make these problems more transparent, but will not come anywhere close to solving them, as I explore further in the next district example.

Beachside School District: Doing the Hard Work

Beachside is a much larger school district than Westview, with more than 200,000 students, one of the largest and most diverse populations of students in the country. The City of Beachside is a large, densely populated area. It is a very diverse city. Ten percent are Black, 11% are Asian, 49% identify as Hispanic, and 30% identify as other ethnicities. The characteristics of Beachside School District's student population stand in marked contrast to those of the residents: 73% of Beachside students are Hispanic (not White or Black), 11% are Black, only 9% are White, and just over 6% are Asian, Pacific Islander, or Filipino. Almost 82% of Beachside schools are Title I eligible.

Beachside is a highly decentralized district, separated into regions, with subject area coordinators designated for each region. Although it has consistently increased the percentage of proficiency among students in most subgroups over the past four years, the district still has struggled to meet the mandates of NCLB, and in fact has never made AYP itself. Additionally, while some subgroups have met the criteria for AYP year after year, no subgroup is anywhere near 100% proficient in either language arts or mathematics.

Beachside started experimenting with benchmark assessments in 2000, when the district adopted a curriculum for elementary reading offered through the state that included periodic assessments. This curriculum represented the first time that the district had adopted standardized tests to be used across all elementary schools. "Prior to that," one Beachside official notes, "mostly, schools were using teacher-developed materials, or test prep, or end-of-chapter tests, but nothing was done in a systematic way to collect data." The new assessments were given and hand-scored by teachers. To make the assessment data more useful to teachers and principals, a district employee developed a spreadsheet program into which the test data could be entered. Over time it evolved into a database connected to the district's student information system; teachers were able to generate reports showing which students were progressing as expected, which students were starting to struggle, and which were at a critical point of need.

In mid-2001, a new superintendent arrived with very strong views of where the district should be headed. He called for implementing a standards-based curriculum, improving instruction through professional development, offering teachers school-site coaching, and instituting periodic assessments. From his perspective, it was time to expand the benchmark assessment system to include more grade levels and subject areas. The developer of Beachside's home-grown tracking and benchmark system had by that time left the district and did not have the capacity to expand the system he had helped launch. The district had also been warned in an audit against building too many of its own structures from scratch because it could cost more time and money than buying products from outside vendors. Instead, the district contracted with Test Whiz to design and write a series of benchmark assessments for multiple grade levels. The following year, Beachside later recontracted with Test Whiz for three years of additional service at a fixed cost, with an annual option to renew. ·

The terms of the contract were discussed and agreed to by both sides beforehand. According to district officials, however, Test Whiz was unprepared for the size and complexity of the district. As a consequence, one district official reported, "The system was unusable for more than a year." Beachside district staff had to spend an extraordinary amount of time teaching Test Whiz about the district and helping the company adapt its products to the district's unique needs; for example, the fact that the district had year-round schools. After three years, the district signed a new contract with a new vendor; that firm, too, was unprepared for the district's distinctive challenges. According to several administrators, the district then had to spend a whole year backtracking. As one individual commented, "We had to start all over with the new company."

In its bid for a renewed contract, Test Whiz had banked on the district paying a much higher price. The new price estimate, $9 million, was a third higher than the $6 million the district had been paying. Also, there were still aspects of the system that were not working. Specifically, under Test Whiz, teachers were responsible for scanning the test score data themselves, but the equipment that the district had purchased was not up to the demands of the system, and Beachside's strong teachers' union strenuously objected to this use of teachers' time. Furthermore, the individuals we spoke with viewed the system as disconnected from the deeper set of changes required if the achievement gap was to be addressed in any significant way. The Chief Instructional Officer in Beachside put it this way:

> Changing instruction is the hard work. Putting periodic assessments into the system is a snap compared to the larger issue of helping people understand how to use data and how to create the conditions for helping teachers be reflective about their practice. That's professional

development in itself. It's conversations about removing barriers, it's about the principals being present and observing their teachers. It is examining the quality of a grade level meeting and pressing on that quality. It's not letting people off the hook simply because they gave the test, but getting them to look at the data. No, that is the hard work before us.

As in the case of Westview, Beachside officials also acknowledged the role of racist and class-based stereotypes in countenancing lower achievement among some groups and a district culture "where it has been OK to look at data through the lens that it is the kids have the problem" rather than looking critically at district and school policies and practices.

The implementation of the benchmark assessment system also depends on the strength of the union in the district and its involvement in the process. In Beachside, union officials appeared to have considerable input into the planning and use of formative assessment systems—specifically, when the assessments would be given, and whether teachers or the vendor would be responsible for scanning answer sheets. The union was adamantly opposed to an approach where teachers scanned the test scores themselves. Although the district had little sense beforehand that there might be an uproar, the strength of the union is likely one reason why Beachside was eventually forced to establish a contract with a vendor that provided scanning services rather than relying on teachers for this work. Part of what won the second vendor the contract was its solution to this issue, which involved having FedEx pick up answer sheets from each school and return them to a central location for scanning and uploading to the system.

The Beachside case further reveals the complex web of district policy and practice that intersect with the technological tools private firms are introducing in the context of NCLB. As in the case of Westview, district officials in Beachside viewed contracts with firms like Test Whiz as one slice of what necessarily must be a larger set of systemic changes that involved professional development, collaboration, and respect for teachers' primary responsibility for classroom instruction. In Beachside as in Westview, effective implementation of the system required substantive learning and change on the part of the firm itself. The ability of firms to learn and adapt to diverse district contexts helps frame and define district-level usage of the system and ultimately, its interactions with teachers around the system. At the same time, district context must play a large part in determining whether to lease a product off the shelf from an established firm, or to enter into partnership with a developer to build a system from scratch. This is illustrated by the decision made by our third case, Chesterville School District, which decided to create a system in-house tailored to its specific needs.

Chesterville School District: Building In-House

The Chesterville School District is a large, urban district with over 100,000 students. Along with the community that surrounds it, Chesterville has undergone sustained growth in recent years, doubling in student population since 1990. Unlike Westview and Beachside, the majority of the students in the district are White. The percentage of Chesterville students enrolled in Title I programs also stands in marked contrast to both Westview and Beachside, although it has jumped dramatically with the increase in population. Much like Beachside, the Chesterville district has never made AYP. Indeed, the percentage of schools making AYP within Chesterville has dropped steadily and dramatically over the past four years, from a high of near 75% in school year 2003 to 2004 to the current low of roughly 40% in year 2006 to 2007.

For years prior to 2001, Chesterville was what some researchers have called "data rich and information poor."[16] For example, in the elementary schools, teachers created detailed, handwritten profile cards for each student, on which they collected information about that child's performance in mathematics and literacy. However, as one official noted, "other than spreading all these cards out on the living room floor, there was really no way of grouping children to make informed instructional decisions." Each level of schooling was also at a different point with regard to the collection of data. While the elementary schools had their profile cards, the middle schools were referred to by some as "assessment-free zones" in which no formative data whatsoever were collected.

An initiative called Project SUCCESS was introduced to low performing elementary and middle schools within the district beginning in school year 2001 to 2002. Project SUCCESS bills itself as a comprehensive school improvement program with seven components, one of which is "evaluation and outcomes." Chesterville implemented new curriculum and periodic assessments as part of the initiative. Project SUCCESS did not come with a benchmark assessment system, and as a result, the district hired a developer to produce a basic program to track the scores from the tests. The tests were all taken by hand and run through a Scantron machine to be scored. The data then had to be transferred to the database program. Thus, there was a very slow turnaround of information, and the technology was in use only by schools that were struggling. By the start of the 2003 school year, only three out of 27 middle schools were participating in Project SUCCESS.

It was at this point that the director of middle school programs decided that she needed a way to track and improve performance in her middle schools across the board, and seized upon the already existing Project SUCCESS assessments as a good way to start. However, she also wanted a more complex database system that would allow the tests to be taken online and an updated, improved capability for analysis and additional reports.

She began to investigate off-the-shelf assessment systems, but what she found was either prohibitively expensive or did not allow for the district's existing Project SUCCESS assessments to be used. Additionally, she needed something that would allow for the evolution of her program, and as another official noted, "if you were dealing with a commercial product, they would never change it. You'd have to adapt what you did to the commercial product." Instead, Chesterville officials asked the programmer who had built the program used to record scores for the Project SUCCESS schools if he could expand its capabilities and make the assessments available online to all students, and not just those in struggling schools. Not only was he able to expand it, but the work he did cost much less than any estimates Chesterville had received from off-the-shelf vendors. Although Chesterville still leased the system from the developer, two of the officials we spoke to estimated that the system, now known as Gold Star, costs them less than $5 per student per year.

Over the next three years, local demand for Gold Star skyrocketed. The system itself evolved through the suggestions of teachers and central office staff members, who began to request adjustments and additions that would make it easier for them to manipulate and understand the data they collected through the assessments. Staff from all levels of the district also participated in expanding the range of assessments available, both by writing items and by participating in the item-review process. It is now a comprehensive benchmark assessment system, similar to off-the-shelf products, yet customized to Chesterville's specifications. The system is widely used in elementary and middle schools and has begun to expand into the high schools.

Although Gold Star is similar to Test Whiz in many ways, Chesterville's experience is distinct from that of Beachside and Westview. Officials spoke very positively of the responsiveness of the developer, of Gold Star itself, and of the changes in practice the system had helped to facilitate. For example, although there were initial technical problems with Gold Star, they were fixed very quickly after a simple series of visits the programmer made to schools using the system. Further, in speaking of the effects of the system, one official noted that it had actually helped teachers to break down some of their existing stereotypes. Because of the immediate availability of data, and the ability to see individual item analysis, teachers began to realize that children who had been previously assumed to be of "low ability" were actually doing much better on some objectives than those assumed to be of "higher ability." The system helped teachers not only change perceptions, but also understand how to build up support for students in crucial areas.

Chesterville's positive experience with Gold Star might be attributed to the fact that the impetus for the system was somewhat organic and came from the ground up rather than externally. Further, the fact that Gold Star was built and not bought off-the-shelf allowed for input from a much wider variety of school-level stakeholders, and may have contributed to less initial resistance toward the system and a quicker adoption.

Chesterville's unique structure and context allowed for this option in ways that neither Beachside's nor Westview's would have done. For instance, with Beachside's strong and active union playing a major role in all teacher-related business, it is unlikely that building a system would have been as quick or easy for its officials. The district might have had to formally negotiate the building of the system in a way that Chesterville, which has no teachers' union, did not. Similarly, in Westview, a district which had not struggled as much with its AYP goals, the local demand for data might not have been as urgent as it was in Chesterville, a district whose AYP performance had worsened every year since that standard's initiation.

Additional evidence to support the idea that customization is not always best can be found in the cost structure of the systems in Beachside and Chesterville. Both districts paid an annual licensing fee, based on the number of students and teachers, for the use of their systems; officials in both districts said the fee fell in the range of $0 to $5 per student annually. Beachside's system came with a long list of different report formats available to teachers and administrators, which would reveal different things about the data. Chesterville, on the other hand, had to pay an additional fee for each new report officials wanted. Thus, rather than being available at a fixed price, the annual cost of Chesterville's system varied based on the changes the district made to it each year. In a district the size of Beachside, a fluctuating annual cost may not have been worth the level of customization it offered, especially if it meant sacrificing other benefits of choosing a large, established vendor—such as the unique scoring system Beachside's second provider ultimately offered.

Conclusion

The events in these three districts cannot be assumed to generalize to all districts, but they do suggest some problems in the underlying assumptions of market-based education services. First, sanctions and mandates may create the incentive for districts to test more frequently, to include special education students in the testing, and look at data. On their own, however, they do not provide answers on how districts should address these problems, nor do they provide any real indicators of why these problems exist in the district in the first place.

The software is designed to make school districts more efficient. The fact remains that while the software is new, these "reforms," like other kinds of solutions pressed on schools, are being layered onto rather than replacing deeply institutionalized and broader structural inequalities. In Westview, where Test Whiz had been implemented across many schools, there were still students left behind—students whose teachers were excused from looking critically at their own practice, on the basis of assumptions about what students placed in special needs classrooms could achieve.

Further, there is some evidence to suggest that the new private-sector solutions could be exacerbating problems in districts. Districts such as Beachside are paying significant sums of money to firms contracted ostensibly to help them make their processes more efficient so that they can focus on the core work of teaching and learning. Yet if they have to invest a lot of time teaching those same firms, they are investing both time and money in the effort—scarce resources in virtually every school district.

Once the decision has been made to use a benchmark assessment system, there is no easy or standard way to determine whether the most cost effective and productive choice would be to construct one from scratch or lease one off-the-shelf. While constructing a system may win over stakeholders as it did in Chesterville, it may also be impossible given the political constraints and the resources of the district in question. A district may spend millions of dollars implementing a system only to realize that there is a seemingly insurmountable roadblock standing in the way of full adoption.

In summary, these three stories suggest the need for considerable caution on the part of districts racing to install benchmark assessment systems in order to meet the mandates of NCLB. For the testing industry, this is an exciting time as the mandates of NCLB and other policy pressures create incentives for local purchases. The problem is not that private firms are involved in the design and delivery of testing and measurement services. They always have been and probably always will be. Yet at the same time, as the role of these firms in testing grows and evolves, concerted action is needed to help districts evaluate the full implications of their purchasing decisions and assess whether the software product is a good investment. If a district is not able to muster the resources or make the changes required of practice at all levels, it runs the risk of allowing the assessment system to become a mechanism for unnecessary summative exams.

Finally, as a strategy for helping schools and districts develop a more fine-grained and nuanced picture of their performance, draw appropriate conclusions from the data, and use the data to revise district strategy, benchmark assessment systems hold considerable promise. Thoughtful attention by districts of the appropriate role of for-profit firms in developing and managing these systems is important. This should include consideration of the importance of developing internal district capacity, sustaining the work over time, and employing the data in the service of urgent equity issues.

CHAPTER 7

Working for Transparency

At a time of increasing private sector activity in the design, delivery, and evaluation of K–12 educational services and products, this book provides evidence of the paradigm shift occurring from public to private management in public education. There is a quiet revolution occurring in the relationship between the public and private sector in K–12 education that is not being publicly discussed and is likely to have significant implications for disadvantaged children. Private, for-profit firms are becoming the major suppliers to local school systems for an array of instructional services and products.

The firms gaining prominence under the new educational privatization are drawing on political networks, new technologies, and capital investments to become the major suppliers to school systems of an ever-growing array of services, from professional development to test score analysis to after-school programming. The for-profit business framework is increasingly becoming the model for education, and it runs through the NCLB legislation, creating new inconsistencies and tensions in the law. The outcomes of this most recent chapter of business involvement in public education likely will fundamentally shape the future of public education in the United States.

The K–12 education market, which only a decade ago Wall Street analysts termed sluggish, is exploding through the rapid influx of capital investments and federal education, state, and local revenue linked to accountability mandates. First, education policy increasingly is being linked to the financial market and the importance of speculative capital in spurring innovation and improving social outcomes. Federal education policy, in the form of the No Child Left Behind Act (NCLB), has given themes of accountability and choice an even more central place in national and local discourse around public education. More tangibly, NCLB has helped firms providing an array of accountability products—including test development, after-school tutoring, and prepackaged, online curriculum—to make fast and deeper inroads into local markets. The involvement of the private sector is further facilitated by two additional factors: technological change and the global economy make it possible for national and international firms, with expansive resources, to offer services to local districts quickly and efficiently—on their own terms.

The new educational privatization is promoted as a means to increase access to varied and high quality education for disadvantaged children, increase the accountability of the organizations that work with children, and increase the liberty of parents to choose educational experiences matched to their children's needs. Under the new educational privatization, for-profit firms are cast and identified in policy as bringing needed expertise, innovation, and cost efficiencies to the problems of public education. Given these claims, there is a compelling need for more transparency around what these firms are doing, and the implications of their influence for public policy in education and the educational opportunities of disadvantaged youth.

In this book, I have explored a frame for analyzing the new privatization that cuts across two bodies of literature. As I discussed in chapter 1, I draw on ideas from critical studies of markets and education policy and contemporary ideas from the new institutionalism. In what follows, I revisit this frame, its core components, and the insights that it provides. In the second section of the chapter, I turn to a more practical set of considerations, by discussing problems in current trends in education policy, and by identifying levers for strengthening policy.

Theory in Use

In Table 7.1, I offer a frame for examining the consequences of new privatization through the theoretical lens that I described in chapter 1. The consequences are institutional in the sense that they reflect effects on organizational fields—how roles are being cast, relationships reformed, what new strategies are defining the work. They also are institutional in their focus on maintenance of established practices and the privileging of dominant ideas. While framed by the new institutionalism, the consequences also bear directly on the equity issues that are central concerns in critical studies of education markets (and for the present author). These include (1) reproduction of structural inequalities; (2) reproduction of established practices of schooling that contribute to these inequalities; and (3) the possibilities for increased influence on the part of less powerful groups in policy discourse.

In arguing the value of this frame, I have four main points. First, we need to look at organizational fields. Much of the action that is shaping education

Table 7.1 Studying the New Privatization

1. Organizational Fields
    Shift in kinds of organizations and individuals involved in the work
    Recasting of roles, relationships, and interdependencies
    (Re)definition of practices

2. Institutional Processes
    Maintenance of established policies and practices
    Masking of deeply rooted schooling inequities
    Possibilities for increased influence on educational meanings and processes

3. Field Effects
    Policy discourse—what problems/solutions are privileged
    New organizational forms—e.g. hybrid organizations
    Political resources—new alliances, sources of information

is happening through a redefinition of organizational fields. Second, larger cultural ideas, specifically those based on neoliberal thinking, are shifting the gravity of public policies and these shifts have direct consequences for local policy discourse and in this regard, are important field effects. Third, corporations and market ideas are changing education, but corporations are also trying to look like education—often in highly traditional and discredited ways. Fourth, as all of this is happening, pressures and conflicts within the field are building, which in turn is creating the space for less powerful actors to have some influence on definitions of educational meanings and processes.

Public and Private

Institutional perspectives on educational policy and practice can draw attention to for-profit and not-for-profit vendors' expanding role in local governance. Districts and states historically have relied on outside vendors for functions related to standardized tests, such as test preparation and score reporting. But now districts and states also are paying outside vendors to assist them in the overall design, operation, and evaluation of instructional reforms. These developments demand conceptual frameworks for studying educational policy that place nongovernmental organizations and their linkages with governmental agencies at the center of the policy process. The level of analysis becomes the organizational field and the array of organizations, both public and private operating in that field.

In my article "The New Educational Privatization" I identified four core activities as central to the contracting that forms around the mandates of NCLB: test development and preparation, data analysis and management, remedial services, and content area-specific programming.[1] In this book, having identified these emergent fields, I looked inside of them in order to map the kinds of companies attracted to different segments, the organizing principles that they brought into their interactions with districts, and the tensions and possibilities that these interactions created.

In thinking about the new privatization as an organizational field, I asked several questions. One question concerned what kinds of firms are being attracted to the education industry as a consequence of increasing privatization and the shift toward neoliberal thinking. I also asked how firms are interacting with districts, and what are the nature of the interdependencies. These questions helped me to delineate several features of the new privatization; for example, shifts in pricing and the importance of technology.

A second question concerned how, through these developments, the roles of various actors—parents, private firms, district staff —are being recast.[2] My analysis provided further illustration of how neoliberal education policy shifts the expected roles of individuals and organizations in policy implementation; how parents are expected to contribute, what constitutes good government, and what constitutes expertise in addressing the achievement gap. These shifts grow out of the circular logic of market education. They help change the terrain of what people are expected to do. The reframing of roles underway involves a narrowing effect, a shift toward a more technical and atomistic orientation of public responsibilities.

In my analysis, and consistent with the new institutional frame, I had a particular interest in who was helping to do the political work of the new privatization. I noted how individuals and organizations that straddled the worlds of markets and policy serve as carriers. For example, former government officials that move to jobs in the private sector have helped the private sector see where the revenue sources lie. I also offered the example of how through their criteria for education ventures, investors blend ideas about education policy with ideas of the market. Further, in seeking to understand some of the influences on the new privatization, I examined and then argued the critical function of education policy texts (and specifically the role of second layer policies) in authoring and legitimizing these changes.

Reproducing Problematic Practices

Corporations and market ideas are changing education, but corporations also are trying to look like education—often in highly traditional and discredited ways. In prior work, I have argued that scholarship that applies institutional theory to education also has offered explanations for why schools and districts that are located in very diverse settings and that may have little interaction nevertheless adopt policies and practices that are very similar.[3] I have spent a part of this book showing how market thinking and corporate models are becoming institutionalized in education policy.

However, as noted, there is another side to this coin: namely, the tendency of for-profits to take on educational structures and rhetoric and traditional curricular practices in order to legitimize themselves as both conduits for public money and genuine educational players. Firms adopt practices and design products to signal their legitimacy as providers of public services and in order to legitimize their role as extensions of the state. They look to the practices of other firms, to the language of policy, to established routines and practice used by districts as cues for what they should be doing. To offer a few examples, after-school programs hire public school teachers as tutors, organize sessions around homework help, use worksheets, and take attendance. Virtual school providers have staff development days, and staff developers. Firms assign managers titles that sound a lot like those used in regular school districts, such as curriculum developer and staff developer.

Thus, while for-profit firms certainly influence education policy and impose corporate values in their interactions with districts, the influences are multidirectional. As for-profit firms interact with school districts, they assimilate and adopt the established practice of the State. This isomorphism is reflected in a number of different arenas: curriculum approaches, instructional formats, and functions such as the design of professional development. To put it another way, corporate influence on public education is only part of the story. The State continues to have a significant influence on firms that design and deliver services, because of the very established nature of its policies and practices. This raises a number of issues that have not received much attention in policy debates and should. Proponents of privatization argue that by involving for-profit private firms more in the design and delivery of instructional services, we can make available significant alternatives to state-run education, increasing innovation in the design and delivery of public services. The developments that I have described suggest the possibility of a different scenario. What large, for-profit firms may end up delivering in K–12 education is more of the same—more traditional curriculum in the form of worksheets, more staff development disconnected from classroom realities and teachers' needs, more layers of administration (regional offices, chief instructional officers) that remove policy from practical concerns. The case studies in the preceding chapters point to many examples of for-profit firms mimicking what some districts do or what some schools do. Rather than break the mold, private firms can in fact reinforce tradition.

Further, the consequences of these dynamics can be very insidious by helping to create the appearance of real change in the absence of substantive policy action to address inequalities.[4] At the time of writing, there is much policy discussion about the problem of public governance and how it contributes significantly to the achievement gap. Certainly, there is much to criticize in government's actions. However, institutional theory can inform understanding of how for-profit firms interact with institutionalized environments of public schools to shape policy outcomes and the reproduction of inequalities. The very same organization that uses slogans such as "personalized instruction" or "expanding access and opportunity" for the disadvantaged is at the same time participating in corporate planning that will favor boilerplate curriculum and increase class size to reduce costs, and engage in niche marketing to students whose ensured academic success will help sell the product. Institutional theory helps us see how firms can adopt the equity language of public policy (access, participation, choice) and even the structures of public policy (special education director, the purchase of test preparation materials, reading curriculum) while "protecting" their core technologies and practices from any significant changes.

Consider these examples. The firm that is approved as a supplemental education service provider and has a contract with the state and participates in its compliance activities does not make services available to English learners or students with disabilities. The firm that identifies as a choice option under NCLB, a school that purportedly expands choices for economically disadvantaged students, nevertheless encourages its staff to *discourage* families "without means" from enrolling. The firm that markets itself as helping districts become more efficient also designs products that cost districts significant sums of money with little assurance of usage. In much of the literature on corporate influence in education, the emphasis has been on how corporations are changing public education. In fact, the dynamics may be much more conservative although at significantly greater cost because of the expanding scope of services purchased and numbers of districts involved.

Contradictions and Openings

However, convergence between practices of the state and for-profit firms is not inevitable. In my work, I encountered a few instances in which, at least over the short term, for-profit firms offered alternative practices that interrupted at least temporarily established policy routines. For example, for-profit firms in the online testing market have designed software that eliminates district staff as a middleman in data requests. The traditional state model of restricting access to raw standardized test score data to district officials with formal responsibility for accountability, or research and evaluation is not democratic and does not support the kind of informed dialogue that is needed to improve instruction. Through the design of software, for-profit firms can help districts reconceptualize norms about who should have access to data.[5]

The possibilities of interrupting established State practices also apply to supplemental education services and virtual charter schools. In economically disadvantaged communities, the safety and care of children after school is an enormous concern. Families in these communities frequently rely on older siblings to care for younger siblings. For-profit firms that offer families after-school programming in the home and on the computer create alternatives for families who, because of practical and financial constraints, and safety concerns, cannot have their children participating in after-school tutoring in school or a community setting.

As a final example, schooling inequities derive in large part from residential segregation by race and class. Families with the financial resources exercise choice options by buying real estate in communities with good schools. Virtual schooling reinforces the ideas that there are different kinds of charter schools that can be honored and encouraged by school districts. Sometimes the traditional public school model of having children physically attend a school does not accommodate the needs of students and their right to an adequate public education. This is particularly the case when students have social/emotional disabilities or physical impairments that make learning at home preferred and less frightening.

Lasting Resources

Larger cultural ideas are becoming part of public policies; the presentation and organization of policy in this regard represents important field effects. Recent institutional theorizing also provides an expanded lens for examining how reforms aimed at strengthening classroom teaching contribute to shifts in the broader policy environment. Field theorists view the settings for examining policy effects as broader than those typically presented in the policy literature, which tends to concentrate on policy effects inside schools and governing agencies. They are particularly interested in the effects that interactions across organizations have on the larger reform environment. How has the discourse linked to the policy problem shifted? What are the cultural and institutional effects of the reform? Is there evidence that new organizational forms are emerging as a result of the reform, or do we see new categories of policy actors?

The concept of field level effects provides an expanded lens for examining the impact of market-oriented education policies. At this writing, the future of NCLB is unclear. Even though the law purportedly was built through bi-partisan support, it is like the war the Iraq, closely associated with President Bush—whose approval ratings are at an all time low. The issue that we need to consider is that even if NCLB is not reauthorized or changes significantly, from the perspective of privatization proponents and supporters of market-oriented policy, some important objectives will have been achieved. A broader array of organizations has entered the K–12 education industry than was previously the case; there is more competition in the market at least for the short term. The industry itself has started to attract players with revenue and political capital at their disposal, such as software companies and producers of home entertainment and computer games. The activity in the market has spurred some new investor interest as manifested both in the high level of merger and acquisition activity and in the investments being made by firms such as Knowledge Universe.

Further, while aspects of NCLB may be eliminated or radically revised, the developments chronicled in the preceding chapters appear to have helped establish new organizational forms and power blocs that will be able to sustain interest even if the privatization elements of NCLB are dismantled. As described in chapter 3, one of the effects of the new educational privatization has been the emergence of market-oriented philanthropies whose organizational form straddles the world of philanthropy and capital investment. These foundations-cum-investment firms are injecting a corporate approach in their grant-making activities. They are funding nonprofits but doing so on the condition that these nonprofit charter schools function more like for-profit firms, evaluating reforms in terms of rate of return, considering the "competition"—other charter schools—as they design their programs. These networks also are playing a major role in pushing for policy changes at the federal, state, and local level to sustain investment and interest in the ideas over time. For example, the New Schools Venture Fund played a major role in reducing the cap on charter schools in California. The Educational Industry Association is, through its lobbying and political work around supplemental education services, redefining after-school programming as part of a broader privatization agenda that also includes charter schools and vouchers.

These kinds of field effects—the establishment of new professional categories, increase in perceived legitimacy of an idea—increase or shift in kinds of firms working independently or jointly on a problem up to this point have not been focal in policy research. Neither have they been at the forefront of debates around the effects of NCLB. I believe that as a profession, policy researchers need to pay more attention to these kinds of institutional policy effects. Through the lens of institutional theory, we can begin to see how interactions across the public and private sector establish the underlying conditions in which public policy is designed and implemented. For-profit firms are important not only because they are assuming broader responsibilities as providers of instructional services, but also because, through these interactions, they contribute to shifts in the institutional environment of public education—redefining who are considered key professionals, what kinds of organizations are considered legitimate providers and therefore have rights to public revenues, what makes a public school public, what can be considered as a legitimate format for publicly funded after-school programming and so forth. These changes—the redefinition—can happen alongside of the mimicking of established practices. In this regard, as in other respects, the institutionalization of educational privatization carries contradictions.

These effects and these dynamics are not occurring without conflict. In education, we tend to view policy conflict and contradiction as detracting from successful policy implementation. Institutional theorists offer an alternative view on the role of ideological conflict in social change.[6] From their perspective, where there is deep ideological disagreement (such as dissent about the value of high-stakes testing in instructional improvement), there is also ambiguity. Longstanding approaches can come under scrutiny (such as the value of evaluating student progress at one point in time). The ideas that people have taken for granted no longer seem as secure. Because things do not sit right, there is more press and support to ask hard questions about what constitutes best practice. From this perspective, where we see heated public debates about public policy, we can assume that strategic opportunities also exist. Under these conditions, organizations that lack institutional legitimacy or conventional resources such as money can introduce changes in the design and delivery of educational policy.

The preceding chapters offer some examples of how organizations and individuals outside of the mainstream are interrupting and transforming the developments in contracting. As online testing systems become more widespread, teachers' unions are seeking to have a greater say in their design. District officials are seeking to redesign contracts with for-profit firms that maintain their authority over data and that help them maintain the capacity for the work over time. In the area of supplemental education services, parents are beginning (individually and in some places collectively) to articulate concerns about the quality of information that they receive on after-school programs. Instructors, often drawing on their own resources, are finding ways to differentiate curriculum or to make programming more responsive to students' needs; for example, by offering home-made meals at the end of the tutoring session.

Future Work

This book takes a step in the direction of situating local forms of educational privatization, such as virtual charter schools and after-school programming, in the context of broader market logics and traces some of the implications. What this book cannot do, and what I hope others will do, is twofold. First, in-depth qualitative research is needed in order to examine the interplay between local practice, government policy, and corporate activity. The cases I present above can only scratch at the surface of the complex local political, human, social, and instructional dynamics that work in and through privatization schemes. They offer a window onto the conditions through which firms either reproduce problems or in a few instances, provide alternatives to inequitable practices. Here too, much more work is needed to understand under what conditions it may make sense to contract education services to for-profit firms and how to structure the relationships in ways that expand access and participation to high quality programming.

In addition, while I do have national data on several for-profit firms, this data is partial. I do not have large scale quantitative data on either district or vendor practices that would provide a comprehensive and representative picture of the changes described. Developing this kind of database would be a worthwhile project and could provide a context for the case studies described above. Economic data could also provide more insight into the incidence of the trends that I have noted, the cost considerations (how much districts are spending on these firms) and the resource implications for other kinds of instructional services traditionally provided by districts. Put differently, when money flows to private firms for market based education services, what does not get funded? Finally, I have argued that recent developments in institutional theory offer education researchers important insights for understanding contemporary policy and practice. However, more work is needed that incorporates insights from institutional theory into a critical policy framework. The blending of these two perspectives is more possible given the new institutionalism's greater focus on power and agency. Although some of the insights that emerge from continued integration of institutional perspectives and education research will be specific to education, other themes—many discussed in this book—may operate in other sectors and domains of social policy. Institutional theory may provide valuable leverage for understanding developments in education; yet by applying emergent constructs to the case of education, education researchers also can elaborate and strengthen contemporary institutional thinking.

Policy Problems and Possibilities

What needs to happen in order to minimize the negative consequences of the new educational privatization for least advantaged students? What kinds of institutional arrangements seem promising as tools for preventing profit agendas from trumping quality and equitable programming?

For several decades now, the topic of educational accountability has dominated K–12 policy discussions. By stronger accountability, policymakers typically mean strengthening the levers, such as the tests and sanctions, rather than broadening the scope of who is to be made accountable for student outcomes. But in the debates so far, there has very little talk about the track record of NCLB in holding private firms accountable for achievement outcomes. Instead, any discussion of program impact is in reference to conducting general evaluations of the program, without specific mention of assessing those firms that provide the services and therefore receive public funds.

In this book, I have pursued three interrelated arguments around the intensifying and evolving nature of contracting activity in K–12 education. First, the actors are shifting. Relative to past statutes, neoliberal education policy invites firms to play a far wider range of roles and responsibilities for meeting the needs of schools, in particular in reducing the achievement gap. Second, the interests are shifting. With NCLB, the financial interests of the private sector (and neoliberal thinking) have become wedded closely to Federal education policy as reflected in the design of the law. Third, these changes have happened without commensurate attention to how these firms will be monitored. In the next section, I identify the fundamental problems and possibilities generated by these trends and identify principles for policy action.

Profits and Equity

The message we hear from current Federal education policy is that, now more than ever before, the public sector needs the private sector. The assumption is that the financial interests of for-profit firms and the social agenda of public education can converge. From this perspective, maximizing profit and achieving more equitable outcomes are not mutually exclusive, but rather mutually enforcing. Evidence from the book suggests that in the absence of monitoring and oversight, the agenda of making a profit can override the public interest of improving access to and participation in quality public education. These risks are apparent when large, after-school tutoring firms schedule tutoring sessions in ways that minimize costs rather than maximize student engagement. We see these risks when virtual charter schools adopt policies that make it difficult for working families and the very poor to enroll in their programs. We see these risks when virtual charter school providers increase class size to 49 students for one teacher, again as a means to cut costs. These risks are apparent in the stories of families of children with disabilities who are unable to gain access to appropriate after-school programming even though by policy their children are eligible.

Lack of Transparency

The more economic incentive there is, the greater the tendency for for-profit firms to want to keep their finances and operations out of public view. When firms are privately held, they have to disclose very little to the public. When public companies go private or when public companies are acquired, it becomes increasingly difficult for the public to assess both the strength and value of these firms in any systematic or in-depth manner. The firm essentially is allowed to disappear from public view. Whether and how the entity of being private, not having to report to shareholders, shapes access and quality is not well understood. Some might argue that when firms go private, they have more freedom to innovate and respond to customers rather than shareholders. In my evaluation, based on the evidence presented in the book, the greater the role of policy in legitimizing and expanding revenues for for-profit firms, the greater the need for private firms to keep their operations opaque and the greater the tendency of large for-profit corporations—some of them public, some of them private—to acquire smaller firms. This means that as revenues for the new educational privatization grow, there will be moves toward the privatization of public information. I refer here not only to the expanding role of private firms in the control and management of public information, but also to a trend in which the movement of public revenue in and out of corporations becomes more opaque. In an era defined by calls for more transparency in government, the contribution and the costs of companies in the K–12 education industry ironically stay hidden from view.

Private Uses of Public Policy

Another problem concerns the commercial uses of education policy by private firms. Stephen Ball makes this point when he talks about the retailing of policy.[7] Policy becomes a tool through which firms sell their products and services. There is, of course, a different way to think about policy, one that I would argue has been largely marginalized as of late: the idea that policy is more than a means for stimulating the economy and promoting competition. It may be inevitable that policy will work in the interest of private firms. The real danger comes when education policy is used to rationalize these interests, as I think has started to happen with NCLB. There is a kind of circular argument that emerges. Policy creates demand for products and services that will help schools and districts comply with mandates. Policy also becomes a tool for ensuring and maintaining over time the revenues that flow to the vendors of these products and services.

As its stands now, firms profiting under NCLB have minimal to no responsibility for these populations. More to the point, government regulations are used to rationalize and stabilize the financial interests of firms—with a deemphasis of the rights of the least advantaged populations. Thus, in the SES regulations, states are forbidden from establishing absolute limits on what providers can charge based on the logic that doing so will interfere with market competition. To offer other examples, states have no funds to evaluate private providers; the providers are not required to show objective measures of performance; districts have no say over curriculum; private providers are not obliged to work with the most expensive students while districts are required to; requirements for highly qualified teachers are expressly forbidden. This is a regulatory framework that effectively contributes to enhancing the private firms' bottom line.

Uneven Political Influence

The third problem is that while educational privatization typically is thought of as freeing educational services from governmental regulations or creating new markets as alternatives to government-delivered services, in fact somewhat of the reverse also is likely to be true. State policies can create incentives and pressures for public sector providers to use private sector services. Vendors have sought to leverage NCLB mandates as part of their marketing strategies. As they invest in new products, the importance of maintaining policies that will enable them to reap financial returns on their investments grows.

In the emerging world of K–12 education contracting, powerful interest groups are forming, establishing new strategic alliances and recruiting new members. Their activities so far have occurred largely behind the scenes and out of the spotlight of the NCLB debate. These associations, such as the Education Industry Association, and EduVentures are highly organized, well funded, well connected, and very knowledgeable about policy and the stakes involved in the reauthorization. They have lobbied successfully for policy that will protect the interests of their members. These groups are firmly grounded in the ideology of the market model of education reform. These firms are working to change and introduce the next chapter of these ideas and to ensure their members—large, for-profit firms—have the flexibility and rights to use public resources in ways that they see fit.

The problem is not that these trade-groups exist or even that they are powerful. The problem is that the resources and influences of those representing the interests of the industry far surpasses that of other stakeholders, such as classroom educators, economically disadvantaged families, and nonprofit community organizations. As the policy context for-profit firms are remade, the influence of these firms increases. Meanwhile, as discussed in chapter 1, through new spending regulations and budget shifts, federal policy marginalizes models of collective parent and community participation and diminishes them through the reduction of financial resources. Who shapes education policy, who decides where revenues flow and the restrictions on that flow reflects and turns on level of resources of institutions who can afford to lobby Congress over extended periods of time.

Niche Marketing to the Poor

The fourth problem concerns the long-term strategies and interests of large, for-profit firms that are content, for now, to sell services and products under different brand names. All signs point, however, to trends in which large, established firms capture much of the business of a single school district, albeit through an array of atomistic contracts. This raises issues of monopolies, power asymmetries, and ethical business practices. There is another lurking related issue here. Buoyed by the mandates of NCLB, firms are seeking to develop a niche market among very low-income families, seeking increased market share and market penetration among the economically disadvantaged. They are sending their representatives into low-income communities to learn more about how these families live and, purportedly, what they want, so as to lay a better foundation for selling products and services to them. They are using marketing channels that will help them integrate the sale of their products better into the community, involving and contacting churches in advertising their programs as in the case of SES, offering in-kind contributions to low-income families such as free computers, and forming strategic alliances with organizations with credibility in these communities. Firms are using the language of civil rights to frame their marketing efforts as expanding parents' choices and giving them more choices as consumers. Yet in the world of retailing, there are many examples of firms using their influence and capital to sell low-income families things that they neither want nor need, like cigarettes and junk food. Supermarket chains offer lower quality food (especially meat and produce) at higher prices in poor neighborhoods. Banks that decide to put ATMs in poor neighborhoods charge higher rates.

Criteria for Strengthening Accountability for Private Firms[8]

Finally, I consider several criteria for designing governance arrangements given the changing nature of privatization in K–12 compulsory education. The force of policy recommendations is strongest when supported by a collective process whereby different stakeholders participate and provide input. With the hope that they might inform public deliberation, I offer four principles for policymaking that emerge from my analysis.

Economic Entanglements

Any effort to improve accountability for private firms under NCLB must address or at least acknowledge the larger contours and trends in the economic and political environment.[9] Under the Bush administration, numerous regulatory changes have been introduced to protect the financial interests of industries by eliminating or changing federal regulations that cost employers and large companies money. For example, business lobbyists have argued for tighter restrictions on employees taking family and medical leave, citing economic losses to industry of reduced work hours. Large banks are evaluating credit and debt applications in ways that raise troubling issues around consumer protection, and the need for more judicious practices on the part of the industry when approving loans. Advocacy groups, such as environmental groups and employee protection groups have charged that under the current administration federal agencies responsible for regulating business practices are responding sluggishly if at all to complaints.

The design and logic of NCLB is deeply entangled with broader economic policy. If policymakers are to address the current tensions in protecting the rights of children under Title I to high quality instruction, they need to address and advocate for changes in this larger arena. This can be accomplished in part by leveraging what is happening in public school districts across the country which have been at the forefront of recognizing and challenging the centrifugal forces of some education policy and economic policies. Communities across the United States and globally are questioning in tandem the burden of state policy and the spread of privatization in education.[10]

This work also involves action on the part of the academic community to pay deliberate attention to the underlying logic of policy trends. It involves helping the public see the drift that pulls policies (located in different sectors, such as health, education, and social work) in the same direction. By looking at the big picture, and looking across segments of public policy in our work, avenues for collective action become more possible.

More Transparency and Accountability

Policy is needed that provides institutional incentives for holding private firms accountable to the public goals of equity, participation, access, and quality in education. As a condition for receiving federal education funds, private firms must assume and be held responsible for ensuring appropriate and adequate supply of services to historically underserved populations, such as English learners, students with disabilities, and students living in communities with high concentrations of poverty.

More stringent rules are needed that will enable valid comparisons, both across different kinds of firms (such as the track records of various

SES vendors in contributing to average gains of student achievement) and comparison among publicly designed and delivered and privately designed and delivered programs. At the minimum, in segments of the industry such as SES, for-profit firms should be required to use a common standardized benchmark for assessing the academic progress of students. Further, if it is important for public schools to be held accountable for having expected outcomes with students, similar standards with equally clear measures should be required of private providers. With the profit motive providing obvious incentives to compromise educational quality in class sizes, teacher qualifications, and standardization rather than differentiation of curriculum, it is doubly imperative—especially in an incentives-driven model—to insert policy mechanisms that adequately encourage the provision of high quality offerings, set firm minimal standards of quality, and establish measures of accountability for performance. This is the especially true as for-profit providers draw limited federal funds away from the core offerings of public schools in high-needs areas.

Policy guidance that partly exempts private firms from upholding students' civil rights while earning millions of dollars in public revenue is unethical. Ensuring compliance with civil rights mandates remains a public responsibility and there is a considerable gray area as new forms of contracting emerge. The problem is exacerbated by the fact that developing appropriate and meaningful services for historically underserved populations can be expensive, and therefore firms and the associations that represent them are likely to see little in the way of financial rewards or incentives for serving these populations.

The federal government can play a very aggressive role in establishing and enforcing the rights of these populations to access the financial resources intended for their benefit, as can the courts. In the context of SES, in the context of virtual charter schools that serve as choice options, in the context of assessment systems that incorporate very high stakes, students have the right to appropriate, high quality public schooling resources even when and *especially when* these resources flow in and through intermediary organizations, such as for-profit firms.

Design for Collaboration

The current design of the law moves in the opposite direction, pitting local government against education service providers around control of Title I funds. In the case of SES, for example, Title I funds flow to private providers rather than to local school districts when districts have not made AYP. Alternative frameworks are needed that encourage collaboration and co-operation among providers and local schools and governments. We have few levers or models available to encourage this collaboration. The design of NCLB compounds rather than reduces these tensions because it assumes that the relationship between private firms and public agencies primarily is unidirectional. Involving private firms (SES vendors, charter school operators, testing firms) in the design and delivery of Title I is framed as reforming public agencies and making them more efficient, while those private firms are not similarly subject to reform themselves.

Because of differences in local context, increasing collaboration may ultimately boil down to local efforts to create better contracts between education service providers and local governments. Tighter rules around contracting serve to make both public officials and private firms more accountable for outcomes. For example, there need to be clear restrictions barring public officials who award contracts to private firms aimed at helping their education agencies comply with NCLB mandates from then going on to assume lucrative positions in the industry.

Further discussion and development of these principles is needed. Designing strategies for improving the use of public funds must simultaneously move beyond conventional wisdom while carefully weighing what is politically and technically possible. Political philosophers have remarked that in contemporary policy debates, "the central question is not whether or not choice should be allowed" given that choice already exists in many forms. Instead, they urge us to ask questions such as "What kinds of public choice should be allowed and expanded? On what terms should be allowed? On what terms should it be publicly funded?"[11] For the sake of increased equity, we also need to be asking these questions when we spend public money on privately designed and delivered education services—not necessarily whether we should do so, but under what conditions, and with what specific and substantive regulations?

In examining the need for stronger policy and legal frameworks for protecting issues of equity in public education, it is important not to conflate completely the role of private firms and public agencies in matters of public education governance. The higher level of accountability for the public interest is part of what defines an agency as public. Neither is it appropriate, however, for federal education policy to exacerbate tensions between the public and private sectors around the governance of public education.

Conclusion

In this book, I have argued that more attention be given to hidden developments in K–12 education contracting. We do not expect for-profit, private firms to have the same level of accessibility and transparency as public agencies. Yet, these private, for-profit firms draw on public funds that are designed to serve common interests. Of course, it is important to recognize that private firms have a role to play in public education. They long have acted as suppliers to education and will continue to do so. Under certain conditions, they can contribute to the democratic purposes of education.

But, right now, the center of gravity in public policy is shifting. Ideologies of neoliberalism are remaking education policy to fit the needs of the market. The ideas are pushed as helping public education although the arguments have little empirical basis. The governance of public education is not just another education market. The distinction between public policy and private markets in education, as in other sectors, is very important, and it is worth defending.[12]

Research Design and Methodology

Below I present a summary of the research design and methodology on which the arguments for the book are based. The summary covers the following topics: (1) methodology and perspective; (2) researcher role; (3) key components of data gathering and analysis; and (4) concluding comments.

Methodology and Perspective

The study was based on qualitative research methods, and specifically in-depth interviews, participant observation, and analysis of public and official documents. I began with an orienting interest in new forms of education contracting being triggered by the mandates of NCLB. As qualitative research, the design of the study evolved somewhat over time as the work progressed.[1]

A phenomenological perspective guided the study based on my interest in understanding how various actors experienced and interpreted the new privatization. In addition, as I described in chapter 1, I also employed ideas from the new institutionalism and critical studies of education markets as a frame for understanding developments.[2] The new institutionalism is particularly important given neoliberal trends that afford private firms greater access to public revenues and a wider variety of roles in education. Critical studies of education markets informed my analysis of the social justice implications of institutionalizing processes.

I used both theoretical sampling and nested sampling.[3] The sample was theory driven in the sense that I looked for instances of the new privatization that would allow me to understand it in its different manifestations and from different perspectives. The three instances were supplemental education services, virtual charter schools, and contracts for benchmark assessments.

These were forms of contracting that were nested in broader trends that I had identified in other work as triggered by the mandates of No Child Left Behind (NCLB).[4] I also selected them because they seemed to reflect what I had begun to identify as the defining dimensions of the new privatization. Further, at the outset of my research, these developments had received little attention.

I also used within-case, nested sampling as a design and analytic strategy. Thus, as reflected in appendix B, for each of the types of new privatization, I examined key features which included key actors (what kinds of firms were selling; what was their target group); trends in financial data (based on public documents and as described in more detail below); the policy drivers (what kinds of policy trends were authoring the developments); the key processes involved in the work (pricing, duration of contract, theories of action behind the product); the strategies employed by those involved in the segment (both in selling, purchasing, and using) and the consequences of the trends.

I also employed nested sampling. This was appropriate given the policy issue focus of the study and my theoretical interest in markets as an influence on policy processes. Thus, for each of the cases (for example, virtual schools), I sampled leading firms selling in the market segment, districts purchasing products from them, and the district administrators and school staff within these districts. It was also important in this work to use nested sampling in examining firms' activities. Thus, I examined what firms were doing nationally (and the business models employed across states). However, I also sought understanding of how some of the same firms operated locally—how they interacted with districts, for example.[5]

Researcher Roles

There were aspects of the research that were conducted with the assistance of a research team. In describing aspects of the research, I use the terms *team* or *we* in acknowledgment of this collaboration. The team was composed of graduate students who worked with me on the project as part of their master's theses. These individuals worked on the project at different times and assumed different roles. These roles included designing, collecting, and analyzing survey data; conducting interviews in local settings; note-taking during interviews with executives; analyzing documents and existing research to place developments in historical context; and participating in discussions of the data. In addition to making the act of writing the book less isolating, the team also served the function of triangulation in many aspects of the research in that in general there were two or more individuals analyzing the same data or doing research in the same setting.

In one aspect of the study (supplemental education services), the work was supported in part by a school district. This work was part of a larger study of supplemental education services. In this larger study, my formal role involved helping districts understand the implementation challenges of SES. In the context of this research, we wrote a report for the district that highlighted key findings and triggered some organizational changes in the district. Our ongoing involvement in this district and funding for our work provided advantages in terms of our understanding. In the other districts, our research was conducted at more of a distance in the sense that our efforts were not connected to specific organizational problems that the district itself had identified as important.

Key Components of Data Gathering and Analysis

The study was conducted over a two-and-a-half-year period (from December 2006 to June 2008). The overall study involved three main components:

Evidence on Private Firms

Evidence on the activities of private firms was collected from numerous sources. This included in-depth unstructured interviews with senior executives, analysis of documents and news reports, and field observation of industry events.

In-Depth Unstructured Interviews with Senior Executives

The majority of these interviews were conducted in the summer of 2006 and the summer of 2007. In this phase of the work, 30 interviews were conducted with individuals representing 20 different private firms. I also interviewed five individuals working for market research firms, trade groups, or advocacy groups. In total, approximately 50 hours of interview data were collected in this research. Approximately half of the interviews were conducted by phone; the other half were conducted in person in the context of participant observation of industry related events.

The value of these interviews was twofold. First, it allowed me to capture what was happening in the industry with more complexity than if I had only examined publicly accessible documents such as the SEC documents, trade journals, or company Web sites. Second, it provided a window on the behavior and attitudes of those working *in* the private sector, but *with* the public sector. Representatives from the private sector are not typically included in interview pools in education research. Yet, because of my research focus, their perspective was critical. There were several key informants in this research with whom I cultivated closer relationships and who helped introduce me to others in the industry. I supplemented these interviews with follow-up e-mail exchanges where I asked for clarification and incorporated the responses as interview notes.

Descriptive Analyses of the Financial and Operational Data of Publicly Traded Firms

I also gathered data on financial and operational trends among 18 for-profit K–12 education vendors. I used the same data sources (for example 10-K forms filed the same year) from each firm wherever possible to facilitate comparisons. For the purposes of this study, I defined for-profit education vendors as for-profit organizations that had contracts with public schools or districts to provide education services including but not limited to, assessment tools (test design, reporting management analysis); online curriculum and instructional tools (digitized curriculum, Web-based platforms, computer assisted learning and school management services; e.g., electronic blackboards, online student registration); human resource services (hiring and training of instructional staff); and educational services (professional development, after school programming, online curriculum). In my analysis, I only included those firms that had their main headquarters in the United States. Each firm was identified as a competitor by at least one another firm.

By law, publicly traded firms must file annual and quarterly reports on income with the Security and Exchange Commission (SEC).[6] Firms that are private do not have to report this data. However, private firms with some public debt do have to report financials, though with nowhere near as much detail as publicly traded firms. For each of the publicly traded firms, I retrieved information for the years 2000 to 2007 on reported numbers for the following: annual revenue, gross profits, cost of goods sold, selling, general and administrative expenses, and net income. The documentation that publicly traded firms must report is extensive and is presented in a standard format, facilitating cross-comparisons. In addition, the SEC filings were a major source for identifying which public policies were revenue sources for the new privatization firms because the statements name the sources. The text accompanying the financial statements also provided information on the firm's business model, what they were selling, and their perspective on future demand.

For the private firms, I used company Web sites and financial and operational information complied by sources such as Standard and Poors in order to compile basic information such as absolute revenues and product descriptions. As an aid to future research on the content of these documents, appendix C includes a list of representative firms and their Web site addresses.

Information Collected from Web Sites, Marketing Materials, and Field Observation of Industry Events

The Internet and World Wide Web was another important source of information about firms and their activities. Nearly every firm public or private has a

Web site which provides basic information on its products and services, the firm's history, and its management team. At trade conferences and association conferences, I had further opportunity to have informal conversations with sales staff and in many instances watch or participate in a demonstration of the products and services, including online lessons, and test databases. Several events also hosted panel presentations and workshops where firms' strategies and challenges (for example, in advertising) were further discussed. These presentations were very useful in providing insights on the use of products and services that would otherwise be off-limits to noncustomers. I took field notes on these events and collected documentation.

In my analysis of key features in the industry, I looked across these combined sources of data in order to arrive at a more complete picture of trends in the industry.

Evidence on Policy Trends

Policy Documents   I also used existing policy documents to examine the extent to which federal policy was driving the new privatization and for information about the stance of the current administration towards private sector activity in education services. I drew on these multiple document sources in my analysis. This included analysis of mandates and rules (required actions); guidance (expectations for how people do things), subsidies, and grants (financial incentives); agency budgets (also a means of creating incentives or signaling support or lack thereof for an idea); information (by this I mean the production and dissemination by the federal government of information about the concept or idea and why it is important).[7]

In my analysis of these policy documents, I paid attention to the following: the introduction of new rules, or abolishment of old ones; the tightening or loosening of standards or definitions (for example what constitutes good technical assistance); the increasing or reduction of sanctions; changes in reporting procedures; the introduction of new incentives; the modification of existing ones; new rules about conditions or eligibility for funds.[8]

Small Scale Surveys   Another source of data for analyzing policy trends, in this instance at the state and local level, was structured interview questions in the form of small-scale surveys. We used this data collection strategy in two phases of the study: supplemental education services and benchmark assessments. In both instances, the use of the survey helped provide us with a preliminary map of policy trends. For example, in the context of our work on benchmark assessments, it helped us to begin to identify the extent to which districts were actually purchasing the systems and provided us with a rough indicator of cost.

The SES surveyed involved mapping early implementation patterns in states' responses to the supplemental education services provisions of NCLB. The survey, which was administered by mail and online between September 2005 and January 2006, asked state coordinators to describe policy developments within their state and to share their experiences and views on initial work. The survey included six parts: (1) the professional background of state administrators; (2) state activities around screening, monitoring, and evaluating providers; (3) state activities to disseminate information to parents; (4) state activities to regulate the format and content of SES services; (5) state activities to provide districts with training and technical support around SES; and (6) state participation (if any) in the creation of Department of Education guidance documents. A total of 30 out of 50 state administrators, evenly represented across geographic areas of the United States, responded to the survey for a response rate of 60%. Respondents came from across the United States and included respondents from each of the four U.S. Census Regions: West (24% of the states that responded), Midwest (31% of the states that responded), South (28% of the states that responded), and Northeast (17% of the states that responded). We analyzed the survey data to identify dominant patterns in state activity in each of these areas. There were several open-ended items in the survey. Where we needed more explanation of the responses, we followed up with a brief phone interview.

Survey data also was collected in the analysis of benchmark assessment systems. We collected survey data from 28 of the 30 largest (as measured by student enrollment in 2003–2004) school districts in the United States. The survey was administered online between May 2007 and August 2007. We drew the sample from the 2003 to 2004 survey of the 100 largest school districts as conducted by the National Center for Education Statistics.[9] The smallest district in the sample had over 94,000 students and the largest had over one million. The districts sampled varied in terms of both geographic location, representing the South, Midwest, West, and Northeast regions of the country, and socioeconomic status. Title I-eligible schools can be used as a rough proxy for socioeconomic status of student enrollment. The percentage of schools that were Title I-eligible in the districts we sampled ranged between 9.3% and 97.7%. In nearly three-quarters of the districts, 50% or more of the student population were students of color. Out of a total of 148 people across those districts, 54 (36.54%) responded. We sent surveys to three individuals in each of the 28 districts. We purposely sampled individuals within the districts whom we would expect to play a central role in the purchase of software and hardware. The people most likely to respond were those in the role groups of Technology (32%) and Research, Assessment, and Accountability (32%), although we also received responses from those in Title I Administration (14%), Budget and Finance (13%), and Curriculum and Instruction (9%).

In summary, in two instances surveys were used to help us construct a picture of actual policy responses to the patterns emerging from analysis of federal policy documents and interviews with executives. In both instances, survey responses helped frame our analysis of local practice. For example, in the SES survey, we found a low incidence of states reporting that they were satisfied with how special education students and English language learner students were being served. Building on this data, we sought more descriptive information on these trends in our field research in Riverview. To offer another example, in the benchmark assessment survey, a few districts reported that they were designing benchmark assessments systems in-house. This encouraged us to include this district type in our field research. The survey technique also was appropriate to the extent that it allowed us to describe aspects of the implementation process that could not easily be captured in talking with executives, or analyzing their materials. For example, the executives would not share specifics on what they charged districts for benchmark assessments.

Evidence on Local Settings

The third level of analysis involved case studies of local practice.[10] As noted above, the cases represented different instances of the new privatization. In this aspect of the research, I focused on elements of the new privatization as they occurred and unfolded within specific local sites; settings and contexts linked to place. The research sites were six school systems that had contracted with one or more of the leading firms identified in the first phase of analysis. Three of the communities were located in the Midwest. Two of the communities were located on the west coast. One was located in the Southeast. While all districts in the sample served a high percentage of students living in poverty, they varied in terms of their size and metropolitan status. Two were very large urban school districts; two were small rural school districts; and two were midsized suburban districts. They were districts where public debates were underway about the advantages and disadvantages of privatizing certain district functions. They were districts that had established contracts with one or more of the firms identified and analyzed in the profile of market trends.

Embedded within these cases were subcases. For example, nested within our case study of contracts between virtual school firms and local school districts were smaller cases of two specific virtual schools, and key events within these schools. In all instances, we sought to understand events and processes linked to the district's contracting with the firm from multiple perspectives. In order to do so, there were small numbers of people involved in our field sample, the specific numbers of which varied from case to case. In each of our sites, a minimum of nine interviews were conducted with individuals representing the following groups: district administrators, employees of firms working with the district, school staff and parents in schools within the district that had exposure to the products and services being contracted. All of the interviews in the research on local sites were tape-recorded and logged.

The following provides a brief description of the field research for each of the three cases of the new privatization.

Chapter 4: Supplemental Education Services

Our data sources included end-of-year reports for the years 2004 to 2005 and 2005 to 2006 that were provided by SES firms to the state department of education. These reports itemized the following for each calendar year: (1) the total number of students applying for and receiving full or partial services; (2) the number of students reported making academic progress; and (3) the different costs charged by each firm (measured either by hourly cost per student or a total charge for a day's worth of services). Among the companies that provided services during the 2004 to 2005 or 2005 to 2006 school years, we identified companies that provided supplemental education services to at least one student. Of these providers, we then identified the largest SES providers by total number of students served. For these providers, we compared the costs charged by each company for supplemental education services, the reported pupil–teacher ratios, the availability of the services to special needs and English language learner students, the numbers of parents who selected the provider for their children, and student enrollment levels.

We also spent a year closely observing the tutoring being provided to students in the district. As noted, the findings from this portion of the study were compiled as part of a one-year evaluation of SES that we conducted for the district. Three of the four providers we studied each had significant market share in the district over a two-year period. The fourth was a small, local provider. Because the design of the law does not require every firm to provide English language learner and special education services, we included in our sample two firms that reported that they did have services that were accessible and appropriate for those populations. We selected sites to observe that were representative of the district's student demographics (particularly race and socioeconomic status). One of the four vendors provided in-home, online instruction. For this vendor, we observed SES tutoring through an "access" function provided and monitored by the vendor. For each vendor, we observed two to four different tutoring sessions at one or two different tutoring sites and interviewed one to three program employees, including managers and tutors. In these observations, we used a semistructured observation protocol with some close-ended items, asking, for example, whether curriculum planned was the same as the curriculum actually in use, the duration of the instructional period, actual attendance, whether individual achievement plans (IAP) were available or in use, and whether instruction was differentiated based on English language learner or special education needs. We also participated in and observed several district-level meetings focused on SES.

In addition, we conducted three separate focus groups with the following groups: SES vendors, principals of SIFI schools (schools in need of improvement and eligible for services), and SES coordinators (individuals designated to coordinate SES services at the school) and district officials. At one school site, we also interviewed nine parents of children eligible for service (including those who enrolled and those that did not) in an attempt to understand their experiences with SES. We also analyzed a broad range of documents used by the district, by schools, or by vendors in the program. These included contracts between provider and district, district budget information, minutes from advisory council meetings, district working protocol for observing contract compliance, formal curriculum provided to the state by vendors, copies of relevant policies (e.g., on recruitments and incentives, complaint forms). At the school level it included the curriculum in use locally, supplementary materials, teacher guides, assessment tools, and individualized achievement plans (IAPs) that the district requires vendors to use with students.

Chapter 5: Virtual Charter Schools

The research in the virtual charter schools occurred over a six-month period from May 2007 to October 2007. The focus of this field research was two virtual charter schools, which I described in chapter 5. Each school had contracts with one or more of the providers identified in the first phase of my work as a leading firm in this area.

The focus of my field research in part was to describe and document what virtual charter schools look like. What does it mean to attend, work in, or be a parent of a child in a virtual school? To date, there is little if any descriptive research on these schools. I developed cases of each school based on in-depth interviews with district employees and school staff, and through document analysis. For each school, I obtained and analyzed policy documents such as district budgets, strategic plans, quantitative data related to student demographics and achievement, district memoranda, and data from the district's Web site and the firm's Web site.

In each school, I began by obtaining and reviewing descriptions of the schools, news reports, course descriptions, and the planned curriculum for reading, mathematics, and social studies for specific grade levels. These descriptions included detailed instructions to parents on the objectives of each unit and supplementary materials to be used. It would have been very useful to actually see a lesson in action. However, I was discouraged by the district from contacting parents to request visits. To compensate for this lack of "real time" observation data, I conducted extended interviews with teachers, asking about their classroom experiences and the curriculum in use, as well as examples of how they worked with students. With three exceptions, all of the interviews were conducted by phone; the others were conducted at district offices. In total, I was able to interview 13 individuals across two schools: three parents, five teachers, and five school administrators.

Chapter 6: Benchmark Assessments

As noted, we started the study of benchmark assessments with a survey of district practice. The survey data provided broad patterns in district usage, but provided little in the way of contextualized knowledge of how local political, economic, and social histories interact with and shape the implementation of testing technology. To investigate more microlevel influences, we selected three communities, each of which contracted with a firm that provided assessment solutions. The three firms represented were identified in the survey as leading firms in the field. The districts differed in size from fewer than 50,000 students to more than 200,000 students.

We developed cases of each district based on in-depth interviews with district employees. We used a snowball sampling strategy—seeking individuals who did different kinds of work in the district (staff development, test analysis, budget preparation) and who were identified as familiar with the software that was being leased. In the interviews, we sought to understand the impetus and history of the district's testing contracts and perceived challenges in working with vendors and strategies for addressing these challenges. We analyzed policy documents such as district budgets, strategic plans, quantitative data related to student demographics and achievement, policies regarding purchasing, and policy data from the district's Web-site.

In one case (Westview), we conducted a higher number of interviews and also conducted observations of school and district practice. Because of resource constraints, we were unable to take the same approach in the other two districts. However, in these districts, we conducted repeated phone interviews with key informants in each of the sites and had numerous e-mail exchanges to clarify information obtained in interviews.

As noted, an important impetus behind the field research component was to understand the new privatization and its patterns in local perspective—from the perspective of those working at the street-level of contracting—who were involved in the establishment of the contracts, or involved in service delivery, or who were the intended beneficiaries of the contracts. This work was critical for understanding the complex processes involved in contracting, the context in which these interactions took place, and some of the ways in which local communities resisted or adapted to broader trends.

Conclusion

Out of concern for the power disparities between the local school systems and the large national firms participating in my research, and in order to maintain the confidentiality of all respondents, I use pseudonyms or generic terms, such as, parent, for all those that I interviewed, and in the local research, for the names of the districts, firms, and their products.

In my analysis of how these developments are unfolding in practice, I focus mostly on effects on districts and local policy more than classroom practice. Particularly given the absence of classroom level data, this book is not intended to answer such questions as how the curriculum of for-profit after-school firms compares with that of large textbook publishers, or how virtual school teachers interact with children. However, it *is* meant to trigger these kinds of questions and as a first step in this research direction.

New Privatization Trends and Questions Conjoined

SEGMENTS	After school Programming	On-line Instruction	Testing
Which firms are selling to districts?			
What trends in financial data?			
What are policy drivers?			
What political activity surrounds?			
What are the firms' strategies?			
What equity issues are raised?			

Characteristic Companies

Company	Website	Industry	Est.
Blackboard	Blackboard.com	Application Software	1997
Ecollege	Ecollege.com	Internet Services	1996
Educate	Educate-inc.com	Education Services	2003
Club Z!	ClubZtutoring.com	Education Services	1995
Connections	Connectionsacademy.com	Internet Services	2001
Edison	Edisonproject.com	Education Services	1992
Houghton Mifflin	Hmco.com	Publishing	1832
Huntington Learning	Huntingtonlearning.com	Education Services	1992
K12	K12.com	Education Services	1999
Kaplan	Kaplan.com	Education Services	1972
Knowledge Universe	Knowledgeu.com	Education Services	2007
McGraw Hill	Mcgraw-hill.com	Publishing	1989
Pearson Education	Pearsoned.com	Publishing	1998
Plato	Plato.com	Application Software	1963
Princeton Review	Princetonreview.com	Education Services	1996
Renaissance Learning	Renlearn.com	Home Entertainment	1986
Schoolnet	Schoolnet.com	Application Software	1998
White Hat Management	Whitehatmgmt.com	Education Services	1998

Notes

Chapter 1

1. There are a number excellent books and articles that treat the rise of market models in social policy and the problems created by them; e.g., Leys, C. (2003). *Market-driven politics: Neoliberal democracy and the public interest.* New York: Verso; Jessop, B. (2002). *The future of the capitalist state.* London: Polity; Marglin, S. (2008). *The dismal science: How thinking like an economist undermines community.* Cambridge, MA: Harvard University Press. Marglin provides an excellent summary of the evolution of the economic thinking that undergirds neoliberalism.

2. On the rise of privatization in the provision of social services in the United States, see Sclar, E. (2000). *You don't always get what you pay for: The economics of privatization* (pp. 1–20). London: Cornell University Press.

3. To cite two recent examples, see Princeton Review. (2006). *Annual Report: Form 10K.* Retrieved August 2007, from http://www.10KWizard.org; Educate Inc. (2007). *Annual Report: Form 10K.* Retrieved September 2007, from http://www.educate.com

4. Harvey, D. (2005). *A brief history of neoliberalism.* Oxford: Oxford University Press.

5. For a discussion of what separates classical liberalism from neoliberalism, see Apple, M. W. (2006). *Educating the "right" way: Markets, standards, God, and inequality* (p. 60). New York: Routledge. Also see, Apple, M. (2000). *Official knowledge: Democratic education in a conservative age* (2nd ed.). New York: Routledge.

6. See Sclar, E. (2000, pp. 132–144), for an example of this argumentation in his discussion of mayor-led privatization of the Indianapolis city services.

7. On the legitimization of neoliberalism, see Jessop, B. (2002). *The future of the capitalist state.* London: Polity.

8. Bourdieu, P., & Wacquant, L. (2001). NewLiberalSpeak: Notes on the new planetary vulgate. *Radical Philosophy, 105,* 2–5.

9. Ball, S. (2007b, September 5,). *Education PLC.* Paper presented at the British Education Research Association. Institute of Education, London. Personal communication.

10. For examples of this argumentation, see the publications of the promarket Reason Foundation (reason.org) and Cato Institute (cato.org). One example is a brief authored by Governor Mitchell Daniels (2006). Reforming government through competition. *Annual Privatization Report.* (p. 21). Los Angeles: Reason Foundation.

11. See CRS (2006, p. 12), for a discussion of examples of the Federal privatization agenda beginning with President Ronald Reagan through President George W. Bush as well as recent congressional action which includes, e.g., P.L. 104-193, sec. 104; P.L. 106-554, sec. 1.

12. Belfield, C. R., & Levin, H. (2002). *Education privatization: Causes, consequences and planning implications.* New York: International Institute for Education Planning, UNESCO. See also, Henig, J. R. (1989). Privatization in the United States: Theory and practice. *Political Science Quarterly, 104,* 649–670.

153

13. Murphy, J. (1998). *Pathways to privatization in education*. Greenwich, CT: Ablex.
14. Agron, A. (2001, September). 7th privatization/contract services survey. *American School and University Magazine*, 27–31.
15. Beales, J. (1994). *Doing more with less: Competitive contracting for school support services*. Los Angeles: The Reason Foundation. Reflecting this perspective, Janet Beales (1994) said:

    In the area of support services, school administrators are finding some budgetary relief by turning to the efficiencies of the private sector for help. By contracting with private companies for busing, maintenance and food service, schools can do more with less. Reducing costs, increasing revenues and tapping new reserves of capital investment can help school administrators focus on their core responsibility: educating children. (p. 68)

16. Molnar, A., Wilson, G., & Allen, D. (2004). *Profiles of for-profit education management companies, sixth annual report, 2003–2004*. Tempe, AR: Arizona State University, Educational Policy Studies Laboratory.
17. Molnar, A. (2005). *School commercialism: From democratic ideal to market commodity* (p. 93). New York: Routledge. For other work on commercialism in education, see Bracey, G. W. (2002). *The war against America's public schools: Privatizing schools, commercializing education*. Boston: Allyn & Bacon.
18. President, Personal interview, July 5, 2006.
19. Chubb, J. E., & Moe, T. M. (1990). *Politics, markets, and America's schools* (p. 2). Washington, D.C.: The Brookings Institution.
20. Fuhrman, S., Goertz, M., & Duffy, M. (2004). Slow down, you move too fast: The politics of making changes in high-stakes accountability policies for students. In S. Fuhrman & R. Elmore (Eds.), *Redesigning accountability systems for education* (p. 245). New York: Teachers College Press. Also see, McDonnell, L. (2005). NCLB and the Federal role in education: Evolution or revolution. *Peabody Journal of Education, 80*(2), 19–38.
21. Stone, D. A. (2002). *Policy paradox: The art of political decision-making* (p. 285). New York: W.W. Norton.
22. Districts that do not make test score targets can apply for waivers. This allows them to be SES providers. If waiver is approved, the district can serve as a provider of SES.
23. U.S. Department of Education. (2001). *Title I: Improving the academic achievement of the disadvantaged*. Sec. 1111 (j). Washington, D.C.: Author.
24. Committee for Education Funding. (2007). *Budget response 2007*. Washington, D.C.: Author.
25. Stoneman, C. (2000, February 23). Title I and parent information resource center. *First annual review of the family involvement in education*. Washington, D.C.: The National Coalition for Parent Involvement in Education. retrieved November 10, 2007, from http://ncpie.org/pubs/ncpie_first_annual_review_family_involvement_education.pdf
26. U.S. Department of Education. (2001). *NCLB overview*. Retrieved June 2007, from http://www.ed.gov/nclb/overview/intro/execsumm.html
27. See, U.S. Department of Education (2005). *No Child Left Behind. Supplemental educational services. Non-regulatory guidance*. Washington, D.C.: Author.
28. Ibid.
29. U.S. Department of Education (2002c, December). *Federal Register Vol 67, No 231. Title I. Improving the Academic Achievement of the Disadvantaged. Final Regulations*. Washington, D.C.: Government Printing Office.
30. U.S. Department of Education. (2003). *Title IA services for private school children: Non-regulatory guidance* (p. 5). Washington, D.C.: Author.
31. Ball, S. (2007a). *Education Plc: Understanding private sector participation in public sector education*. London: Routledge.
32. Ball, S. (2006). Policy sociology and critical policy research. In S. Ball (Ed.), *Education policy and social class: The selected works of Stephen J. Ball* (p. 20). New York: Routledge.
33. Apple, M. W. (1996). *Cultural politics and education*. New York: Teachers College Press.
34. Lipman, P. (2004). *High stakes education: Inequality, globalization, and urban school reform*. New York: Routledge.
35. Ball, S. (Ed.). (2005). *Education policy and social class: The selected works of Stephen J. Ball* (pp. 143–156). New York: Routledge.
36. Privatization 'Philly Style': What can be learned from Philadelphia's diverse provider model

of school managsement (updated edition with important new finsings, June 2006). Research for Action. Retrieved August 30, 2008, from http://researchforaction.org/publication/details/37

37. Wells, A. S. (Ed.). (2002). *Where charter school policy fails: The problems of accountability and equity* (pp. 1–29). New York: Teachers College Press.
38. Apple (2006).
39. See, for example, Henig, J. R., Holyoke, T., Lacreo-Paquet, N., & Mostner, M. (2003). Privatization, politics, and urban services: The political behavior of charter schools. *Journal of Urban Affairs, 25*, 37–54. For a useful synthesis of regime theory as applied to education, see Bulkley, K. E. (2007). Bringing the private into the public: Changing the rules of the game and new regime politics in Philadelphia public education. *Educational Policy, 21*(1), 155–184. Also see, Burns, P. (2003). Regime theory, state government and a take-over of urban education. *Journal of Urban Affairs, 25*, 285–303.
40. See, for example, Burns (2003).
41. Ball (2007a) also makes a related point.
42. Whitty, G. (1997). Creating quasi-markets in education: A review of recent research on parental choice and school autonomy in three countries. *Review of Research in Education, 22*, 3–47.
43. Wells (2002, p. 13).
44. Henig, J. (1994). *Rethinking school choice: Limits of a market metaphor* (p. 5). Princeton, NJ: Princeton University Press.
45. Also see Brighouse, H. (2004). What's wrong with privatising schools? *Journal of Philosophy of Education, 38*, 629–630. Brighouse can conceive of ways that limited forms of partial privatization may have positive consequences. However, he maintains that adopting full privatization will exacerbate inequalities because children (particularly in parent choice initiatives) will have to rely on parents' resources, including access to information, which are inequitably distributed.
46. Levin, H. M. (1987). Education as public and private good. *Journal of Policy Analysis and Management, 6*, 641–643.
47. Ibid. In later work, Levin develops these arguments further, including discussion of the costs of some forms of privatization. See, for example, Levin, H. M. (2001). *Privatizing education: can the marketplace deliver choice, efficiency, equity, and social cohesion?* Boulder, CO: Westview Press; Levin, H. (2006). Déjà vu all over again. *Education Next*, 1–7.
48. In my treatment of the literature, I have focused on some areas of consensus in the literature on the limits of market model as applied to education policy. It is important to note, however, that even within those who look critically at education and markets, there are important differences of opinion. Among others, there is the issue of how much to use education policy and regulation to correct for the limitations of the market model. How can policy be used to minimize negative consequences and maximize the good that may come from reforms such charter schools, vouchers, and choice? On productive roles that policy and regulations can play in improving choice, charter schools, standards, and accountability, see Wells (2002); Elmore, R., & Fuller, B. (1996). *Who chooses? Who loses? Culture, institutions, and the unequal effects of school choice* (pp. 187–201). New York: Teachers College Press. For discussion of the limits of policy in solving the problems of market-oriented reforms, see Apple (2002) and Ball (2006). Stambach and David (2005) examine gender relations in school choice debates. Another set of issues focus on how we think about the role of families and communities in this dynamic (see Stambach, A., & David, M. (2005). Feminist theory and education policy: How gender has been 'involved' in school choice debates. *Signs, 30*, 1633–1658). In some of the literature there is much discussion about the importance of the community within schools. See, for example, Meier, D. (2002). *In schools we trust: Creating communities of learning in an era of testing and standardization*. Boston: Beacon Press. Others have argued the point that policy communities in education can be regressive and racist and deserve careful scrutiny before we protect them. See for example, Gillborn, D. (2005). Education policy as an act of white supremacy: Whiteness, critical race theory and education reform. *Journal of Education Policy, 20*, 485–505. Others have focused on the tension between respecting the democratic processes and purposes in education and the rights of families to choose alternatives to state-run education. See Levin (2001), Apple (2002), and Wells (2002) on this point.
49. See, for example. Burch, P. (2007a). Educational policy and practice from the perspective of institutional theory: Crafting a wider lens. *Educational Researcher, 36*(2), 84–95; Burch,

P. (2007b, March). The professionalization of instructional leadership in the United States: Competing values and current tensions. *Journal of Educational Policy, 22*(2), 195–214; Burch, P. (2006). The new educational privatization: Educational contracting in the era of high stakes accountability. *Teachers College Record, 88*(2), 129–135.

50. Rowan, B. (2002). *The ecology of school improvement: Notes to the school improvement industry in the United States.* Ann Arbor: Consortium for Policy Research in Education, University of Michigan, Ann Arbor. Rowan also develops these ideas in H. D. Mayer & B. Rowan (Eds.). (2001). *The new institutionalism in education* (pp. 87–102). Albany: SUNY Press.

51. In the subfield of education policy research, David K. Cohen was one of the first to make the point that the policy environment includes the "non-governmental system." See, Cohen D. K. (1982). Policy and organization: The impact of state and federal educational policy on school governance. *Harvard Educational Review, 52*(4), 474–499.

52. There are a number of excellent collections that present empirical work on institutional processes of organizations. See, for example, Zucker, L. (Ed.). (1988). *Institutional patterns and organizations: Culture and environment.* Cambridge, MA: Ballinger; Scott, R. W. (1988). *Institutions and organizations.* Thousand Oaks, CA: Sage; Powell, W. W., & DiMaggio, P. (1991). *The new institutionalism in organizational analysis.* Chicago: University of Chicago Press.

53. Ogawa, R. T. (1992). Institutional theory and examining leadership in schools. *International Journal of Educational Management, 6,* 14–21.

54. The literature that uses regime theory to examine contracting makes a related basic point. It talks about how under certain conditions contract relationships can have a stabilizing effect on district policy and how established interests ("employment regimes") can exert strong pressures on districts during the contracting process. See, Bulkley (2007), for a discussion of this literature.

55. Metz states, "offering the same education to all appears the essence of fairness—unless one has a sense of the interactive processes that transform the same structures and procedures into the diverse daily lives of schools in differing communities." In Metz, M. H. (1989). Real school: A universal drama amid disparate experience. *Politics of Education Association Yearbook, 75*–91. See also, Metz, M. H. (2008). Symbolic uses of NCLB: Reaffirmation of equality of educational opportunity or delegitimization of public schools? In A. Sardovnik et al. (Eds.), *No Child Left Behind and the reduction of the achievement gap: Sociological perspectives on federal educational policy.* New York: Routledge.

56. Apple and Pedroni also make and develop this point. See, Apple, M. W. & Pedroni, T. (2005). Conservative alliance building and African American support of vouchers. *Teachers College Record, 107,* 2068–2105.

Chapter 2

1. Education Industry Association. (n.d.a.). *Overview of the education industry association.* Retrieved August 6, 2008, from http://www.educationindustry.org/tier.asp

2. For a few examples, see Farkas, G., & Durham, R. (2006, February 23–24). *The role of tutoring in standards-based reform.* Paper presented at the conference, Will Standards-Based Reform in Education Help Close the Poverty Gap? University of Wisconsin, Madison, 2006.; Sunderman, G. L. (2006). Do supplemental educational services increase opportunities for minority students? *Phi Delta Kappan, 88*(2), 117–122; Lacireno-Paquet, N. (2004). Do EMO-operated charter schools serve disadvantaged students? The influence of state policies. *Education Policy Analysis Archives, 12*(26). Retrieved October 16, 2007, from http://epaa.asu.edu/epaa/v12n26/

3. In the case studies of market-based education services that follow, I explore these and other issues in greater detail.

4. See Appendix A for a detailed discussion of the research design. The names of those I interviewed nor their companies, are not identified, to ensure confidentiality.

5. I draw here on a distinction made by Joseph Murphy between specialty services providers and educational management organizations. Murphy, J. (1996). *Privatization of schooling: Problems and possibilities.* Thousand Oaks, CA: Corwin Press.

6. Hentschke, G. C. (2005). *New areas of educational governance: The impact of international*

organizations and markets on educational policymaking. Los Angeles: Center on Educational Governance, University of Southern California.

7. I first made this argument in Burch, P. (2006). The new educational privatization: Educational contracting in the era of high stakes accountability. *Teachers College Record, 88*(2), 129–135.

8. Flam, S., & Keane, W. (1997). *Public schools/private enterprise: What you should know and do about privatization.* Lancaster, PA: Technomic.

9. Stein and Bassett (2004a) also make this point. By their estimates, the annual sales of printed materials related to standardized tests nearly tripled between 1992 and 2003, jumping from $211 million to $592 million. See Stein, M., & Bassett, E. (2004a). *Staying ahead of the curve: A value chain analysis of the K-12 assessment market.* Boston: Eduventures.

10. In Appendix A, I define terms such as *gross profit margins* for the reader who is unfamiliar with the terminology of companies' financial statements.

11. SchoolNet. *Product description.* Retrieved February 7, 2007, from http:www.schoolnet.org

12. Ibid.

13. Flam and Keane (1997).

14. Murphy, J., Glimer, S. W., Weise, R., & Page, A. (1998). *Pathways to privatization in education.* Greenwich, CT: Ablex.

15. Stein and Bassett (2004a). This figure is based on estimates for the broader tutoring market, elementary grades through college, and includes those companies who only sell directly to parents.

16. Ibid.

17. Renaissance Learning. (n.d.). *Product overview.* Retrieved June 1, 2008, from https://www.capitaliq.com/CIQDotNet/company/longBusinessDescription

18. Florida Center for Reading Research. *Wilson reading system.* Retrieved May 1, 2008, from http://www.fcrr.org/FCRRReports/PDF/wilson.pdf

19. Smith, S., & Lipsky, M. (1999). Non-profits for hire: The welfare state in the age of contracting. *Contemporary Sociology, 23*(4), 584–585.

20. K-12. (2007b, December 10). *S-1/A.* Herndon, VA: Author.

21. Educate Inc. (2004b March 14). *10-K.* Baltimore, MD: Author; Educate Inc. (2006, March 16) *10-K.* Baltimore, MD: Author; Educate Inc. (2007b, April 3). *10-K.* Baltimore, MD: Author.

22. Educate Inc. (2007a, March 16). *10-K.* Baltimore, MD: Author.

23. Ibid.

24. Ibid.

25. Rowan (2002).

26. For a useful synthesis of research, which probes ideologies behind the rise of technology in education see, Ferneding, K. A. (2003). *Questioning technology: Electronic technologies and educational reform.* New York: Peter Lang.

27. Press coverage of educational management organizations as compared to firms representing industry segments represents another rough indicator of the visibility of firms' operations to the public. Over the first eight years of operation, the activity of Edison Schools was referenced 542 times in *Education Week.* In contrast, since its establishment in 1999, K-12, Inc., a supplier of virtual schooling, was referenced 154 times.

28. Molnar (2005) also makes this point.

29. Edison Inc. (2003, September 9). *10-K.* New York: Author.

30. Ibid.

31. Chief Executive Officer, personal communication, June 30, 2006.

32. Chief Executive Officer, personal communication, June 28, 2006.

33. Vice President, personal communication, July 20, 2006.

34. President, personal communication, June 28, 2006.

35. Ball (2007, p. 10) describes this approach in his analysis of education privatization in the UK as "savior discourse."

36. Princeton Review. (2004, December 3). *10-K.* New York: Author; Princeton Review (2007, April 2). *10-K.* New York: Author; Princeton Review. (2008, March 17). *10-K.* New York: Author.

37. Educate Inc. (2007, May 10). *10-K.* Baltimore, MD: Author.

38. Pearson. (n.d.). *Our News.* Retrieved July 1, 2007, from http:/www.pearson.com

39. President, personal communication, June 28, 2006.

Chapter 3

1. In his in-depth examination of the Edison Schools model, Kenneth J. Saltman cogently argues the need to "shift the frame of the debate on effectiveness that dominates the popular and academic conversation about Edison" (p. 69) and to pay closer attention to the effect of the EMO model on democratic outcomes; Saltman, K. (2005). *The Edison schools: Corporate schooling and the assault on public education*. New York: Routledge.
2. For an early example of this approach, see, Chubb, J., & Moe, T. (1990). *Politics, markets and America's schools* (p. 36). Washington, D.C.: Brookings Institution.
3. I would like to thank Carl Frederick, University of Wisconsin—Madison, Department of Sociology, for his research assistance here.
4. See, for example, O'Toole, J., & Meier, K. (2004). Parkinson's Law and the new public management: Contracting determinants and service-quality consequences in public education. *Public Administration Review, 64*(3), 342–352; Marlow, M. I. (2001). Bureaucracy and student performance in US public schools. *Applied Economics, 33*(10), 1341–1350; Smith, K. B., & Meier, K. J. (1994). Politics, bureaucrats and schools. *Public Administration Review, 54*(6), 551–558.
5. My focus here is on studies of contracting that focus on efficiencies. See chapter 1 for reference to literature that employs regime theory to examine education contracting.
6. There are several reports that examine the evidence on the effectiveness of EMOs and reach this conclusion. For early arguments on the limits of the evidence and evidence of limited effects, see Shaul, M. S. (2002, October). Public schools: *Insufficient research to determine effectiveness of selected private education companies* [GAO-03-11]. Washington, D.C.: General Accounting Office. For more recent examples of reports reaching this conclusion, see Gill, B., Hamilton, L., Lockwood, J. R., Marsh, J., Zimmer, R., Hill, D., & Pribesh, S. (2005). *Inspiration, perspiration and time: Operation and achievement in Edison Schools*. Santa Monica, CA: RAND Corporation; Comprehensive School Reform Quality Center. (2006). *Report on education service providers. Executive summary*. Washington, D.C.: American Institutes for Research.
7. See, for example, McLaughlin, M. W., Irby, M., & Langman, J. (1994). *Urban sanctuaries: Neighborhood organizations in the lives and futures of inner city youth*. San Francisco: Jossey-Bass; Honig, M. I. (2004). The new middle management: Intermediary organizations in education policy implementation. *Educational Evaluation and Policy Analysis, 26*, 65–87. Spillane, J. P., & Thompson, C. L. (1997, Summer). Restructuring conceptions of local capacity: The local education agency's capacity for ambitious instructional reform. *Educational Evaluation and Policy Analysis, 19*(2), 185–203.
8. Confessore, N. (2003, July/August). Welcome to the machine: How the GOP disciplined K Street and made Bush supreme. *Washington Monthly, 35*(7/8), 30–37.
9. Ibid.
10. Those included among the group of former officials moving to for-profit firms selling services and products linked to the mandates of NCLB included the Secretary of Education, two former Chief of Staff, four Directors, six Assistant Secretaries, two Deputy Secretaries, and one Under Secretary. These individuals were hired by firms such as Chartwell Education Group, Dutko Worldwide, the Akin Group, Alliance for School Choice, White Hat Management, Kaplan, and Knowledge Universe. The remaining 13 assumed positions at universities, foundations, and think tanks.
11. Chartwell Education Group. (n.d.). Retrieved October 1, 2007, from http://www.chartwelleducation.com/
12. Ibid.
13. Ibid.
14. Dutko Worldwide. (n.d.a). *Practice Areas: Education*. Retrieved June 8, 2007, from http://www.dutkoworldwide.com/
15. Davis, M. R. (2003, April 16). Doing the "right" thing: The man in charge of making the No Child Left Behind Act a reality, a true-believer conservative, may be developing a taste for shades of gray. *Education Week*. Retrieved November 12, 2007, from http://www.edweek.org/ew/articles/2003/04/16/31hickok
16. Ibid.
17. Dutko Worldwide. (n.d.). *Latest News*. Retrieved October 1, 2007, from www.dutkoworldwide.com/media_center/latest_news/1048

18. Ball (2005).
19. Vice-President, personal communication, July 11, 2006.
20. Education Industry Association. (2006). *Enterprising Educators. Newsletter of Education Industry Association, 15*(2), 1.
21. Field notes (Patricia Burch), Education Industry Association Conference, Denver, Colorado, July 2006.
22. Education Industry Day. (n.d.) *Highlights and program.* Retrieved March 2006, from http://www.educationindustry.org/tier.asp?sid=4
23. Education Industry Association. (2008, January 8). *Education principles and policies for the next U.S. president: Recommendations of the Education Industry Association.* Rockville, MD: Author.
24. Education Industry Association, personal communication through EISlist@lists.education-industry.org, October 2007.
25. New Schools Venture Fund. (n.d.). *About us.* Retrieved April 1, 2006, from http://www.newschools.org
26. NewSchools Venture Fund. (n.d.). *Our portfolio.* Retrieved August 26, 2008, from, http://www.newschools.org/portfolio/submit-a-business-plan
27. Harvard Business Review. (2000, October 13). *Case 9-301-038. NewSchools Venture Fund*, p. 4.
28. Ibid, p. 3.
29. Ibid, p. 6.
30. Apple (2002, p. 199).
31. Riley, J. (2008, February 9). Movie man: An interview with Reed Hastings. *Wall Street Journal*, p. A9.
32. Stein, M. (2004). *Testing in flux: Future directions in the pre-K-12 assessment market* (p. 12). Boston: Eduventures; Jackson, M., & Bassett, E. (2005). *The state of the K-12 state assessment market.* Boston: Eduventures.
33. Ibid.
34. School Improvement Industry. (n.d.). *Our editor's resume: Marc Dean Millot.* Retrieved June 4, 2008, from http://www.siiwonline.com/Resume.html

Chapter 4

1. For examples of work pointing to these transformations, see Davies, S., & Aurini, J. (2006). The franchising of private tutoring: A view from Canada. *Phi Delta Kappan, 88*(2), 123–128; Burch, P., Steinberg, M., & Donovan, J. (2007). Supplemental educational services and NCLB: Policy assumptions, market practices, emerging issues. *Educational Evaluation and Policy Analysis, 29*(2), 115–133; Bray, M. (1999). *The shadow education system: Private tutoring and its implications for planners.* Paris: International Institute for Educational Planning.
2. Unless less is needed, an LEA must spend equal to 20% of their Title I Part A funds on choice related transportation or supplemental education services, or a combination of the two.
3. See, Burch, P. et al. (2007); and Burch, P. (2007c). Supplemental educational services under NCLB: Emerging evidence and policy issues. *Educational Policy Research Unit.* Retrieved from http://epsl.asu.edu/epru/documents/EPSL-0705-232-EPRU.pdf
4. For examples of this work, see, Heinrich, C. J., Meyer, R. H., & Whitten, G. (2007, November). *Supplemental education services under No Child Left Behind: Who signs up, and what do they gain.* Paper presented at the annual meeting of the American Educational Research Association, New York; Sunderman, G. L., & Kim, J. (2004). *Increasing bureaucracy or increasing opportunities? School district experience with supplemental educational services.* Cambridge, MA: The Civil Rights Project at Harvard University; Sunderman, G. L., Kim, J. S., & Orfield, G. (2005). *NCLB meets school realities: Lessons from the field.* Thousand Oaks, CA: Corwin Press; Heistad, D. (2006). *Analysis of 2005 supplemental educational services in Minneapolis public schools: An application of matched sample statistical design.* Minneapolis, MN: Minneapolis Public Schools.
5. See appendix A for a more detailed description of the research design. All names, including the name of the district, parents, and district managers are pseudonyms to protect confidentiality.

6. I first was introduced to the term *shadow education* in an article by Scott Davies and Janice Aurini (2006) who use the term to help categorize tutoring that happens after school and that is closely tied to the school curriculum.

7. I first made this argument in Burch et al. (2007).

8. See U.S. Department of Education. (2003). *Supplemental educational services. Non-regulatory guidance*. Retrieved November 20, from http://www.ed.gov/nclb/choice/help/ses/guidance. html; U.S. Department of Education. (2002, September). *No child left behind: A desktop reference*. Washington, D.C.: Office of Elementary and Secondary Education. Retrieved November 20, 2006, from http://www.ed.gov/admins/lead/account/nclbreference/reference.pdf

9. Sclar (2000).

10. For example, in 2002, in a statement accompanying the release of guidance for including faith-based and community organizations in SES, Secretary of Education Rod Paige noted that

   the guidance makes it very clear that local school districts must provide equal opportunity and cannot discriminate against any organization that wants to help children and is willing to do so under the law's strict requirements. We must put the welfare of children first, and these measures will ensure that all hard-working and effective organizations have the opportunity to help children in their communities....

   Paige continued,

   Across our nation, we see a great need for experienced and proven providers to step up to the plate and offer supplemental services. Faith-based and community groups frequently have a strong track record—often developed on a shoestring budget—of helping communities and community members succeed. It is critical that we all join forces to ensure that no child is left behind.

   U.S. Department of Education. (2002a). *President Bush unveils new guidance empowering faith-based and community groups to provide extra academic help to low-income students*. Retrieved January 3, 2007, from http://www.ed.gov/news/pressreleases/2002/12/12122002. html

11. The section on national level trends in the SES market is a condensed version of an argument that appeared in Burch et al. (2007).

12. Educate Inc. (2004). *Annual Report: Form 10K*. Retrieved September 2007, from http://www. educate.com

13. The market also is highly segmented geographically. The level of available SES revenues is higher in some regions of the United States than in others. For example, the Southwest region experienced a 63% increase in SES funds available from FY 2001 to FY 2005. The West region experienced a 52% increase in SES funds available from FY 2001 to FY 2005. During this same time period, the New England region and the South region experienced growth in SES funds of 33% and 47%, respectively.

14. Sclar (2000).

15. See U.S. Department of Education (2002a); U.S. Department of Education (2005b). Also see, Sunderman, G. L., & Kim, J. (2004). *Increasing bureaucracy or increasing opportunities? School district experience with supplemental educational services*. Cambridge, MA: The Civil Rights Project at Harvard University; or, Sunderman, G. L., & Kim, J. S. (2006). Implementing supplemental educational services: Implications for school districts and educational opportunity. In Wong, K. K., & Rutledge, S. (Eds.), *System-wide efforts to improve student achievement* (pp. 63–93). Greenwich, CT: Information Age.

16. U.S. Department of Education (2002a); U.S. Department of Education (2005b).

17. Ibid.

18. Specifically, the regulatory guidance states; "Under Section 1116(e)(5)(C) of Title I, a supplemental educational service provider must meet all applicable Federal, State, and local civil rights laws (as well as health and safety laws)." With respect to Federal civil rights laws, most apply generally to "recipients of Federal financial assistance." A supplemental educational service provider, merely by being a provider, is not a recipient of federal financial assistance. As a result, the above-referenced federal civil rights laws are not directly applicable to a provider unless the provider otherwise receives federal financial assistance for other purposes. The regulatory guidance states that two laws that "*may* [emphasis added] apply to supplemental

educational service providers despite the fact that a provider is not a recipient of Federal financial assistance." This includes U.S. Department of Education. (2005c). *Title II of the Americans with Disabilities Act of 1990*, and Sec C3 VII of the Civil Rights Act of 1964, which prohibits discrimination in employment on the basis of race, color, religion, sex, or national origin.

19. See Burch(2007c), for a synthesis of this literature and its findings.
20. Burch et al. (2007).
21. I use the term *policy discourse* here in the sense defined by Stephen Ball, "Policy discourses are about what can be said, and thought, but also who can speak, where, when and with what authority" (2005, p. 48).
22. The competition also led vendors to structure tutoring schedules based on billing rather than instructional motivations. For example, one provider had less frequent but longer sessions because then attendance was not as much of an issue. The rationale, according to the director of program, was that it was easier for children to show up and the provider could reduce administrative costs by billing once for a two-hour session rather than twice for two one-hour sessions.
23. Elmore, R. F. (2004). *School reform from the inside out: Policy, practice, and performance.* Cambridge, MA: Harvard Education Press.
24. I would like to thank Annalee Good, who assisted greatly in the field research, and offered useful feedback on several versions of the chapter.
25. Field Notes (Patricia Burch), March 22, 2007.
26. Field Notes (Patricia Burch), March 6, 2007.
27. For examples of this argumentation,see Reason Foundation (http://www.reason.org/education) in particular policy briefs written by Lisa Snell, Director of Education and Child Welfare.
28. The discussion of parents' experiences draws on interview data collected by May Hara, University of Wisconsin—Madison. See, Hara, M. (2007). *Everything has a price tag: Parent responses to supplemental educational services.* Unpublished master's thesis, University of Wisconsin—Madison, 2007.

Chapter 5

1. Tucker, B. (2007, June). *Laboratories of reform: Virtual high schools and innovation in public education.* Washington, D.C.: Education Sector. Retrieved June 1, 2007, from http://www.educationsector.org/research/research_show.htm?doc_id=502307
2. Clark, T. (2001, October). *Virtual schools: Trends and issues; A study of virtual schools in the United States.* San Francisco, CA: West Ed, Distance Learning Resource Network.
3. K-12. (2007, July). Annual Report S-1. Herndon, VA: Author.
4. I would like to thank Joseph Donovan who assisted with background research for this chapter.
5. The former estimate is provided by Clark (2001). However, K12, a for-profit organization that provides a virtual curriculum to home schooled students and cyber charters, estimates that approximately $4,800 to $5,000 per student needs to be allocated.
6. For examples, see, Hassel, B. C., Godard, M. G., & Public Impact. (2004). *How can virtual schools be a vibrant part of meeting the choice provisions of the No Child Left Behind Act?* Washington, D.C.: U.S. Department of Education. Retrieved October 6, 2007, from http://www.ed.gov/about/offices/list/os/technology/plan/2004/site/documents/Hassel-Terrell-; National Association of State Boards of Education. (2001). Any time, any place, any path, any pace: Taking the lead on e-learning policy. Alexandria, VA. Retrieved May 10, 2006, from http://nasbe.org/Organization_Information/e_learning.pdf; Patrick, S. (2006, June). Clicking to class: The state of virtual schools. *Converge Magazine.* Retrieved November 27, 2007, from http://www.convergemag.com/story.php?id=101886
7. K-12. (2007, July). *Annual Report S-1* (p. 10). Herndon, VA: Author.
8. Cavanaugh, C. S. (2001). The effectiveness of interactive distance education technologies in K-12 learning: A meta-analysis. *International Journal of Educational Telecommunications, 7*(1), 73–88. Retrieved April 15, 2006, from http://www.unf.edu/~ccavanau/CavanaughIJET01.pdf
9. Kozma, R., Zucker, A., Espinoza, C., McGhee, R., Yarnall, L., Zalles, D., et al. (2000, November). *The online course experience: Evaluation of the Virtual High School's third year of implementa-

tion, 1999–2000. Menlo Park, CA: SRI International. Retrieved March 5, 2006, from, http://www.sri.com/policy/ctl/assets/images/VHS_Online_Experience.pdf

10. See, for example, Southern Regional Education Board. (1999). Distance learning policy laboratory: *Current initiatives and priority issues*. Retrieved August 2007, from http://www.electroniccampus.org/policylab/docs/initiatives.asp; National Association of State Boards of Education. (2001).

11. See Apple (2002, p. 194), who discusses the use of Internet based home schooling by Conservative Christians.

12. The rise of virtual charter schools also is very closely tied to developments in state chartering laws and to state laws regarding interdistrict transfer.

13. U.S. Department of Education. (2004e, July). *The impact of the new Title I requirements on charter schools: Non-regulatory guidance*. Washington, D.C.: Author. Retrieved August 2007, from http://www.ed.gov/policy/elsec/guid/charterguidance03.pdf; U.S. Department of Education. (2007, August) *Improving basic programs operated by local education agencies*. Title I, Part A, Sec 1003. Washington, D.C.: Government Printing Office. Retrieved December 2007, from http://www.ed.gov/programs/titleiparta/. In order to be eligible, for student transfer, the virtual school must be a public elementary or secondary school. The school also cannot have been identified for school improvement, corrective action, or restructuring.

14. See Hassel et al. (2004).

15. U.S. Department of Education. (2001d). *Elementary and Secondary Education Act of 1965, as amended, Title II, Part D—Enhancing Education Through Technology*. Retrieved October 7, 2007, from http://www.ed.gov/policy/elsec. Sec. 2403.

16. Ibid.

17. Committee for Education Funding. (2007). *Budget response 2007*. Washington, D.C.: Committee on Education Funding.

18. Collins, S. R. (2004). *e-Learning frameworks for NCLB*. Retrieved October 7, 2007, from http://www.ed.gov/about/offices/list/os/technology/plan/2004/site/documents/S.Collins-e-LearningFramework.pdf

19. Hassel et al. (2004).

20. Committee for Education Funding (2007).

21. Ball (2005, p. 48).

22. Apple (2002, p. 209).

23. Home School Legal Defense Association. (2002). The problem with Home-based Charter Schools: HSLDA's position in the home school charter debate. *Current Issue Analysis*. Retrieved August 4, 2007, from http://www.hsdla.org. See also, Klicka, C. J. (2002, January/February). Charter schools: The price is too high. *The Home School Court Report*, 17(1).

24. Ibid.

25. *eSchool News*. (2006, October 1). Districts' virtual schools run afoul of state rules. eSchool News: Technology news for today's K-20 educator. Retrieved September 4, 2007, from http://www.eschoolnews.com/news/showStory.cfm?ArticleID=6610; Human, D. (2007, February 19). Virtual schools face opposition from teachers: State considers legislation banning two of Ball State's charter schools. *The Ball State Daily News Online* Retrieved. November 27, 2007, from http://media.www.bsudailynews.com/media/storage/paper849/news/2007/02/19/News/Virtual.Schools.Face.Opposition.From.Teachers-2727761.shtml

26. See, for example, Wisconsin Education Association Education Council v. Northern Osaukee School District, 2006AP1380, p. 12 (December 5, 2007).

27. Annalee Good provided valuable research assistance in mapping school enrollment patterns and school population characteristics. In our research, we found that other virtual schools in the state also reflected these enrollment patterns (more White, economically advantaged students enrolled in virtual schools).

28. See, Ahearn, E. M., Lange, C. M., Rhim, L. M., & McLaughlin, M. J. (2001). *Project SEARCH: Special education as requirements in charter schools. Final report of a research study: Cross-state analysis of findings and summaries of state case studies*. Alexandria, VA: National Association of State Directors of Special Education; and Wells (2002).

29. The image of invisible work was inspired by the article, Invisible women, invisible work: Women's caring work in developmental disability services. In S. J. Taylor & R. Bogdan (Eds.), *Introduction to qualitative research methods: A guidebook and resource*. New York: Wiley.

Chapter 6

1. Portions of the chapter also appear in: Burch, P., & Hayes, T. (in press). The role of private firms in data-based decision-making. In T. Kowalski & J. Lasley (Eds.), *Handbook of data-based decision making in education*. New York: Routledge.
2. Please see the appendix for a detailed discussion of the research design and data collection activities.
3. Hayes, T. (2007). *Sea change: The proliferation of benchmark assessment systems in U.S. school districts*. Unpublished master's thesis, University of Wisconsin—Madison.
4. Although, the ways in which districts employ the products, as I will note, can end up looking very different depending on the district.
5. Villano, M. (2006). Assessing formative assessment. *Technology and Learning, 26*(6), 8–12.
6. Black, P., & William, D. (2004). The formative purpose: Assessment must first promote learning. In M. Wilson (Ed.), *Towards coherence between classroom assessment and accountability* (pp. 20–50). Chicago: University of Chicago Press.
7. Edusoft. (n.d.). *Description of product*. Retrieved April 10, 2007, from http:///www.edusoft.com
8. Riding the wave of technology. (n.d.). *District-wide applications*. Retrieved January 8, 2008, from http://www.sandi.net/dwa/dwa_what.htm
9. CTB/McGraw Hill. (n.d.). *K-12 products*. Retrieved July 20, 2007, from http://www.ctb.com/products/category_home.jsp
10. Enhancing Education through Technology Act, 2001, Sec. 2402-2403.
11. Personal correspondence, August 1, 2007.
12. See, Metz (1989), for example.
13. The sample was limited to all 30 school districts (excluding Puerto Rico and Hawaii) with a student population greater than 94,000 according to the NCES report, National Center for Education Statistics (2006, September).Characteristics of the Largest 100 Public Elementary and Secondary School Districts in the United States, 2003–2004. As reflected in Table 2.1, we received a response from at least one official in 93.33% of the 30 school districts surveyed. Out of a total of 148 people across those districts, 54 (36.54%) responded. The people most likely to respond were those in the role groups of Technology (32.69%) and Research, Assessment, and Accountability (32.69%), although we also received responses from those in Title I Administration (15.38%), Budget & Finance (13.46%), and Curriculum & Instruction (9.25%). There are several primary patterns suggested by the survey data.
14. All names of districts, firms, and those interviewed are pseudonyms to protect confidentiality.
15. Tracy Hayes collaborated in the research and writing in this section of the chapter. See, Hayes, T. (2007). *Sea change: The proliferation of benchmark assessments systems in U.S. school districts* Unpublished master's thesis, University of Wisconsin—Madison.
16. Halverson, R., Prichett, R., Grigg, J., & Thomas, C. (2005). *The new instructional leadership: Creating data-driven instructional systems in schools*. Paper prepared for the annual meeting of the National Council of Professors of Educational Administration, WA.

Chapter 7

1. Burch (2006).
2. Ball (2006).
3. Burch (2006).
4. Metz (1989, 2008).
5. However, the case studies of benchmark assessments systems suggest that there are challenges to ensuring that equal access is ensured.
6. See, for example, Fligstein, N. (1990). *The transformation of corporate control*. Cambridge, MA: Harvard University Press.
7. Ball (2007).
8. I would like to thank Gail Sunderman, Matthew Steinberg, and members of the Spring 2008 Educational Policy Studies Seminar for their comments and suggestions on earlier drafts of this portion of the chapter.

9. The importance of examining the linkages between education policy and economic policies receive thorough treatment in Anyon, J. (2005). *Radical possibilities: Public policy, urban education, and a new social movement*. New York: Routledge.

10. For a discussion of the efforts by some parents to challenge policies of neoliberalism see, Lipman, P. (2004). *High stakes education: Inequality, globalization and urban school reform*. New York: Routledge Falmer; Apple, M. (2006); and Saltman, K. (2005). *The Edison Schools*. New York: Routledge.

11. See, for example, Reich, R. (2007). Common schooling and educational choice as a response to pluralism. In W. Feinberg & C. Lubienski (Eds.), *School choice policies and outcomes: Philosophical and empirical perspectives on limits to choice in liberal democracies*. Albany, NY: SUNY Press. Comments by Stephen Macedo (October 24–26), *Values, charters and choice*, presented at a conference hosted by the Spencer Foundation, Values and Evidence in Education Reform, Chicago, also posed these questions in relationship to debates on school choice.

12. In thinking about this, I have benefited much from the work of Sclar (2000).

Appendix A

1. Bogdan, R., & Biklen, S. K. (1992). *Qualitative research for education: An introduction to theory and methods*. Boston: Allyn & Bacon; Bogdan, R., & Taylor, S. (1998). *Introduction to qualitative research methods*. New York: Wiley.

2. For examples of others' work in this area, see Coburn, C. E. (2004). Beyond decoupling. Rethinking the relationship between the institutional environment and the classroom. *Sociology of Education, 77*(3), 211–244; and Anagostopoulos, D., & Rutledge, S. (2007). Making sense of school sanctioning policies in urban high schools: Charting the depth and drift of school and classroom change. *Teachers College Record, 109*(5), 1261–1291.

3. Miles, M. B., & Huberman, A. M. (1994). *Qualitative data analysis: An expanded source book*. Thousand Oaks, CA: Sage.

4. Burch (2006).

5. Ultimately, the focus of my work was on a firm's activities nationally and locally because of my interest in NCLB as a driver of trends, and in local school districts. However, the changes described are rooted in internationalizing trends in the K-12 education industry. Hentschke (2005), makes this point in his useful analysis of internationalizing trends in the industry of higher education, and how organizations such as the University of Phoenix are describing their schools in terms of a global campus. Also, see Ball (2007) on internationalizing trends in education contracting.

6. The financial and operational data of publicly traded firms can be searched via Web-based platforms such as Hoovers (http://www.hoovers.com) and 10KWizard (http://www.tenkwizard.com).

7. I included in the last category archived information from the U.S. Department of Education's Web site on the Department's current and former employees.

8. I draw here on typology and discussion by Bardach, E. (2005). *A practical guide for policy analysis: The eightfold path to more effective problem solving* (2nd ed., pp. 123–131). Berkeley, CA: CQ Press.

9. National Center for Education Statistics (2006).

10. Miles and Huberman (1994).

Bibliography

Agron, A. (2001, September). 7th privatization/contract services survey. *American School and University Magazine*, 27–31.

Ahearn, E. M., Lange, C. M., Rhim, L. M., & McLaughlin, M. J. (2001). *Project SEARCH: Special education as requirements in charter schools. Final report of a research study: Cross-state analysis of findings and summaries of state case studies*. Alexandria, VA: National Association of State Directors of Special Education.

Alliance for Children, Inc. v. City of Detroit Public Schools, 475 F. Supp. 2d 655 (U.S. District Court for Eastern District of Michigan 2007).

American Home School Association. (2006). *Resource listings from the National Home Education Network*. Retrieved August 20, 2007, from http://www.americanhomeschoolassociation.org/resources.html

American Institutes for Research, & Education Industry Association. (2005). *The promise and challenge of supplemental educational services: The providers' perspective*. Washington, D.C.: American Institutes for Research.

Anagostopoulos, D., & Rutledge, S. (2007). Making sense of school sanctioning policies in urban high schools: Charting the depth and drift of school and classroom change. *Teachers College Record, 109*(5), 2356–2372.

Anyon, J. (2005). *Radical possibilities: Public policy, urban education, and a new social movement*. New York: Routledge.

Apple, M. W. (1996). *Cultural politics and education*. New York: Teachers College Press.

Apple, M. W. (2000). *Official knowledge: Democratic education in a conservative age* (2nd ed.). New York: Routledge.

Apple, M. W. (2006). *Educating the "right" way: Markets, standards, God, and inequality*. New York: Routledge.

Apple, M. W., & Pedroni, T. (2005). Conservative alliance building and African American support of vouchers. *Teachers College Record, 107*, 2068–2105.

Ball, S. J. (Ed.). (2005). *Education policy and social class: The selected works of Stephen J. Ball*. London: Routledge.

Ball, S. J. (2006). Policy sociology and critical policy research. In S. J. Ball (Ed.), *Education policy and social class: The selected works of Stephen J. Ball* (p. 20). New York: Routledge.

Ball, S. J. (2007a). *Education Plc: Understanding private sector participation in public sector education*. London: Routledge.

Ball, S. J. (2007b, September 5). *Education PLC*. Paper presented at the British Education Research Association. Institute of Education, London.

Bardach, E. (2005). *A practical guide for policy analysis: The eightfold path to more effective problem solving* (2nd ed., pp. 123–131). Berkeley, CA: CQ Press.

Basset, E., Burdt, C., Jackson, J., Gallagher, S., & Poroy, B. (2005, May). *The education investor: First quarter 2005*. Boston, MA: Eduventures.

Beales, J. (1994). *Doing more with less: Competitive contracting for school support services*. Los Angeles: The Reason Foundation.

Beales, J. R., & O'Leary, J. (1993). *Making schools work: Contracting options for better management*. Los Angeles: Reason Public Policy Institute.

Belfield, C. R., & Levin, H. M. (2002). *Education privatization: Causes, consequences and planning implications* (Fundamentals of Educational Planning, No.74). Paris: United Nations Educational, Scientific and Cultural Organization, International Institute for Educational Planning.

Black, P., & William, D. (2004). The formative purpose: Assessment must first promote learning. In M. Wilson (Ed.), *Towards coherence between classroom assessment and accountability* (pp. 20–50). Chicago: University of Chicago Press.

Bogdan, R., & Biklen, S. K. (1992). *Qualitative research for education: An introduction to theory and methods*. Boston: Allyn & Bacon.

Bogdan, R., & Taylor, S. (1998). *Introduction to qualitative research methods*. New York: Wiley.

Bourdieu, P., & Wacquant, L. (2001). NewLiberalSpeak: Notes on the new planetary vulgate. *Radical Philosophy, 105*, 2–5.

Bracey, G. W. (2002). *The war against America's public schools: Privatizing schools, commercializing education*. Boston: Allyn & Bacon.

Bradach, J., & Tempest, N. (2000). *New schools venture fund*. Cambridge, MA: Harvard Business School.

Bray, M. (1999). *The shadow education system: Private tutoring and its implications for planners*. Paris: International Institute for Educational Planning.

Brighouse, H. (2004). What's wrong with privatizing schools. *Journal of Philosophy of Education, 38*, 629–630.

Bulkley, K. E. (2007). Bringing the private into the public: Changing the rules of the game and new regime politics in Philadelphia public education. *Educational Policy, 21*(1), 155–184.

Burch, P. (2006). The new educational privatization: Educational contracting in the era of high stakes accountability. *Teachers College Record, 88*(2), 129–135.

Burch, P. (2007a). Educational policy and practice from the perspective of institutional theory: Crafting a wider lens. *Educational Researcher, 36*(2), 84–95.

Burch, P. (2007b, March). The professionalization of instructional leadership in the United States: Competing values and current tensions. *Journal of Educational Policy, 22*(2), 195–214.

Burch, P. (2007c, May). *Supplemental educational services under NCLB: Emerging evidence and policy issues*. Retrieved June 5, 2007, from http://epsl.asu.edu/epru/documents/EPSL-0705-232-EPRU.pdf

Burch, P., & Hayes, T. (in press). The role of private firms in data-based decision-making. In T. Kowalski & T. Lasley (Eds.), *Handbook of data-based decision making in education*. New York: Routledge.

Burch, P., Steinberg, M., & Donovan, J. (2007). Supplemental educational services and NCLB: Policy assumptions, market practices, emerging issues. *Educational Evaluation and Policy Analysis, 29*(2), 115–133.

Burns, P. (2003). Regime theory, state government and a take-over of urban education. *Journal of Urban Affairs, 25*, 285–303.

Cantelon, J. (2002, August 13). Virtual charter schools face opposition from unlikely source. *CNSNews.com: Cybercast News Service*. Retrieved August 2007, from http://www.cnsnews.com/ViewNation.asp?Page=//Nation//archive/[200208//NAT20020813b.html

Cavanaugh, C. S. (2001). The effectiveness of interactive distance education technologies in K-12 learning: A meta-analysis. *International Journal of Educational Telecommunications, 7*(1), 73–88.

Center for Digital Government. (2002, October) *Virtual schools forum report: A report on the virtual schools—A policy forum*. Retrieved August 2007, from http://www.centerdigitalgov.com/center/media/DenverVSF_FINAL.doc

Center on Education Policy. (2006, March). *From the capital to the classroom: Year 4 of the No Child Left Behind Act*. Washington, D.C: Center on Education Policy.

Chartwell Education Group. (n.d.). Retrieved October 1, 2007, from http://www.chartwelleducation.com/

Chicago Public Schools. (2007). *SES tutoring programs: An evaluation of year 3 in the Chicago Public Schools*. Chicago: Chicago Public Schools.

Childress, S., & King, C. (2005, December). *New schools venture fund in 2004: At a crossroads*. Cambridge, MA: Harvard Business Publishing.

Chubb, J. E., & Moe, T. M. (1990). *Politics, markets, and America's schools.* Washington, D.C.: Brookings Institution.

Clark, T. (2001, October). *Virtual schools: Trends and issues; A study of virtual schools in the United States.* San Francisco, CA: West Ed, Distance Learning Resource Network.

Clearinghouse on Educational Policy and Management. (n.d.). *Virtual schools. Trends and issues: School choice.* Retrieved September 4, 2007, from http://eric.uoregon.edu/trends_issues/choice/virtual_schools.html

Coburn, C. E. (2001). Collective sense-making about reading: How teachers mediate reading policy in their professional communities. *Educational Evaluation and Policy Analysis, 23*(2), 145.

Coburn, C. E. (2004). Beyond decoupling: Rethinking the relationship between the institutional environment and the classroom. *Sociology of Education, 77*(3), 211–244.

Cohen, D. K. (1982). Policy and organization: The impact of state and federal educational policy on school governance. *Harvard Educational Review, 52*(4), 474–499.

Collins, S. R. (2004). *White Paper: e-Learning Frameworks for NCLB.* Retrieved October 7, 2007, from http://www.ed.gov/about/offices/list/os/technology/plan/2004/site/documents/S.Collins-e-LearningFramework.pdf

Committee for Education Funding. (2007). *Budget response 2007.* Washington, D.C.: Committee on Education Funding.

Comprehensive School Reform Quality Center. (2006, April). *Report on education service providers: Executive summary.* Washington, D.C.: American Institutes for Research.

Confessore, N. (2003, July/August). Welcome to the machine: How the GOP disciplined K Street and made Bush supreme. *Washington Monthly, 35*(7/8), 30–37.

Congressional Research Service. (2006). *Privatization and the federal government: An introduction.* Washington, D.C.: Author. Retrieved April 2008, from http://www.fas.org/sgp/crs.

Coulson, A. J. (1999). *Market education: The unknown history.* New Brunswick, NJ: Transaction. CTB/McGraw Hill. (n.d.). *K-12 products.* Retrieved July 20, 2007, from http://www.ctb.com/products/category_home.jsp

Daniels, M. (2006). *Reforming government through competition.* Los Angeles: The Reason Foundation. Retrieved December 10, 2006, from http://www.reason.org/apr2006/apr2006_daniels.shtml

Davies, S., & Aurini, J. (2006). The franchising of private tutoring: A view from Canada. *Phi Delta Kappan, 88*(2), 123–128.

Davis, M. R. (2003, April 16). Doing the "right" thing: The man in charge of making the No Child Left Behind Act a reality, a true-believer conservative, may be developing a taste for shades of gray. *Ed Week.* Retrieved November 12, 2007, from http://www.edweek.org/ew/articles/2003/04/16/31hickok

Denzin, N. K., & Lincoln, Y. S. (1994). *Handbook of qualitative research.* Thousand Oaks, CA: Sage.

DiMaggio, P. D. (1988). Interest and agency in institutional theory. In L. Zucker (Ed.), *Institutional patterns and organizations: Culture and environment* (pp. 3–21). Cambridge, MA: Ballinger.

Dutko Worldwide. (n.d.a). *Practice Areas: Education.* Retrieved June 8, 2007, from http://www.dutkoworldwide.com/

Dutko Worldwide. (n.d.b). *Latest News.* Retrieved October 1, 2007, from http://www.dutkoworldwide.com/media_center/latest_news/1048

eClassroom. (n.d.a). *About eClassroom.* Retrieved August 2007, from http://www.eclassroom.com/about/About.learn

eClassroom. (n.d.b). *News.* Retrieved August 2007, from http://www.eclassroom.com/news/News.learn

eClassroom. (n.d.c). *Products and services.* Retrieved August 2007, from http://www.eclassroom.com/products/Products.learn

Edison Inc. (2003, September 9). *10-K.* New York: Author.

Educate Inc. (2004a). *Annual Report: Form 10K.* Retrieved September 2007, from http://www.educate.com

Educate Inc. (2004b, March 14). *10-K.* Baltimore, MD: Author.

Educate Inc. (2006, March 16). *10-K.* Baltimore, MD: Author.

Educate Inc. (2007a, March 16). *10-K.* Baltimore, MD: Author.

Educate Inc. (2007b, April 3). *10-K.* Baltimore, MD: Author.

Educate Inc. (2007c, May 10). *10-K.* Baltimore, MD: Author.

Educate Inc. (2007d). *Annual Report: Form 10K*. Retrieved September 2007, from http://www.educate.com

Education Industry Association. (n.d.) *Overview of the education industry association*. Retrieved August 6, 2008, from http://www.educationindustry.org/tier.asp

Education Industry Association. (2006). Enterprising educators. *Newsletter of Education Industry Association, 15*(2), 1.

Education Industry Association. (2008, January 8). *Education principles and policies for the next U.S. president: Recommendations of the Education Industry Association*. Rockville, MD: Author.

Education Industry Day. (n.d.) *Highlights and program*. Retrieved March 2006, from http://www.educationindustry.org/tier.asp?sid=4

Edusoft. (n.d.). *Description of product*. Retrieved April 10, 2007, from http:///www.edusoft.com

Eduventures. (2003, August). *Learning markets & opportunities 2003: New models for delivering education and services drive pre-K-12 and postsecondary sector growth*. Boston, MA: author.

Eduventures. (July 2006). *Closing the achievement gap: Opportunity and improvement*. Paper presented at the Education Industry Association Annual Conference, Denver, Colorado.

Elluminate. (n.d.) *Elluminate community*. Retrieved August 2007, from http://www.elluminate.com/community/

Elmore, R. F. (2004a). Conclusion: The problem of stakes in performance-based accountability systems. In R. F. Elmore & S. H. Fuhrman (Eds.), *Redesigning accountability systems for education* (pp. 274–296). New York: Teachers College Press.

Elmore, R. F. (2004b). *School reform from the inside out: Policy, practice, and performance*. Cambridge, MA: Harvard Education Press.

Elmore, R. F., & Fuller, B. (1996). *Who chooses? Who loses? Culture, institutions, and the unequal effects of school choice*. New York: Teachers College Press.

eSchool News. (2004, August 16). Grants to Bennett's K-12 Inc. challenged. *eSchool News: Technology news for today's K-20 educator*. Retrieved August 2007, from http://www.eschoolnews.com/news/showstory.cfm?ArticleID=5220

eSchool News. (2006, October 1). Virtual schools again in spotlight District-run online schools run afoul of state regulations. Retrieved October 4, 2007, from http://www.eschoolnews.com/news/top-news/index.cfm?i=41301&CFID=1251340&CFTOKEN=68783391

eSchool News: Technology news for today's K-20 educator. Retrieved September 4, 2007, from http://www/eschoolnews.com/news/showStory.cfm?ArticleID=6610

Farkas, G., & Durham, R. (2006, February 23–24). *The role of tutoring in standards-based reform*. Paper presented at the conference, Will Standards-Based Reform in Education Help Close the Poverty Gap? University of Wisconsin, Madison.

Feinberg, W., & Lubienski, C. (Eds.). *School choice policies and outcomes: Philosophical and empirical perspectives on limits to choice in liberal democracies*. Albany, NY: SUNY Press.

Ferneding, K. A. (2003). *Questioning technology: Electronic technologies and educational reform*. New York: Peter Lang.

Fitz, J., & Beers, B. (2001, June). *Education management organizations and the privatization of public education: A cross-national comparison of the USA and the UK* (Occasional paper no. 22). New York: Columbia University, National Center for the Study of Privatization in Education.

Flam, S., & Keane, W. (1997). *Public schools/private Enterprise: What you should know and do about privatization*. Lancaster, PA: Technomic.

Fligstein, N. (1990). *The transformation of corporate control*. Cambridge, MA: Harvard University Press.

Florida Center for Reading Research. (n.d.). *Wilson reading system*. Retrieved May 1, 2008, from http://www.fcrr.org/FCRRReports/PDF/wilson.pdf

Foley, E. (2001). *Contradictions and control in system reform: The ascendancy of the central office in Philadelphia schools*. Philadelphia, PA: Consortium for Policy Research in Education.

Franklin, B. M., Bloch, M. N., & Popkewitz, T. S. (2004). *Educational partnerships and the state: The paradoxes of governing schools, children, and families*. New York: Palgrave Macmillan.

Fuhrman, S., & Elmore, R. F. (Eds.). (2004). *Redesigning accountability systems for education*. New York: Teachers College Press.

Fuhrman, S., Goertz, M., & Duffy, M. (2004). Slow down, you move too fast: The politics of making changes in high-stakes accountability policies for students. In S. Fuhrman & R. Elmore (Eds.), *Redesigning accountability systems for education* (pp. 245–274). New York: Teachers College Press.

Gill, B., Hamilton, L., Lockwood, J., Marsh, J., Zimmer, R., Hill, D., et al. (2005). *Inspiration, perspiration, and time: Operations and achievement in Edison schools*. Santa Monica, CA: RAND.

Gillborn, D. (2005). Education policy as an act of white supremacy: Whiteness, critical race theory and education reform. *Journal of Education Policy, 20,* 485–505.

Giroux, H. (2002). Schools for sale: Public education, corporate culture and the citizen-consumer. In A. Kohn & P. Shannon (Eds.), *Education Inc: Turning learning into a business* (pp. 105–118). Portsmouth, NH: Heinemann.

Gold, E., Christman, J. B., & Harold, B. (in press). Blurring the boundaries: Private sector involvement in Philadelphia public schools. *American Journal of Education.*

Halverson, R., Prichett, R., Grigg, J., & Thomas, C. (2005). *The new instructional leadership: Creating data-driven instructional systems in schools*. Paper prepared for the annual meeting of the National Council of Professors of Educational Administration, Washington, D.C.

Hara, M. (2007). Everything has a price tag: Parent responses to supplemental educational services. Unpublished master's thesis, University of Wisconsin–Madison.

Harvard Business School. (2000, October 13). *Case 9-301-038. New schools venture fund*. Cambridge, MA: Author.

Harvey, D. (2005). *A brief history of neoliberalism*. Oxford: Oxford University Press.

Hassel, B. C., Godard, M. G., & Public Impact. (2004). *How can virtual schools be a vibrant part of meeting the choice provisions of the No Child Left Behind Act?* Washington, D.C.: U.S. Department of Education. Retrieved from http://www.ed.gov/about/offices/list/os/technology/plan/2004/site/documents/Hassel-Terrell-VirtualSchools.pdf

Hassel, B. C., Godard Terrell, M., & Public Impact. (2004). *U.S. increasing options through e-Learning*. Paper presented at the Department of Education Secretary's No Child Left Behind Leadership Summit.

Hayes, T. (2007). *Sea change: The proliferation of benchmark assessment systems in U.S. school districts.* Unpublished master's thesis, University of Wisconsin–Madison.

Heinrich, C. J., Meyer, R. H., & Whitten, G. (2007, November). *Supplemental education services under No Child Left Behind: Who signs up, and what do they gain*. Paper presented at the annual meeting of the American Educational Research Association, New York.

Heistad, D. (2006). *Analysis of 2005 supplemental educational services in Minneapolis public schools: An application of matched sample statistical design*. Minneapolis, MN: Minneapolis Public Schools.

Henig, J. R. (1989). Privatization in the United States: Theory and practice. *Political Science Quarterly, 104,* 649–670.

Henig, J. R. (1994). *Rethinking school choice: Limits of the market metaphor*. Princeton, NJ: Princeton University Press.

Henig, J. R., Holyoke, T., Lacreo-Paquet, N., & Mostner, M. (2003).Privatization, politics, and urban services: The political behavior of charter schools. *Journal of Urban Affairs, 25,* 37–54.

Hentschke, G. C. (2005). *New areas of educational governance: The impact of international organizations and markets on educational policymaking*. Los Angeles, CA: Center on Educational Governance, University of Southern California.

Hill, P. T., & Lake, R. (2006, September). *Charter school governance*. Paper presented at the National Conference on Charter School Research, Vanderbilt University, Nashville, TN.

Hill, P. T., Pierce, L. C., & Guthrie, J. W. (1997). *Reinventing public education: How contracting can transform America's schools*. Chicago: University of Chicago Press.

HomeSchoolChristian.com (n.d.a). *Affiliates and advertisers*. Retrieved August 2007 from http://homeschoolchristian.com/allaffiliates.html

HomeSchoolChristian.com. (n.d.b). *Leadership position papers: K12 letter to local homeschoolers*. Retrieved August 2007, from http://homeschoolchristian.com/Position/K12Letter.html

Home School Legal Defense Association. (2002, June 26). The problem with home-based charter schools: HSLDA's position in the charter school debate. *Current Issue Analysis*. Retrieved October 31, 2007, from http://www.hslda.org/docs/nche/000010/200206260.asp

Home School Legal Defense Association. (2003, August). *Virtual charter schools*. Retrieved August 20, 2007, from http://www.hslda.org/docs/nche/Issues/C/CharterSchools.asp

Honig, M. I. (2004). The new middle management: Intermediary organizations in education policy implementation. *Educational Evaluation and Policy Analysis, 26,* 65–87.

Human, D. (2007, February 19). Virtual schools face opposition from teachers: State considers legislation banning two of Ball State's charter schools. *The Ball State Daily News Online*. Retrieved

November 27, 2007, from http://media.www.bsudailynews.com/media/storage/paper849/news/2007/02/19/News/Virtual.Schools.Face.Opposition.From.Teachers-2727761.shtml

Jackson, M., & Bassett, E. (2005). *The state of the K-12 state assessment market*. Boston: Eduventures.

Jessop, B. (2002). *The future of the capitalist state*. London: Polity.

K-12. (2007a, July). *Annual Report S-1*. Herndon, VA: Author.

K-12. (2007b, December 10). *S-1/A*. Herndon, VA: Author.

K12. (n.d.) *About K12*. Retrieved August 2007, from http://www.k12.com/about_k12/about_k12_overview/index.html

Klicka, C. J. (2002, January/February). Charter schools: The price is too high. *The Home School Court Report, 17*(1). Retrieved July 1, 2006, from http://www.hslda.org/courtreport/V18N1/V18N101.asp

Kozma, R., Zucker, A., Espinoza, C., McGhee, R., Yarnall, L., Zalles, D., & Lewis, A. (2000, November). *The online course experience: Evaluation of the Virtual High School's third year of implementation, 1999–2000*. Menlo Park, CA: SRI International.

Lacireno-Paquet, N. (2004). Do EMO-operated charter schools serve disadvantaged students? The influence of state policies. *Education Policy Analysis Archives, 12*(26). Retrieved from http://epaa.asu.edu/epaa/v12n26/

Learning Point Associates. (2002, April). E-Learning policy implications for K-12 educators and decision makers. *Policy Issues, 11*. Retrieved August 20, 2007, from http://www.ncrel.org/policy/pubs/html/pivol11/apr2002d.htm

Levin, H.M. (1987). Education as public and private good. *Journal of Policy Analysis and Management, 6*, 641–643.

Levin, H. M. (2001). *Privatizing education: can the marketplace deliver choice,efficiency, equity, and social cohesion?* Boulder, CO: Westview Press.

Levin, H. (2006). Déjà vu all over again. *Education Next, 6*(2) 1–7.

Leys, C. (2003). *Market-driven politics: Neoliberal democracy and the public interest*. New York: Verso.

Lipman, P. (2004). *High stakes education: Inequality, globalization, and urban school reform*. New York: Routledge Falmer.

Lipton, E. (2006, June 18). Former anti-terror officials find industry pays better. *New York Times*, p. 11. Retrieved Septmember 26, 2008, from http://www.nytimes.com/2006/06/18/washington/18lobby.html?_r=1&oref=slogin

Macedo, S. (2006) *Values, charters and choice*. Presented at a conference hosted by the Spencer Foundation. Values and Evidence in Education Reform. Chicago. October 24-26.

Mandinach, E. B., Rivas, L., Light, D., Heinze, C., & Honey, M. (2006, April). *The impact of data-driven decision making tools on educational practice: A systems analysis of six school districts*. Paper prepared for the meeting of the American Educational Research Association, San Francisco, CA.

Mandlawitz, M. (2005). *Education budget alert for fiscal year 2006*. Washington, D.C.: Committee for Education Funding.

Marglin, S. (2008). *The dismal science: How thinking like an economist undermines community*. Cambridge, MA: Harvard University Press.

Marlow, M. I. (2001). Bureaucracy and student performance in us public schools. *Applied Economics, 33*(10), 1341–1350.

McDonnell, L. (2005). NCLB and the Federal rolle in education: Evolution or revolution. *Peabody Journal of Education, 80*(2), 19–38.

McLaughlin, M.W., Irby, M., & Langman, J. (1994). *Urban sanctuaries: Neighborhood organizations in the lives and futures of inner city youth*. San Francisco: Jossey-Bass.

Meier, D. (2002). *In schools we trust: Creating communities of learning in an era of testing and standardization*. Boston: Beacon Press.

Metz, M. H. (1989). Real school: A universal drama amid disparate experience. *Politics of Education Association Yearbook*, 75–91.

Metz, M. H. (2008). Symbolic uses of NCLB: Reaffirmation of equality of educational opportunity or delegitimization of public schools? In A. Sardovnik et al. (Eds.), *No Child Left Behind and the reduction of the achievement gap: Sociological perspectives on federal educational policy* . New York: Routledge.

Meyer, H. D., & Rowan, B. (2006). *The new institutionalism in education*. Albany: SUNY Press.

Meyer, J. W., & Rowan, B. (1977). Institutionalized organizations: Formal structure as myth and ceremony. *The American Journal of Sociology, 83*(2), 340–363.

Meyer, J. W., Scott, W. R., Strang, D., & Creighton, A. L. (1988). Bureaucratization without centralization: Changes in the organizational system of US public education, 1940–80. In L. Zucker (Ed.), *Institutional patterns in organizations: Culture and environments* (pp. 139–168). Cambridge, MA: Ballinger.

Mezias, S. J. (1990, September). An institutional model of organizational practice: Financial reporting at the Fortune 500. *Administrative Science Quarterly, 35*(3), 431–457.

Miles, M. B., & Huberman, A. M (1994) *Qualitative data analysis: An expanded source book.* Thousand Oaks, CA: Sage.

Miller/McKeon discussion draft of ESEA reauthorization: Hearing before the Committee on Education and Labor of the House of Representatives, 110th Congress, 1st Session. (2007).

Molnar, A. (2005). *School commercialism: From democratic ideal to market commodity.* New York: Routledge.

Molnar, A., Wilson, G., & Allen, D. (2004, February). *Profiles of for-profit education management companies: Sixth annual report. 2003–2004.* Tempe, AZ: Educational Policy Studies Laboratory, Arizona State University.

Murphy, J. T. (1996). *The privatization of schooling: problems and possibilities.* Thousand Oaks, CA: Corwin Press.

Murphy, J. T. (1991). Title I of ESEA: The politics of implementing federal education reform. In A. Odden (Ed.), *Education policy implementation* (pp. 13–38). Albany: State University of New York Press.

Murphy, J. T., Glimer, S. W, Weise, R., & Page, A. (1998). *Pathways to privatization in education.* Greenwich, CT: Ablex.

Nation At Risk: The imperative for educational reform. Washington DC: The Commission on Excellence in Education, 1983.

National American Council for Online Learning. (n.d.). *About NACOL.* Retrieved August 2007, from http://www.nacol.org/about/

National Association of School Board Educators. (2001). *Any time, any place, any path, any pace: Taking the lead on e-learning policy.* Alexandria, VA: National Association of School Board Educators.

National Association of State Boards of Education. (2001). *Any time, any place, any path, any pace: Taking the lead on e-learning policy.* Alexandria, VA. Retrieved July 2006, from http://nasbe.org/Organization_Information/e_learning.pdf

National Center for Education Statistics. (2006, September). *Characteristics of the 100 largest public elementary and secondary school districts in the United States: 2003–2004* (NCES Rep. No. 2006-329). Washington, D.C.: National Center for Education Statistics. Retrieved December 19, 2006, from http://nces.ed.gov/pubsearch/pubsinfo.asp?pubid=2006329

Newman, A. (2004). *Closing the equity gap: Addressing NCLB compliance with access infrastructure software.* Boston: Eduventures.

New Schools Venture Fund. (n.d.a). *About us.* Retrieved April 1, 2006, from http://www.newschools.org

New Schools Venture Fund. (n.d.b). *Investment process.* Retrieved April 1, 2006, from http://www.newschools.org/work/investment-process

Noam, G. (2002). *After school education: Approaches to an emerging field.* Cambridge, MA: Harvard Education Press.

No Child Left Behind Act of 2001, 155 Stat. 1425 (2001).

Ogawa, R. T. (1992). Institutional theory and examining leadership in schools. *International Journal of Educational Management, 6*, 14–21.

O'Toole, L. Jr., & Meier, K. (2004). Parkinson's law and the new public management: Contracting determinants and service-quality consequences in public education. *Public Administration Review, 64*(3), 342–352.

Patrick, S. (June 2006). Clicking to class: The state of virtual schools. *Converge Magazine.* Retrieved November 27, 2007, from http://www.convergemag.com/story.php?id=101886

Patrinos, H. A. (2005, October). *Education contracting: Scope of future research.* Paper prepared for the conference "Mobilizing the private sector for public education," A Program on Education Policy and Governance, Harvard University–World Bank conference, Cambridge, MA. Retrieved October 2007, from http://www.hks.harvard.edu/pepg/conferences/MPSPEpapers.htm

Pearson. (n.d.) *Our News*. Retrieved July 1, 2007, from http:/www.pearson.com

Pennsylvania Coalition of Charter Schools. (2007, June 11). *Pennsylvania cyber charter schools and AYP: The complete story...*Retrieved August 2007, from http://www.pachartercoalition.com/main/news_information/news_20070611.html

Potter, A., Ross, S. M., Paek, J., McKay, D., Ashton, J., & Sanders, W. L. (2007). *Supplemental educational services in the state of Tennessee: 2005–06 (2004–2005 student achievement results)*. Memphis, TN: University of Memphis, Center for Research in Education Policy.

Powell, W. W., & DiMaggio, P. (1991). *The new institutionalism in organizational analysis*. Chicago: University of Chicago Press.

Princeton Review. (2004, December 3). *10-K*. New York: Author.

Princeton Review. (2006). *Annual Report*. Retrieved August 2007, from www.10KWizard.org.

Princeton Review. (2007, April 2). *10-K*. New York: Author.

Princeton Review. (2008, March 17). *10-K*. New York: Author.

Reading School District v. Pennsylvania Department of Education, 875 A.2d 1218 (Pa. Commw. 2005).

Reich, R. (2007). Common schooling and educational choice as a response to pluralism. In W. Feinberg & C. Lubienski (Eds). *School choice policies and outcomes: Philosophical and empirical perspectives on limits to choice in liberal democracies*. Albany, NY: SUNY Press.

Renaissance Learning. *Product overview*. Retrieved June 1, 2008, from https://www.capitaliq.com/CIQDotNet/company/longBusinessDescription

Reason Foundation. (2006). *Transforming government through privatization*. Los Angeles, CA: Reason Foundation.

Rickles, J. H., & White, J. A. (2006). *The impact of supplemental educational services participation on student achievement*. Los Angeles: Los Angeles Unified School District.

Riding the Wave of Technology. (n.d.). *District-wide applications*. Retrieved January 8, 2008, from http://www.sandi.net/dwa/dwa_what.htm

Riley, J. (2008, February 9). Movie man: An interview with Reed Hastings. *Wall Street Journal*, p. A9.

Rowan, B. (2002). The ecology of school improvement: Notes on the school improvement industry in the United States. *Journal of Educational Change, 3*(3), 283–314.

Rowan, B. (2006a). The school improvement industry in the United States: Why educational change is both pervasive and ineffectual. In H. D. Meyer & B. Rowan (Eds.), *The new institutionalism in education* (pp. 67–85). Albany: SUNY Press.

Rowan, B. (2006b). Varieties of institutional theory: Traditions and prospects for educational research. In H. D. Meyer & B. Rowan (Eds.), *The new institutionalism in education* (pp. 15–33). Albany: SUNY Press.

Saltman, K. J. (2000). *Collateral damage: Corporatizing public schools—A threat to democracy*. Lanham, MD: Rowman & Littlefield.

Saltman, K. J. (2005). *The Edison schools: Corporate schooling and the assault on public education*. New York: Routledge.

School Improvement Industry. (n.d.). *Our editor's resume: Marc Dean Millot*. Retrieved June 4, 2008, from http://www.siiwonline.com/Resume.html

SchoolNet. *Product description*. Retrieved February 7, 2007, from http:www.schoolnet.org

Sclar, E. (2000). *You don't always get what you pay for: The economics of privatization*. Ithaca, NY: Cornell University Press.

Scott, W. R. (2001). *Institutions and organizations*. Thousand Oaks, CA: Sage. Second edition

Scott, W. R., & Christensen, S. (1995). *The institutional construction of organizations: International and longitudinal studies*. Thousand Oaks, CA: Sage.

Scott, W. R., Meyer, J. W., & Boli, J. (1994). *Institutional environments and organizations: Structural complexity and individualism*. Thousand Oaks, CA: Sage.

Sharkey, N. S., & Murnane, R. J. (2006, August). Tough choices in designing a formative assessment system. *American Journal of Education, 112*(4), 572–588.

Shaul, M. S. (2002, October). *Public schools: Insufficient research to determine the effectiveness of selected private education companies* (No. Document GAO-03-11). Washington, D.C.: U.S. General Accounting Office.

Shipps, D. (1997). The invisible hand: Big business and Chicago school reform. *The Teachers College Record, 99*(1), 73–116.

Silverman, J. (February 6, 2007). Virtual charter school growing fast. *Northwest News Channel 8*.

Retrieved November 27, 2007, from http://www.kgw.com/education/localeducation/stories/kgw_020607_edu_charter_schools.58473753.html#

Smith, K. B., & Meier, K. J. (1994). Politics, bureaucrats and schools. *Public Administration Review, 54*(6), 551–558.

Smith, M. L. (2004). *Political spectacle and the fate of American schools: Symbolic politics and educational policies.* New York: Routledge Falmer.

Smith, S., & Lipsky, M. (1999). Non-profits for hire: The welfare state in the age of contracting. *Contemporary Sociology, 23*(4), 584–585.

Southern Regional Education Board. (1999). *Distance learning policy laboratory: Current initiatives and priority issues.* Retrieved August 2007, from http://www.electroniccampus.org/policylab/docs/initiatives.asp

Spillane, J. P. (1998, Spring). State policy and the non-monolithic nature of the local school district: Organizational and professional considerations. *American Educational Research Journal, 35*(1), 33–63.

Spillane, J. P., & Burch, P. (2006). The institutional environment and the technical core in K-12 schools: "Loose coupling" revisited. In H. D. Meyer & B. Rowan (Eds.), *The new institutionalism in education* (pp. 89–100). Albany: SUNY Press.

Spillane, J. P., & Thompson, C. L. (1997, Summer). Restructuring conceptions of local capacity: The local education agency's capacity for ambitious instructional reform. *Educational Evaluation and Policy Analysis, 19*(2), 185–203.

Stambach, A., & David, M. (2005). Feminist theory and education policy: How gender has been 'involved' in school choice debates. *Signs, 30,* 1633–1658.

Starr, P. (1988). The meaning of privatization. *Yale Law and Policy Review, 6*(1), 6–41.

Stein, M. (2004). *Testing in flux: Future directions in the pre-K-12 assessment market.* Boston: Eduventures.

Stein, M., & Bassett, E. (2004a). *Staying ahead of the curve: A value chain analysis of the K-12 assessment market.* Boston: Eduventures.

Stein, M., & Bassett, E. (2004b). *Uncovering K-12 professional development opportunities.* Boston: Eduventures.

Steinberg, M. (2006). Private educational services: Whom does the market leave behind? *Policy Matters, 4*(1), 17–22.

Stone, D. A. (2002). *Policy paradox: The art of political decision making.* New York: Norton.

Stoneman, C. (2000, February 23). Title I and parent information resource center. *First Annual Review of the Family Involvement in Education.* Washington, D.C.: The National Coalition for Parent Involvement in Education.

Strauss, A., & Corbin, J. (1990). *Basics of qualitative research.* Thousand Oaks, CA: Sage.

Stricker, N. (2007, February 17). Push for virtual charter school: Education proposal irks state board. *The Salt Lake Tribune.* Retrieved November 27, 2007, from http://sltrib.com/portlet/article/html/fragments/print_article.jsp?articleId=5248205&siteId=297

Stullich, S., Eisner, E., McCrary, J., & Roney, C. (2006). *National assessment of Title I: Vol.1. Implementation of Title I.* Washington, D.C.: U.S. Department of Education, Institute of Education Sciences.

Sunderman, G. L. (2006). Do supplemental educational services increase opportunities for minority students? *Phi Delta Kappan, 88*(2), 117–122.

Sunderman, G. L., & Kim, J. (2004). *Increasing bureaucracy or increasing opportunities? School district experience with supplemental educational services.* Cambridge, MA: The Civil Rights Project at Harvard University.

Sunderman, G. L., & Kim, J. S. (2006). Implementing supplemental educational services: Implications for school districts and educational opportunity. In K. K. Wong & S. Rutledge (Eds.), *Systemwide efforts to improve student achievement.* Greenwich, CT: Information Age.

Sunderman, G. L., Kim, J. S., & Orfield, G. (2005). *NCLB meets school realities: Lessons from the field.* Thousand Oaks, CA: Corwin Press.

Sunderman, G. L., & Orfield, G. (2006). Domesticating a revolution: No Child Left Behind reforms and state administrative response. *Harvard Educational Review, 76*(4), 526–556.

Taylor, S. J., & Bogdan, R. (Eds.). (1998). *Introduction to qualitative research methods: A guidebook and resource.* New York: Wiley.

teachnology (n.d.). *Current trends in education: School choice.* Retrieved August, 2007, from http://teach-nology.com/currenttrends/school_choice/

The White House. (n.d.). *Head Start policy book: President Bush's plan to prepare all children for kindergarten: Where are we now?* Retrieved October 2007, from http://www.whitehouse.gov/infocus/earlychildhood/hspolicybook/01.html

Trotter, A. (2007, March 29). Getting up to speed. *Edweek*, pp. 10–16.

Tucker, B. (2007, June). *Laboratories of reform: Virtual high schools and innovation in public education.* Washington, D.C.: Education Sector. Retrieved October 2007, from http://www.educationsector.org/research/research_show.htm?doc_id=502307

U.S. Department of Education. (2001a). *Enhancing education through technology act of 2001.* Retrieved June 2, 2007, from http://www.ed.gov/policy/elsec/leg/esea02/index.html

U.S. Department of Education. (2001b). *NCLB overview.* Retrieved June 2007, from http://www.ed.gov/nclb/overview/intro/execsumm.html

U.S. Department of Education. (2001c). *Title I: Improving the academic achievement of the disadvantaged.* Sec. 1111 (j). Washington, D.C.: Government Printing Office.

U.S. Department of Education. (2001d). *Elementary and Secondary Education Act of 1965, as amended, Title II, Part D—Enhancing Education Through Technology.* Retrieved October 7, 2007, from www.ed.gov/policy/elsec

U.S. Department of Education. (2002a). *President Bush unveils new guidance empowering faith-based and community groups to provide extra academic help to low-income students.* Retrieved November 2, 2006, from http://www.ed.gov/news/pressreleases/2002/12/12122002.html

U.S. Department of Education. (2002b, September). *No Child Left Behind: A desktop reference, 2002.* Washington, D.C.: Office of Elementary and Secondary Education. Retrieved August 2007, from http://www.ed.gov/admins/lead/account/nclbreference/reference.pdf

U.S. Department of Education. (2002c, December). *Federal Register Vol. 67, No. 231. Title I. Improving the academic achievement of the disadvantaged. Final Regulations.* Washington, D.C.: Government Printing Office.

U.S. Department of Education. (2003a). *No Child Left Behind: Supplemental educational services, non-regulatory guidance* (Final draft.). Retrieved August 2007, from http://www.ed.gov/nclb/choice/help/ses/guidance.html

U.S. Department of Education. (2003b, September). *Report cards: Title I, Part A Nonregulatory guidance.* Washington, D.C.: U.S. Department of Education. Retrieved August 2007, from http://doe.sd.gov/ofm/grants/LEAapp/docs/Report%20Cards%20Guidance.pdf

U.S. Department of Education. (2003c). *Title IA services for private school children: Non-regulatory guidance* (p. 5). Washington, D.C.: Government Printing Office .

U.S. Department of Education. (2003d). *Supplemental educational services. Non-regulatory guidance.* Retrieved August 2006, from http://www.ed.gov/nclb/choice/help/ses/guidance.html

U.S. Department of Education (2004a). SES Policy Letter in Reference to LEA Conditions on Providers. Washington, D.C.: U.S. Department of Education. Retrieved August 2006, from http://www.ed.gov/policy/elsec/guidance/stateletters/choice.

U.S. Department of Education. (2004b). *Evaluation of Title I accountability systems and school improvement efforts (TASSIE): First year technical appendix.* Washington, D.C.: Office of the Under Secretary, Policy and Program Studies Service.

U.S. Department of Education. (2004c, July). *The impact of the new Title I requirements on charter schools: Non-regulatory guidance.* Washington, D.C.: Author. Retrieved August 2007, from http://www.ed.gov/policy/elsec/guid/charterguidance03.pdf

U.S. Department of Education. (2004d, September). *Choosing a school for your child.* Washington, D.C.: Office of Innovation and Improvement. Retrieved August 2007, from http://www.pueblo.gsa.gov/cic_text/education/choosingschool/choosingschool.htm

U.S. Department of Education. (2004e, July). *The impact of the new Title I requirements on charter schools: Non-regulatory guidance.* Washington, DC: U.S. Department of Education. Retrieved August 2007, from http://www.ed.gov/policy/elsec/guid/charterguidance03.pdf

U.S. Department of Education. (2005a). *Supplemental education services non-regulatory guidance.* Washington, D.C.: U.S. Department of Education. Retrieved August 2006, from http://www.ed.gov/policy/elsec/guid/supsvcguid

U.S. Department of Education (2005b). *No Child Left Behind. Supplemental educational services: Non-regulatory guidance.* Washington, D.C.: Government Printing Office.

U.S. Department of Education. (2005c). *Title II of the Americans with Disabilities Act of 1990.* (Sec C3, VII of the Civil Rights Act of 1964). Washington, D.C.: Government Printing Office.

U.S. Department of Education (2006a). *Question and answer on the participation of private schools in providing supplemental education services (SES) under No Child Left Behind.* Washington, D.C.: Government Printing Office. Retrieved March 2007, from http://www.ed.gov/policy/elsec/guid/cnpe/sesguidance.html

U.S. Department of Education. (2006b). *Letter to chief state school officer on district affiliated entities serving as an SES provider.* Washington, D.C.: Government Printing Office. Retrieved March, 2007, from http://www.ed.gov/policy/elsec/guid/

U.S. Department of Education. (2007, August) *Improving basic programs operated by local education agencies.* Title I, Part A, Sec 1003. Washington, D.C.: Government Printing Office. Retrieved December 2007, from http://www.ed.gov/programs/titleiparta/

Villano, M. (2006). Assessing formative assessment. *Technology and Learning, 26*(6), 8–12.

Virtual Sage, & Connections Academy. (May 16, 2006). *Connections Academy and Virtual Sage announce agreement: Leading virtual public school provider to license custom high school courses.* Retrieved August 2007, from http://www.connectionsacademy.com/pdfs/20060516_VirtualSageAgreement.pdf

Ware, A. (1989). *Between profit and state: Intermediate organizations in Britain and the United States.* Cambridge, UK: Polity.

Washington Parents Association. (2003, February 27). *Fact sheet: How virtual charter schools threaten public schools.* Retrieved August 20, 2007, from http://www.homeschooling-wpa.org

Wayman, J. C., & Stringfield, S. (2006). Technology-supported involvement of entire faculties in examination of student data for instructional improvement. *American Journal of Education, 112*(4), 549–571.

Wells, A. S. (2002). Why public policy fails to live up to the potential of charter school reform: An introduction. In A. Stuart Wells (Ed.), *Where charter school policy fails: The problems of accountability and equity* (pp. 1–28). New York: Teachers College Press.

Wenger, Y. M. H., Mindy B. (2007, February 6). Online class bill heads to Senate: Poor students largely left out, Democrats say. *Northwest NewsChannel 8.* Retrieved November 27, 2007, from http://www.kgw.com/education/localeducation/stories/kgw_020607_edu_Charter_schools.58473753.html/

Whitty, G. (1997). Creating quasi-markets in education: A review of recent research on parental choice and school autonomy in three countries. *Review of Research in Education, 22,* 3–47.

Whitty, G., Power, S., & Halpin, D. (1998). *Devolution and choice in education: The school, the state and the market.* Buckingham, UK: Open University Press.

Williams, W. (1982). The study of implementation. In W. Williams (Ed.), *Studying implementation: Methodological and administrative issues* (pp. 1–17). Chatham, NJ: Chatham Press.

Wisconsin Education Association Education Council v. Northern Osaukee School District, 2006AP1380, p. 12 (December 5, 2007).

Wong, K. K., & Rutledge, S. (Eds.). *System-wide efforts to improve student achievement.* Greenwich, CT: Information Age.

Zimmer, R., Gill, B., Razquin, P., Booker, K., & Lockwood, J. R. (2007). *State and local implementation of the No Child Left Behind Act: Vol. 1. Title I school choice, supplemental educational services, and student achievement.* Washington, D.C.: RAND.

Zucker, L. (Ed.). (1988). *Institutional patterns and organizations: Culture and environment.* Cambridge, MA: Ballinger.

Index

barriers to small firms, 59, 64, 67
case study, 63–75
compliance with law, 62
curriculum, 68–70
demand growth, 65–66
district as direct serve provider, 63–64
dominance of national firms, 57, 63–66
emerging market, 56–57
English language learners, 61–62, 72–75
gray areas, 61–62
Individuals with Disabilities Act, 60
limited information for parents, 70–71
limits on government, 59–60
market share, 57
mergers and acquisitions, 57–58
No Child Left Behind Act, 59, 60
patterns in provider activity, 64–65
policy discourse, 66–68
power asymmetries, 71–72
student joining incentives, 67–68
students with disabilities, 72–75
supplemental education services
coordinators, 66
targeting states with greatest revenues, 58
voice in local policy, 67–68
neoliberalism, 55
No Child Left Behind Act, 9, 55
shadow privatization, 55–76

T
Technology
virtual schooling
financial benefits, 79–81
Test development and preparation, 24–25
Testing, x, xi, *see also* Benchmark assessment
systems

Textbook publishers
future risks, 37–38
mergers and acquisitions, 37–38
power asymmetries, 37
Theoretical sampling, 137–138
Transparency, 133–134
lack of, 130
need for, 119
new privatization, 2
Tutoring industry, shadow privatization, 55–76
21st Century Learning Grant, 34

V
Vendors, new roles, 33
Virtual schooling, xii, 77–97, 145–146
Christian conservatives, 83–84
confuses meaning of local, 84–85
development, 77–78
district policy decisions, 96
equity, 78–79
federal policy, 81–83
for-profit firms
local context, 85–95
home schooling, 83–84
No Child Left Behind Act, 81–83
possibilities, 83–85
private financial investment, 80–81
profitable expansion, 80
relationships' opacity, 95–97
residential segregation, 125
technology, financial benefits, 79–81
Vouchers, reproducing inequalities, 14

W
Whittle, Chris, 4–5
Within-case, nested sampling, 138

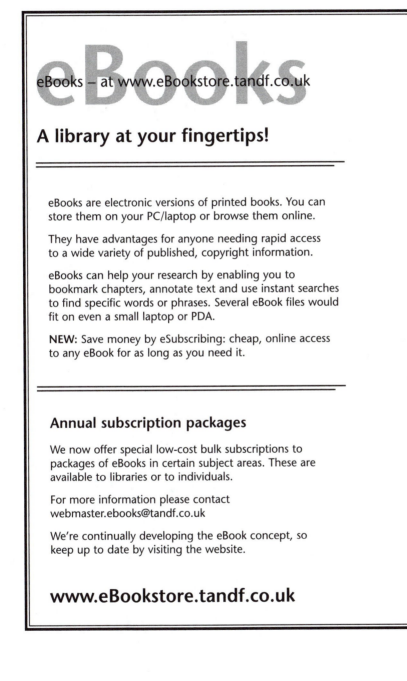